Politician's Dilemma

California Series on Social Choice and Political Economy

Edited by Brian Barry (1981 to 1991), Robert H. Bates,
James S. Coleman (from 1992), and Samuel L. Popkin

Politician's Dilemma

Building State Capacity in Latin America

Barbara Geddes

UNIVERSITY OF CALIFORNIA PRESS
Berkeley · Los Angeles · London

University of California Press
Berkeley and Los Angeles, California

University of California Press, Ltd.
London, England

Library of Congress Cataloging-in-Publication Data

Geddes, Barbara.
   Politician's dilemma: building state capacity in Latin America / Barbara Geddes.

      p.   cm.—(California series on social choice and political economy; 25)
   Includes bibliographical references and index.
   ISBN 0-520-07250-2 (alk. paper)
      1. Latin America—Politics and government—20th century.   2. Bureaucracy—Latin
   America—History—20th century.   3. Civil service reform—Latin America—History—
   20th century.   I. Title.   II. Series.
      JL958.G44   1994
      351'.001'098—dc20   93-14439
                                                                                 CIP

Printed in the United States of America
9 8 7 6 5 4 3 2 1

The paper used in this publication meets the minimum requirements of American
National Standard for Information Sciences—Permanence of Paper for Printed Library
Materials, ANSI Z39.48-1984. ☺

Parts of chapter 3 are reprinted from *Comparative Politics*, with permission from
City University of New York.
Parts of chapter 5 are reprinted from the *American Political Science Review*,
with permission from the American Political Science Association.

To my parents
Jack and Estelle Frye,
from whom I absorbed my interest in politics and
my drive to understand events in the world,
and my children
Dylan, Danielle, Darcy, and Demetria

Contents

Figures and Tables

FIGURES

TABLES

Acknowledgments

Einstein said, "What a person thinks on his own, without being stimulated by the thoughts and experiences of other people, is even in the best cases rather paltry and monotonous." How much more true for the rest of us.

Among the people whose thoughts have stimulated my own are several teachers, colleagues, and friends to whom I owe not only many of the ideas and insights in this book, but much that I now take for granted as my own unique way of thinking about the world. I am also very grateful to several teachers for the personal encouragement they offered to an insecure reentry student embarking on what was at the time an unusual path for a woman with several children.

My debt to Ken Jowitt is hard to measure. From my earliest days at Berkeley, Ken offered enthusiastic recognition and unrestrained moral support. In the intellectual domain, he demonstrated that fine-lined, graceful, and compelling arguments could be constructed from the cluttered rococo of comparative politics. His intellectual worldview has shaped my own and this book, though he may not recognize it expressed in a foreign idiom. He has also been a steadfast friend.

My debt to Chris Achen is no less great. Conversations and classes with Chris caused me to think about building arguments up from primitive terms, about logic, and about evidence in ways that have shaped everything I have done since then. If my work persuades anyone, it will be because he pushed me to strengthen the social science girders that support it. I am grateful to him for reading callow early versions of work on a subject of no particular interest to him with unfailing seriousness, pressing me to do it better, and, above all, for laughing at my jokes.

David Collier first encouraged me to become an interloper in the field of Latin American politics and thus saved me from becoming an expert on an East European country that no longer exists. For this, he deserves my deepest gratitude. For his unfailing interest, enthusiasm for new ideas, and kindness over the years, I also thank him.

Edson Nunes first sparked my interest in Brazil. Talks with him were one of the most fruitful parts of my graduate education. Many of the ideas in chapter 3 first emerged during conversations with Edson while we were both students. I am also greatly indebted to him for introducing me to his friends and colleagues at the Instituto Universitário de Pesquisas do Rio de Janeiro and for easing my transition into Brazilian life.

Bob Bates was the first person "outside the family" to read the entire manuscript. He has my deep gratitude for his enthusiasm about the project, as well as his penetrating and insightful comments on the work.

Many others have also contributed to this study, often in greater measure than they realize. Eve Wallenstein first introduced me to the doubtful pleasures of political science. Barry Ames, Margaret Levi, and Artur Ribeiro Neto read carefully and commented helpfully on the entire manuscript. Steph Haggard, Jeff Frieden, David Lake, and George Tsebelis have read and commented on large portions of it. I have found conversations with each of them invaluable for developing and honing my ideas. I have also had the benefit of comments on various chapters from Gary Bonham, Gary Cox, Peter Evans, Frances Hagopian, Bob Kaufman, Linda Lewin, Eric Nordlinger, and Eliza Willis.

I should also express my gratitude to the UCLA Political Science Department for providing both a congenial place to work and encouragement for the synthesis of comparative politics and economic models of politics that I have tried to accomplish in this book. I have especially enjoyed the intellectual stimulation, raucous atmosphere, and ribald jokes of the Tuesday political economy lunches.

Although this project began as a dissertation, most of that grand opus has over the years found its way to the cutting room floor. I wish I could thank the Inter-University Consortium for Political and Social Research (ICPSR) or some other central data collection organization for providing the data that made the new chapters possible, but unfortunately I had to carry out the tedious and time-consuming task myself. I have grown old hunting through dusty archives and moldy microfilm for fugitive bits of information needed to test various arguments, especially in chapter 6.

Without the energy, intelligence, and persistence of several research assistants at various points along the way, data collection would have taken even longer than it did. I owe a great debt to Glen Biglaiser, David Drake, Tony Gill, Melodye Hannes, Carlos Juárez, Kimberly Niles, and Cheryl Schonhardt-Bailey. Each of them did much more than he or she was paid for.

I received material help during the course of working on this project from the Latin American Studies Center at the University of California, Berkeley, and the Tinker Foundation; the American Association of University Women; and the Council on International and Comparative Studies, the International Studies and Overseas Program, the Academic Senate, and the Latin American Center at UCLA. The American Association of University Women deserves special thanks. It was the only national funding agency willing to support field research tailored to fit the needs of a woman with children. The AAUW's flexibility allowed me to make several short fieldwork trips rather than stay away from my family for an unacceptably long time.

One's greatest debts are often closest to home. Throughout the time I have known him, John Zaller has read and improved everything I have written. He has read this entire manuscript, some of it repeatedly, always with an eye to the underlying logic. Much of what is felicitously expressed, I owe to him. For this, for his serenity, cheerful disposition, and unfailing reasonableness, and for providing me with an excuse for having another child, I thank him.

ONE

The State

The state has been brought back in. It now lumbers through the halls of academe, a great clumsy creature that no one quite knows what to do with. Some have suggested putting it back out, but that, as often happens with strays let in from the cold, has proved difficult to do. Theoretically unwieldy as "the state" has proved to be, the role states[1] play in influencing, managing, and sometimes transforming economics and societies compels the attention of social scientists. Increasingly, researchers have endeavored to take into account the use by national leaders of the unparalleled resources and power of the state to change society; to foster economic development; to provide citizens with education, medical care, sanitation, roads, and other amenities of modernity; and even to alter age-old social structures and cultural patterns.

Such state-led development has rendered inadequate old theories, both those that assumed an automatic diffusion of modernization via markets and spontaneous cultural change, and those that viewed political outcomes as the result of class struggle. At one time, comparativists looked primarily to traits of the domestic society and culture or to

1. The word "state" is used here to refer to regimes, governments, specific administrative agencies, and even individuals who act on behalf of governments. This usage is, I think, consistent with that in much of the literature, despite many efforts to define the state in a more precise manner. Talking about "the state" is a shorthand way of talking about the actions of individuals whose power derives from their positions in government. When dealing with the state as a political actor, one must refer to actions carried out by human beings. Even the state conceived as an expression of class interests "requires an *organization* which, since it cannot be other than a social network of people, exists in its own right and possesses interests of its own" (Cardoso 1979, 51).

1

characteristics of the international environment for explanations of economic development and change. They tended to view the state as simply reflecting outcomes caused by the struggle among private interests to secure policies beneficial to themselves. Now, however, most scholars working on these issues, no matter what their theoretical and ideological commitments, believe that governments can and often do act independently of underlying socioeconomic forces. In consequence, observers have recognized the need for theories to explain the state's role in bringing about change.

Scholars working on a remarkably wide spectrum of questions[2] have concluded that states are loci of power, resources, and interests. They have shown that state officials sometimes have policy preferences independent of those of major social and economic groups in society, and that these officials can sometimes, by virtue of their positions in government, use state power and resources to pursue their own ideas and interests. In other words, government policies often reflect the interests and economic ideologies of state officials, rather than those of domestic or foreign economic elites or powerful organized middle- and working-class groups. These policies in turn create the incentives that shape the day-to-day choices of individuals in society. And these choices then affect the rate of growth, the distribution of the benefits of growth, and, in sum, the way political, economic, and social systems work.

THE STATE IN ECONOMIC DEVELOPMENT

In the study of developing countries, much of the recent interest in the role of the state has arisen from observations that governments sometimes effect radical shifts in economic policy without the support of important interest groups. Observers see such "state" or government autonomy in the most successful new industrializing countries and also in what used to be considered successful post-revolutionary regimes.

The notion of state autonomy, which draws on theoretical constructs developed in structuralist Marxist and realist international relations theory, emerged in the study of developing countries as part of the effort

2. For example, on social revolution, Skocpol 1979; on nonrevolutionary socioeconomic transformation, Trimberger 1978; on economic development in Europe, Gerschenkron 1966, North 1979, Eckstein 1958; on development strategies in the Latin American and Asian newly industrializing countries (NICs), Haggard and Cheng 1987, Haggard 1990, Evans 1979, Rueschemeyer and Evans 1986; on squatter settlements, Collier 1976, Ames 1973; on labor, Goldberg 1986, Collier and Collier 1977, 1979, Katznelson 1986; on the failure of agricultural policy in Africa, Bates 1981.

to understand situations in which a conflict paradigm—that is, an assumption that political outcomes are determined by a clash of interests, with the most powerful interest winning—could not explain major policy shifts. In these situations, the interests injured by the new policies were often those that, shortly before a shift, had appeared to be economically and politically dominant in the country (Trimberger 1977, 1978; Hamilton 1982). In any unmediated struggle among interests, standard political theories, whether Marxist or pluralist, would have expected them to win. And yet they lost.

In Latin America, for example, most governments began to implement industrialization policies that systematically disadvantaged the producers of primary product exports at a time when agriculture and mining remained economically dominant.[3] The more recent history of the region offers numerous additional instances of policy changes that have injured powerful economic groups. Domestic industries, foreign industries, and the organized working class have all failed on various occasions to protect their own interests, despite their considerable political, organizational, and economic resources. No one believes that these groups are weak or uninfluential, but those who propose a focus on the state point out that they have not proved insurmountable obstacles to governments bent on pursuing policies damaging to them.

The interests that benefited from these policy shifts, in contrast to those that lost, were often unorganized, economically weak, and sometimes even weak in terms of sheer numbers of people. If they subsequently developed into powerful interest groups, it was because of the policy shifts initially undertaken by state elites on their own initiative. Manufacturers of inputs for the auto industry in Brazil, for example, have become politically influential since the 1960s. Prior to the state-sponsored implantation of the auto industry and the passage of strict

3. Except for Argentina, the more economically advanced Latin American countries had begun to abandon laissez-faire policies and experiment with state intervention in the economy by the 1930s. Conscious, integrated policies to foster industrialization began in Argentina and Chile in the 1940s, in the other more developed countries during the 1950s, and in most of the poorer countries during the 1960s. Measuring sectoral dominance is extremely problematic, but contribution of the industrial sector to GDP gives a crude indication. Of the nineteen Latin American countries for which data are available, only in Uruguay had industrial production outstripped primary product production by the time policy changes disadvantageous to primary product producers began in the thirties. The transition to industrial dominance over agriculture occurred in Argentina and Brazil during the 1940s, and in Chile and Mexico during the 1950s. In the rest of Latin America, the transition had still not occurred by 1970. In other words, in all but Uruguay and possibly Argentina, the initiation of policies favoring the industrial sector occurred before that sector had attained economic power on its own.

domestic content laws, however, this group was small and insignificant both economically and politically. It owes its current status to the government decision in the 1950s to subsidize and otherwise encourage local production of capital goods and consumer durables. Prior to this decision, the producers of nondurable consumer goods dominated Brazil's private domestic manufacturing sector and the interest organizations that represented it. In spite of its economic importance, however, the traditional manufacturing sector reaped relatively few benefits from the state-sponsored industrialization drive during the 1950s.

Policy shifts that confer benefits on groups insufficiently powerful to have effectively demanded them are not common occurrences, but they do happen from time to time, and, when they do, they can have momentous consequences and are therefore worth trying to understand. Since these policy outcomes could not have been predicted on the basis of known preexisting forces, that is, classes or interest groups, observers posited the existence of some other force to account for them. Just as astronomers deduced the existence of Neptune from perturbations in the orbit of Uranus before they could see the new planet, social scientists inferred the existence of an autonomous force located in the state, even though they could not directly observe it. This new force seemed to depend on state resources and to be guided by the preferences of political leaders.

From positing the existence of an autonomous force made possible by state resources to speculating about the possible effects of such a force on policy was a short step. Several scholars have suggested that state autonomy would aid state intervention to foster rapid economic development or structural adjustment, since it would allow government policymakers to ignore interests injured by particular policies. Both development and adjustment inevitably involve shifting resources among sectors of the economy, geographical areas, and social groups. They also involve a temporary shift of resources from consumption to investment. All of these resource movements impose costs and generate opposition.

Since powerful societal interests, that is, those that benefit most from the status quo, would tend to resist radical changes in policy, several observers have credited more autonomous states with greater flexibility in adapting to crises and rapid changes in the international economy (Haggard 1986; Haggard and Kaufman 1989). They note that policies aimed at creating comparative advantage, taking advantage of new opportunities in the international economy, or adapting to international price shocks often involve channeling resources away from customary uses and into the creation of new productive endeavors. They argue that governments can more readily impose the costs of these transitions if they enjoy some autonomy from the interests being hurt, that is, if their political survival does not depend on support from injured interests.

Autonomy, in this view, frees state elites from the interests vested in earlier stages of development. Thus, autonomy should be especially important when crises precipitate a reexamination of development strategies. Autonomy offers no guarantee that the economic situation will be assessed competently or that decisions in the public interest will be made, but if both do occur, it makes effective action more likely.

The same kind of argument about the utility of autonomy from societal interests has been made about Leninist regimes. Post-revolutionary industrialization drives under Leninist leadership involved an even more radical imposition of costs on large parts of the population. Only governments highly insulated from most societal groups could carry out such policies (Jowitt 1971), and the idea of state autonomy, if not the label, holds no novelty for observers of Leninist political systems.

For scholars interested in explaining why some countries have followed more effective development strategies than others, the notion of state autonomy has seemed a useful starting point, but efforts to develop it have run into snags. State autonomy has not been, and perhaps cannot be, directly observed. Its presence is inferred on the basis of policy outcomes that appear to reflect the preferences of officials, or even of some disembodied national interest (Krasner 1978).[4] "State autonomy" thus explains a situation that appears anomalous if one assumes that government policies generally reflect societal interests.

The fact that state autonomy is inferred from its effects rather than directly observed has made it difficult to study and explain. No one, it seems, is quite sure what "it" actually consists of. State autonomy seems at times to refer to the independence of the state itself, the regime, a particular government, some segments or agencies of the government, or even specific leaders. It seems the phrase can refer to any independent force based in the central government.

Although several authors have discussed the subject (Stepan 1978; Hamilton 1982; Haggard 1986; Rueschemeyer and Evans 1986,

---

4. Eric Nordlinger (1981, 74–98) makes the point that a state could be autonomous even if the preferences of state actors and important societal groups were identical, as long as the preferences of state actors did not derive from societal preferences. Autonomy can only be clearly perceived, however, when policy outcomes diverge from expressed or assumed societal preferences.

63–65; Waisman 1987), no one has confirmed empirically the existence of political or societal characteristics that allow governments to act autonomously. In the absence of such a set of concrete traits by which to identify state autonomy without recourse to its supposed effects, it is impossible to show empirically that it exists and has effects. It also becomes very difficult to explain its historical development. As a result, analyses tend to focus more on the policy outcomes themselves rather than on the state structure that is hypothesized to produce the outcomes.

Nevertheless, by establishing that officials do at times act on the basis of their own ideologies and preferences, the state autonomy literature has performed a useful service. It has set the agenda for further work in the area. Efforts have begun to explain why states intervene in the economy and society, how and why they choose particular policies as the means of intervention, and why some state interventions result in better outcomes than others. The attempt to answer these questions seems stalled, however, at an early and frustrating stage. Insight and description abound, but explanation remains scarce.

Structural arguments, currently the most cogent strand of the state autonomy literature, describe the features of international and domestic situations that would make it rational for states (i.e., governments) to behave autonomously in order to pursue an interest in, for example, national survival or capitalist development (Trimberger 1977; Skocpol and Trimberger 1977–78, 101–13; Skocpol 1979; Cardoso 1969, 1971; Bamat 1977). Such explanations implicitly treat states as rational unitary actors without building any plausible foundation for doing so.

Analysts who attempt to delve into the concrete details of how states behave usually end up moving away from systematic structural explanations and toward ad hoc political and sociological explanations. If one wants to explain a state's preferences regarding development strategies, for example, one needs to know who has power and what they want and believe. Who has power will depend on the outcome of a political struggle that can be "explained" by particular features of the conjuncture and personalities involved. Such an explanation will have few implications for other cases, however.

Thus within the statist literature, one tends to have a choice between systematic structuralist arguments that lack plausible individual-level foundations and plausible individual-level explanations that lack theoretical reach. There is no doubt that the issues raised by the statist literature are important. But studies carried out to date leave doubts about whether the current statist approach is the best theoretical tool for trying to understand the role of states in developing countries. For one thing, most arguments about state autonomy were developed in the context of studies of authoritarian regimes.[5] Now that most developing countries have taken significant steps toward democratization, states still matter, but old arguments may not.

For another, discussions of the state usually assume that states behave as unitary actors. In reality, they often do not. The problem is not that there is "no there there," but that there are too many theres there—each having different capacities, intentions, and preferences. Some parts of the state may express independent preferences while others, often the larger parts, reflect societal interests. Discussions of "the" state offer little theoretical leverage for understanding the sources of the competing interests of different actors within the state.

THE STATE AS A COLLECTION OF
SELF-INTERESTED INDIVIDUALS

Observations of outcomes that seemed to have been caused by autonomous state action were initially taken as challenges to traditional paradigms and theories, especially pluralism, modernization, Marxism, and dependency. But by now, the old paradigms are either enfeebled or revised to the point where further challenges seem pointless, and some analysts have come to feel a need for new theories within which autonomous government actions would cease to be anomalous.

This study proposes such an anchor for the statist perspective: an approach to the state based on a model of rationally self-interested political leaders.[6] By focusing on individual state actors and the different incentives they confront, it suggests an alternative approach to the state that provides a systematic explanation for the different capacities and apparent preferences of different parts of the state. The keystone of the argument is a simple model of politicians and bureaucrats as rational individuals who attempt to maximize career success.[7] The basic idea underlying this model is nicely expressed by Mark Crain and Robert

5. Nordlinger (1981) is an obvious exception.

6. Others, for example Douglass North (1979) and Margaret Levi (1988), have used rational actor models to interpret state actions. Their analyses focus on rulers as revenue maximizers. Though the approach taken here does not use this key assumption, it builds on ideas found in their work.

7. Though novel in the context of the "statist" perspective, the approach used here obviously builds on such works as Mayhew (1974), Fiorina (1977), Arnold (1979), Jacobson and Kernell (1983), Ames (1987), Crain and Tollison (1990), Bates (1989), and Cowhey (1990).

Tollison (1990, 3). "[H]uman behavior in governmental settings is motivated by the same self-interested forces that guide human behavior in private settings. . . . It should be stressed that this is not a dogmatic assertion that politicians and other political actors are self-interested; rather, it is a pragmatic analytical convention."

Since state decisions are made by these human beings, the content of their decisions—including decisions that contribute to reforming the state itself—will reflect *their* interests. Political leaders' interests center on their political careers.

> Normally, personal success in politics . . . will imply concentration of the professional kind and relegate a man's other activities to the rank of sidelines or necessary chores. . . . [I]n modern democracies . . . politics will unavoidably be a career. This in turn spells recognition of a distinct professional interest in the individual politician. . . . Many a riddle is solved as soon as we take account of it. Among other things we immediately cease to wonder why it is that politicians so often fail to serve the interest of their class or of the groups with which they are personally connected.
>
> (Schumpeter 1975, 285)

Whatever additional interests they may have, most political leaders want to remain in office. And, generally speaking, their other goals can only be accomplished while in office. Political institutions determine which strategies for staying in office are likely to work.

If one accepts this view of officials, the route to explaining state or government autonomy ceases to be problematic. One can explain much of the behavior of states as the outcome of rational choices by self-interested officials acting within particular institutional and circumstantial contexts. This approach leads to an explanation of state autonomy grounded in the behavior of individual political actors: officials and politicians will behave in ways that result in state autonomy when it serves their own career interests to do so. When their interests can be furthered by representing particular societal interests, they will do this. Using this approach, degrees or kinds of autonomy can be predicted from institutional features of the regime and other characteristics of the political system, rather than inferred on the basis of policy outcomes. This approach thus creates the possibility of falsifying arguments.

The focus on incentives also offers more leverage for explaining policy outcomes than does the undifferentiated notion of state autonomy. If autonomy is viewed as an attribute of a unitary state, no prediction about state behavior can be made unless state interests or preferences can be identified. Although interests are usefully imputed to states in some schools of thought,[8] attempts to deduce domestic behavior from assumed state interests have failed to produce satisfying results.

It has been argued, most notably by Theda Skocpol (1979), that international threats motivate state officials to act autonomously from dominant classes. The approach taken here, in contrast, emphasizes that state officials have great leeway in choosing how to respond to threats. It suggests that the kind of response state actors select will, whatever else it does, reflect their own domestic political interests. This fact was well understood by European colonizers. Britain's famous divide-and-rule strategy of colonization, for example, was effective precisely because elites in soon-to-become colonized areas chose strategies for responding to the British on the basis of how they would affect competition with domestic rivals. Attention to the domestic interests served by particular responses to outside threats thus helps explain why most Third World elites who faced the threat of colonial military incursion failed to carry out the internal administrative, military, and economic changes that might have given them the strength to meet the challenge. Most so far have also failed to initiate the reforms that would enable them to meet international economic threats more successfully.

Arguments that stress the imperatives created by foreign military and economic threats seem to forget that the world is littered with the corpses of potential and former nations that failed to meet the challenge of international competition (for example, Burgundy, Bavaria, Wales), not to mention the battered victims of economic threats that manage to cling to life despite the policy choices of their leaders. The state autonomy literature might lead one to hypothesize that these failures have been caused by a lack of policy autonomy from dominant groups intent on maintaining their own privileges, but evidence often fails to support this hypothesis (Geddes 1990). These failures have not in general been caused by an inability to ignore the interests of powerful societal groups.

Rather, many failures have been caused by the policies political leaders chose when attempting to respond to international threats and at the same time gain an advantage in the struggle with domestic political rivals. In some cases, such as the presidential efforts to increase bureaucratic capacity analyzed in chapter 6, political rivals (rather than economic elites) have realized the threat to their interests and have success-

---

8. In some Marxist theory, the (capitalist) state is assumed to have an interest in assuring the preservation of capitalism (Poulantzas 1975, 1976). In much of international relations theory, states acting in the international arena are assumed to maximize power or national wealth.

fully blocked reforms. In cases where policy choices have involved the creation of new political resources (such as state enterprises) rather than the redistribution of preexisting ones, political rivals have generally not opposed them. As in other political situations, it is easier to distribute from an expanding pie than to redistribute. The catastrophic problem with these policies is that they have frequently turned out to be much more effective as vehicles for creating political resources useful to incumbent politicians than as strategies for dealing with international economic or military threats.

Commodity marketing boards set up in a number of developing countries provide especially dramatic examples of policies aimed simultaneously at coping with international economic threats and capturing resources for incumbent political leaders. The marketing boards were designed to counteract the threat of foreign control over the marketing of export crops, while at the same time contributing to economic diversification as a means of reducing vulnerability to external price shocks. Monopolies over the marketing of export crops allowed governments to capture resources from the agricultural sector to use in building the industrial sector. The resources spent on manufacturing and infrastructure projects could easily be directed toward regions and projects that would benefit supporters of the current political leadership and thus help maintain the political machinery of incumbents.

The marketing boards succeeded in the sense that they permitted governments to siphon substantial amounts of capital out of the agricultural sector. They worked far less well, however, as tools for reducing economic vulnerability since they had the unintended but predictable consequence of reducing farmers' incentive to export and hence reducing export earnings (Bates 1981; Smith 1969). In many cases, governments established these boards in opposition to dominant agricultural interests and prior to the emergence of powerful industrial interests. This strategy failed to meet the international economic challenge not because of insufficient policy autonomy from interest groups but because the policy instrument chosen turned out to be economically disastrous—though politically quite useful.

Attention to the interests of individual state officials in competition with other politicians yields systematic explanations of the choice of commodity marketing boards as a strategy for dealing with international economic constraints, and for many other policies that would seem irrational if one assumed that state actors are motivated primarily by the need to respond to international threats. To conceive of politicians and officials as motivated primarily by interest in domestic political survival and advancement also provides plausible individual-level arguments about how and under what circumstances officials can be expected to behave autonomously from societal interests.

HOW INSTITUTIONS SHAPE INCENTIVES

If one assumes that the interests of most government decision makers, and of aspirants to that role, center on their political careers, one can expect their policy preferences and their behavior to be shaped by the requirements for advancement imposed by their roles in government and their memberships in the parties, professions, and leadership cliques that structure access to government posts. At the regime level, if we classify governments according to the incentives favoring autonomy that they provide officials, they fall somewhere on a continuum anchored at one end by Leninist regimes and at the other, it could be argued, by oligarchical democracies in undiversified economies. In Leninist regimes, the costs and benefits to officials associated with different behaviors are largely controlled by higher level party officials, and, as a result, officials in these regimes exhibit a remarkable degree of autonomy from societal groups. In democracies in which only members of the economically dominant class may participate, politicians will tend to represent dominant interests since reelection depends only on this narrow group. They have little incentive to behave autonomously and, in fact, face great political dangers if they try to do so. The laissez-faire oriented, limited participation democratic governments of Latin America during the late nineteenth and early twentieth centuries fit this pattern. Among Latin American governments, only Uruguay, the sole Latin American country to enjoy both democracy and universal male suffrage before 1930,[9] and revolutionary Mexico exhibited any noticeable autonomy before the 1930s.[10]

9. The Sáenz Peña Law of 1912 established universal male citizen suffrage in Argentina, but the exclusion of non-citizens denied the vote to the majority of the urban working class. As a result of this provision and the systematic electoral fraud practiced during the thirties and early forties, the class base of political participation in Argentina remained limited until 1946. See Waisman (1987).

10. This discussion is descriptively consistent, up to a point, with those authors who have noted the same change in state behavior and who consequently believe state autonomy to be possible when the mode of production is in transition (Hamilton 1982, ch. 1; Cardoso 1969). In my view, however, their interpretation is an unwarranted generalization from observation of the contrast between state behavior before about 1930, when most Latin American countries' economies depended on primary production of a few crops and minerals and political participation was very limited, and state behavior more re-

As economies developed, however, and the number of urban, organizable potential voters increased, politicians not supported by established interests had an incentive to extend the franchise to excluded groups as a way of enhancing their own competitiveness against more entrenched politicians. Once the electoral system includes voters with more diverse interests, politicians have considerable leeway when it comes to putting together packages of policies to appeal to different aggregations of voters, but their most effective strategy is rarely a simple defense of the interests of the wealthy few. Consequently, it has become common to see elected politicians initiating policies costly to members of the dominant class.

In other words, modern democratic regimes provide self-interested political leaders with reasons for autonomy from dominant groups. These reasons vary, however, over time, across actors, and across countries, as do reasons for autonomy from other groups that have figured less prominently in the literature. Some of this variation can be explained by institutional differences among democracies. Within modern democratic regimes, particular institutions, such as electoral rules and party procedures, determine what kinds of behavior are most likely to contribute to career advancement. By analyzing the institutionally determined incentives facing political leaders, one can explain state actions that might be unexpected from the perspective of more traditional approaches.

This study deals principally with the motivations and incentives of four types of political actor: presidents,[11] legislators, party leaders, and state bureaucrats. Members of each category are assumed to be continually conscious of career interests as they make various policy decisions, but, since actors occupying different institutional roles face different constraints and opportunities, their responses differ.

The career interests of various political actors are discussed in greater detail below, but a sketch of some key assumptions may be useful here. The careers of legislators depend on reelection, so concern with the vote

cently. They see recent instances in which state policies fail to reflect dominant class interests as evidence of division within the dominant class or lack of hegemony, that can presumably be expected to abate once industrial capitalism is consolidated. In contrast, I see the pre-1930 period as a never-to-be-repeated historical phase during which politicians motivated by electoral concerns would have had no reason to respond to any interests other than those of the narrow group able to vote.

11. As this is written, all South and Central American countries have presidential systems, though transitions to parliamentarism are being debated in a few.

in the next election always ranks high in their calculations. Presidents in Latin America, who usually cannot serve consecutive terms and often face a real threat of overthrow, want, first, to complete their terms in office (Ames 1987). Next, they want to maximize their future political power within their parties and their chances of reelection after the constitutionally prescribed time out of office has elapsed. Party leaders pursue career success by maximizing party power and their own power within parties. Bureaucrats prefer, first, security in office, and then, advancement and the material advantages that accompany it. The way these interests impinge on each other and are constrained by other societal forces in specific instances is discussed below.

The time horizons of these actors vary depending on the country and historical period involved, but, on average, Latin American political actors must discount the future fairly heavily because of the high probability that a military intervention will marginalize them. The military ousted 38 percent of all Latin American governments between 1945 and 1982.[12] Furthermore, even when the military remains on the sidelines, a change of the party in power may reduce markedly a politician's or bureaucrat's chances of getting ahead, since success depends heavily on patronage, which presidents monopolize. Consequently, discount rates tend to be high. In other words, the unstable political environment forces rational politicians in office to concentrate on activities that lead to quick results and immediate rewards.

The approach to thinking about the state proposed here focuses on how institutions, especially political institutions, shape the incentives of individuals in government, and how, in consequence, these individuals choose policies. It thus bridges the gap between structuralist arguments and intentional, or rationalist, ones. It moves away from considering the state itself as an actor, as having preferences or interests. Instead, it focuses on individuals whose behavior is shaped by their desire to succeed in political roles and whose capacity to influence other individuals depends on control of state resources. This focus on the interests of political leaders seems completely compatible with observations of autonomous state or government actions. Moreover, I would argue, it explains the *process* through which states sometimes behave autonomously.[13]

12. Calculated from information in Ames (1987, 12). This figure would be even higher if Costa Rica, which has no army, and Mexico, which has experienced no military intervention since 1945, had been excluded.

13. Consequently, I see no point in lumping the statist perspective with other chal-

STATE CAPACITY TO INITIATE CHANGE

Up to this point, discussion has focused on state actors as decision makers, but the implementation of decisions is equally important. Although extensively covered in descriptive and prescriptive literature on economic development, state capacity to translate preferences into actions has received surprisingly little attention in the explicitly statist literature, perhaps because of its roots in Marxist and international relations theory, both of which tend to draw on European experience. To observers of less developed countries, however, it is clear that the articulation of independent state preferences, difficult as that may be to achieve, cannot by itself accomplish anything. Preferences matter very little if officials cannot carry out the policies they choose. The capacity to implement state-initiated policies depends on the ability to tax, coerce, shape the incentives facing private actors, and make effective bureaucratic decisions during the course of implementation. All of these abilities depend in turn on the existence of effective bureaucratic organizations. If one wants to understand states as actors, one needs to look at their bureaucratic innards.

Although several authors have noted the importance of competent bureaucratic organizations (Stepan 1978; Haggard and Kaufman 1989; Haggard 1990), little attention has been paid to the politics of achieving such competence. Bureaucratic competence seems, at least at first glance, to be a universally desirable goal. Yet such reforms have been notoriously difficult to carry out, and effective bureaucratic organizations remain rare in the developing world. Work in the statist tradition offers no suggestion for why a trait so obviously useful when governments intervene extensively in the economy has so often failed to develop. The approach taken in this study, in contrast, leads to the identification of the political conditions that cause bureaucratic capacity to develop and flourish, on the one hand, or stagnate, on the other. One of the central arguments of this study is that the development of bureaucratic competence depends on whether it serves the immediate career interests of the politicians who initiate reforms and choose appointment strategies.

---

lenges to the rationalist approach under the rubric of "the new institutionalism" (March and Olsen 1984).

THE STRUGGLE OVER REFORMS
TO INCREASE STATE CAPACITY

Historically, perception of the need for state capacity developed in tandem with perception of the need for state intervention in the economy. Between the end of World War II and the middle 1980s, governments advocating state-sponsored social and economic change achieved power at one time or another in most developing countries.[14] These governments came to power committed to moving their societies in new directions, armed with plans and programs for doing so, and supported by substantial segments of society. Many of these programs—for example, road building, irrigation projects, the creation of development banks— had nearly universal support. And, although opposition from threatened interests blocked some policies, in most cases the opposition lacked the power to prevent the proposed programs from being initiated. Moreover, although the military eventually ousted some of these governments, few faced serious hostility to their policies from the military at the beginning of their terms. In most instances, militaries supported extensive state intervention to foster development. Thus, the lackluster performance of these change-oriented governments cannot be attributed solely to implacable hostility from dominant groups or the military. Nevertheless, many of the sweeping programs proposed by these leaders never bore the expected fruit.

If opposition from powerful societal and military interests did not prevent the full implementation of most programs, what did? Observation suggests the following reasons: lack of experience, competence, and expertise among personnel charged with carrying out projects; the diversion of needed funds to other uses; and the subversion of reform goals by politicians and bureaucrats uncommitted—for whatever reason—to their achievement.[15] Taken together, these impediments add up to a lack of state capacity to accomplish the tasks involved in state-led change.

Several excellent studies have described the development of state

14. In the middle 1980s, this long secular trend toward more state intervention reversed, and governments in many parts of the developing world, under pressure from changes in the international economy and from international agencies, began advocating less state involvement.

15. No argument is made here that all or even most of these programs and policies were well-conceived by current economic standards or that they would have contributed to long-run economic performance. Rather, the claim is that implementation was often so flawed in the short run that they showed few results at all.

capacity, conceived as expertise in government and the emergence of
consensus among political leaders regarding needed changes (Hirschman 1973; Moran 1974; Tugwell 1975; Fishlow 1980). In these studies,
progress in dealing with public dilemmas takes roughly the following
trajectory: identification of a problem (ideological and technical elements both contribute to identification); early failures because of inadequate understanding, lack of political consensus, and insufficient technical capacity; and renewed efforts, which are at least incrementally
more successful than the initial effort because knowledge has increased,
technical capacity to deal with the problem has improved, and political
capacity, in the sense of the formation of a broader coalition favoring
reform, has developed. Despite their considerable usefulness, however,
these studies do not provide general explanations of when reforms aimed
at enhancing state capacity will occur. In addition, although they realize
that state capacity to implement decisions is crucial, analysts in this
tradition have neglected elements of the argument that would explain
bureaucratic or administrative capacity as distinct from technical expertise.[16] The focus on expertise creates a deceptive sense that lack of
knowledge or know-how is the main impediment to effective state-led
change.

These studies leave the impression that increasing competence and
persuading political leaders that the national interest does indeed lie in
a particular direction will be sufficient to solve problems. And yet many
problems with apparently known solutions remain unsolved. Looking
at issues on which less progress has been made, or even at the same
cases examined by these authors over longer periods of time, brings into
focus the *political interests* that oppose and impede change—including
changes that presidents, legislators, and popular majorities all claim to
want.

Much of the literature has treated the development of expertise and
the creation of more effective government instruments for managing the
economy as primarily technical problems—a matter of setting up schools
to teach skills and figuring out which devices work. But an examination
of the history of such innovations shows that political constraints, rather
than lack of resources or knowledge, have often hindered the development of these apparently neutral capacities. These political constraints,

16. A partial exception, Stepan (1978, 238–39) lists a set of state capacities as
variables that will help explain outcomes in struggles between multinationals and host
country governments, but he makes little attempt to explain them. The same can be said
of Cleaves and Pease García (1983).

as argued throughout this book, are intelligible in light of the political costs and benefits of potential innovations to the politicians who must initiate them.

Those who may impede widely supported reforms include many whose motives are not at first obvious. A look at the nationalization of Chilean copper mines illustrates this point. By the time the mines were nationalized, support for such a move had become overwhelming in Chile. Not a single vote was cast against it in the Chilean legislature (Moran 1974, 147). Most Chileans saw nationalization as an assertion of national sovereignty and also expected it to contribute to Chilean economic success. Theodore Moran (1974) traces the development of the expertise that gave Chileans the capacity to bargain effectively with the transnationals and to run the mines after nationalization. As he demonstrates, political consensus on taking over the mines existed. So did the technical capacity to run them. Nevertheless, in spite of available expertise, the Chilean government led by Salvador Allende mismanaged the mines after nationalization (Valenzuela 1978, 55).[17]

For Allende, the need to consolidate political support in the short run overwhelmed the need for adequate economic performance. In consequence, he allocated managerships in the newly nationalized mines and industries on the basis of a quota system in which the parties that made up his coalition were rewarded in proportion to the number of votes they had received in the most recent election (Valenzuela 1978, 64–65; Castillo 1974). No mechanism existed to ensure that these managers were competent or to prevent Allende from turning posts vital to the Chilean economy into political plums. The performance of the copper mines was critical to the success of Allende's economic program and thus to the viability of his government. And yet the benefits of exchanging managerships for political support exceeded the costs in the very short run. Allende and his coalition partners themselves thus contributed to Chile's disastrous decline in economic performance.

The choice of managers for Chile's nationalized mines and industries is a particularly consequential instance of what I call the politician's dilemma. One can analyze it from the point of view of either the governing coalition or the president. To members of the coalition, the choice of managers was a collective action problem. No party in the coalition

17. No claim is made here that bad management was the only cause of the fall in productivity in the copper mines during Allende's tenure. U.S. refusal to supply spare parts and the atmosphere of revolutionary euphoria that undercut work discipline were at least as important.

wanted to sacrifice the political advantage of having its own managers (and attendant appointment powers), but if all managers were to be chosen for political reasons, the firms would be mismanaged. Mismanagement would increase the probability that the whole coalition would fall, and all members of the coalition would risk losing everything.

Even though all members of the coalition would have been better off if they had all given up some of their political advantage in order to achieve their larger collective goal of remaining in power, in the volatile atmosphere of the early 1970s in Chile, they were unable to do so. Coalition members could not arrive at enforceable agreements that each could trust to prevent others from taking advantage of current political sacrifices in the next election.

From the president's point of view, the choice lay between using the appointment resource as a political or an economic investment. The state would pay the same salary, but the individual who received it, depending on his or her competence and loyalties, might make a greater contribution toward economic performance or toward consolidating political support for the president.[18] The president's survival depended on both economic performance and political support. No one had more to lose than Allende himself from the additional economic strain that would be caused by mismanagement, and yet, with his survival in office immediately threatened, he could not afford to disregard short-term political considerations by choosing managers on the basis of technocratic expertise. The president as well as his coalition partners faced a wrenching conflict between their own need for immediate political survival and longer-run collective interests in economic performance and regime stability. This is the politician's dilemma writ large. And this dilemma, as is shown below, creates many of the obstacles to improving state capacity.

Rather than stressing this political dilemma, most attempts to explain why one government is more capable than another emphasize, as noted above, technical and resource requirements: the availability of funds, which depends on the domestic resource base, tax laws and procedures for enforcing them, and access to foreign capital; the existence of instruments and institutions, such as national development banks, through which the government can manipulate the incentives facing key private

---

18. This is not a mutually exclusive choice. Some party loyalists also have expert credentials. Parties differ, however, in the extent to which they attract supporters with technical and managerial expertise and experience. The parties in the coalition that supported Allende could call on relatively few such supporters.

actors; consensus among leaders regarding goals; and the skill and expertise of officials.

Although these characteristics may be necessary to state capacity, they are not in themselves sufficient. The advice of experts may be ignored, and, as the Chilean case shows, skilled personnel may come up against insurmountable political obstacles to doing the jobs for which they have been trained. In spite of laws and enforcement procedures, taxes may not be collected or, if collected, may be dissipated in patronage or find their way into Swiss banks rather than being spent to pursue national goals. Development banks may award subsidized loans to political supporters rather than to entrepreneurs willing to invest in targeted sectors of the economy. Political leaders may genuinely support some shared set of national goals but still find that the exigencies of political survival cause them to behave in ways that undermine these goals.

To understand these common situations, one needs to examine the incentives facing the individuals who make decisions about whose advice to take, what projects to fund, to whom to give loans, and so on. Where decision makers can best assure their own personal security and advancement by using funds efficiently to implement programs or by hiring experts and following their advice, they will do so. Where they can best further their own interests by exchanging the resources under their control for political support or by simply appropriating them, they will do this. The incentives that face officials depend on the norms, available career rewards, and methods of enforcing the behavior deemed appropriate that have evolved in the offices, professions, institutions, and parties to which they belong. Later chapters consider how such norms, rewards, and methods of enforcement—in other words, incentives—might be changed in ways that would result in greater state capacity.

PLAN OF THE BOOK

Most experts and many political leaders see administrative reform as a key method of increasing state capacity. Chapter 2 reinterprets the struggle over administrative reform as a collective action problem. It discusses solutions to collective action problems that various analysts have proposed and finds that popular movements supporting bureaucratic reform are unlikely to arise spontaneously, even though evidence suggests that most citizens in Latin American countries believe they would benefit from such reforms. It then considers the role of political entrepreneurs in providing collective goods[19] such as administrative reform. It concludes that principal-agent problems[20] prevent the provision of public goods from becoming routinized even in democracies, and that bureaucratic reforms are especially unlikely to be provided because of their cost to politicians themselves. This discussion of potential political entrepreneurs sets the stage for later chapters that focus on the particular circumstances that lead democratic politicians to provide bureaucratic reform as a public good.

Chapter 3 is a case study of the struggle to improve bureaucratic competence and honesty in Brazil between 1930 and 1964. The purpose of this case study is to give the reader a detailed and concrete case with which to compare theoretical arguments. Levels of competence, efficiency, and honesty have varied widely within the Brazilian bureaucracy, but some sectors at some times have been as capable as virtually any in the world. The relatively high level of Brazilian bureaucratic performance, especially in some of the agencies that deal with the economy, developed during a decades-long struggle between those seeking reforms and those whose short-run interests would be hurt by them. During some regimes and administrations, bureaucratic reforms made rapid progress; during others, previous reforms were either rolled back or informally disregarded.

The case study of Brazil shows the persistence of political interests opposed to bureaucratic reform and their links with the democratic political system. It then discusses the creation of an insulated segment of the bureaucracy as a functional substitute for politically infeasible universalistic reforms. This insulated segment of the bureaucracy was responsible for the policies leading to Brazil's most impressive economic gains prior to 1964. The analysis follows the vicissitudes of those parts of the bureaucracy charged with economic development tasks and demonstrates the relationship between insulation from day-to-day partisan political concerns and performance.

Theoretically, this chapter makes a contribution toward understanding and redefining state autonomy. It suggests that the type of autonomy

19. See chapter 2, pp. 27–28, for a detailed discussion of the meaning of collective or public goods.

20. "Principal-agent" or "agency" problems occur when individuals delegated to carry out some task for someone else who pays their salary, or elects them, have interests at variance with those of their employer (or the voters who elected them) that lead them at times to neglect or distort work on the task. See chapter 2, pp. 39–41, and chapter 3, pp. 47–49, for more detailed discussions of the meaning and implications of these terms.

state policymakers need in order to implement policies effectively may not be autonomy from class-based pressures, but rather autonomy from the tide of particularistic demands that has risen as an unintended consequence of certain kinds of representative institutions.

Chapter 4 develops a game theoretic model to explain the failure of the Brazilian legislature to initiate reforms. This model demonstrates that when patronage is distributed unevenly among the larger parties in the legislature—as it is most of the time in Latin American countries— majority party legislators will vote for reforms only under extraordinary circumstances. Consequently, reforms very rarely occur.

If patronage were distributed evenly among the larger parties, however, reforms should occur much more easily. Brazil never experienced equality among the larger parties, and no universal reforms passed the legislature. Thus the model seems consistent with Brazilian evidence, but no general test of the model is possible using only evidence from Brazil.

Chapter 5 turns to the issue of testing the model more generally. It tests the game theoretic model on the South American countries that have experienced substantial periods of democracy since 1930. Case studies of the initiation of reforms in Latin American democracies show that the conclusions of chapter 4 hold in the real world: reforms occur when the larger parties in a political system are approximately equal and thus control approximately equal amounts of patronage. Chapter 5 then goes on to draw several additional conclusions about the effects of different kinds of electoral rules—which shape party systems—on the likelihood of reforms.

Reforms may also be initiated by presidents, who have several reasons for wanting to increase the competence of their administrative machinery. In considering whether to initiate reforms, however, presidents must consider the preferences of other political actors as well as their own; they must behave strategically. Chapter 6 extends the analysis to explain why presidents pursue different appointment strategies. On the basis of an examination of all the larger South American countries, it argues that presidents have reasons to favor appointment strategies that contribute to the growth of state capacity, but are often prevented from following the strategy they would prefer because of more immediate political needs. When military intervention threatens presidents' immediate survival in office—as it did, for example, Salvador Allende's—they must spend all their patronage resources on survival and cannot afford a longer-term investment in building competence.

When presidents are more secure from military intervention, their strategy for improving bureaucratic capacity will depend on their relationship with other members of their parties or coalitions. Although presidents do not face immediate reelection and might, in consequence, refrain from rewarding supporters (whom they will not need in the immediate future), other members of their parties do need supporters. They can be expected to demand that the president distribute the usual spoils to the party faithful as the price of their support for his or her programs in the legislature and bureaucracy.

Presidents who face little competition from rivals within their parties and who can count on disciplined behavior from legislative members of their parties and coalition allies can generally afford to use some of their appointment resources to hire experts and build competent agencies. Presidents who lack the weapon of party discipline, however, and who have had to make deals with and promises to rivals within their parties in order to secure nomination, may have to exchange most of their appointment resources for the support of political allies that they need in order to govern effectively. In brief, strong and secure presidents are more likely to pursue appointment strategies that contribute to the development of bureaucratic competence.

Chapter 7 then turns to a consideration of some of the implications of the arguments made in earlier chapters. It considers, first of all, which particular democratic institutions are most likely to structure the incentives of legislators and presidents in ways that lead them to contribute to building state capacity.

It then turns to one of the murkier areas of research in the study of developing countries: the relationship between authoritarianism and economic performance. It suggests that authoritarianism tempts elites committed above all else to economic development in part because of the disincentives embedded in electoral politics to carrying out capacity-enhancing reforms. Once in power, however, authoritarian leaders face their own problem of how to create incentives conducive to rapid development which, though different from that experienced in democratic settings, is equally intractable. Consequently, authoritarian governments are as likely as democratic to fail in their efforts to foster rapid growth (Remmer 1990 and 1993; Geddes 1993).

Authoritarian governments do often initiate measures that concentrate technocrats in key administrative agencies and insulate them from outside pressures. Their attempts to build state capacity, however, often fail to survive the transitions to democracy that follow authoritarian rule.

Frequent alternations between authoritarianism and democracy seem to provide the worst of all possible contexts for building state capacity. Competence tends to suffer during transitions both to and from military rule. Islands of competence nurtured for decades can be destroyed during a few months by presidents engaged in chaotic struggles to defend themselves against overthrow. At the other end of the cycle, redemocratization brings in its wake hungry parties eager for the spoils they have been denied during the years of military rule.

TWO

Reform as a Collective Good

*Political Entrepreneurs
and Democratic Politics*

Collectives act almost exclusively by accepting leadership—
this is the dominant mechanism of practically any collective
action. . . .
     . . . [S]o far as there are genuine group-wise volitions at
all—for instance the will of the unemployed to receive
unemployment benefit . . . [they] do not as a rule assert
themselves directly. Even if strong and definite they remain
latent, often for decades, until they are called to life by some
political leader. . . . This he does . . . by organizing these
volitions, by working them up and by including eventually
appropriate items in his competitive offering.
                              —*Schumpeter,* Capitalism,
                              Socialism and Democracy

Because of the central role Third World governments play in their economies, competent bureaucracies are widely believed to contribute to
economic development, as well as to the effective delivery of essential
government services. Yet, corruption, inefficiency, and incompetence
remain widespread in the bureaucracies of most Third World countries.
This is true even in democracies, where it might be expected that a
public interest in reform would ultimately lead politicians to enact reforms. This chapter explains why democratic governments have often
failed to respond to this public interest.

THE LATENT INTEREST IN REFORM

In much of Latin America, the need for bureaucratic reform in order to
increase the effectiveness of developmental strategies came to be per-

ceived as more and more urgent as state intervention in economies increased, especially after World War II. Technical experts claimed that government investments would not produce desired effects unless the individuals making and carrying out policies were better trained;[1] presidents regularly proposed administrative reforms as elements of their development strategies; party leaders espoused support for reform; the press railed against corruption and incompetence in the bureaucracy, and campaigned for reform;[2] and ordinary people expressed a desire for more competent and honest government—when given the chance—in their answers to survey questions.

Patronage and corruption were believed to be the cause of much of the incompetence, inefficiency, and unfairness associated with government bureaucracy. Many believed that the incompetence and inefficiency of bureaucrats slowed economic growth and that bribery and favoritism contributed to unfairness in the distribution of the benefits and burdens of development. Personalism in recruitment was also seen as blocking channels of upward mobility for deserving people who lacked personal and political connections. For these reasons, appeals for honesty, rectitude, and fairness in public life found a wide resonance in some parts of populations.

Where it exists, survey evidence reveals high levels of popular concern about corruption and dishonesty. When asked whether "the only really important problem in Brazil is the problem of lack of character and honesty," only 15 percent of those who had an opinion disagreed.[3] When asked what was the most important reason for their party preference, 44 percent mentioned honesty first, more than twice as many as mentioned party program or past record.[4] When asked, "Which one of these do you think our country needs most?" 62 percent answered, "an honest

---

1. For example, Emmerich (1972), IBRD (1961, 14–15), Currie (1966). For discussions of the influence of foreign experts in Brazil, see Siegel (1966) and Graham (1968).

2. For discussions of public statements by politicians and press coverage in Chile, see, for example, Urzúa Valenzuela and García Barzelatto (1971), López Pintor (1972, 103–4); in Venezuela, Brewer-Carías (1975a, 345–521), Petkoff (1978); in Colombia, González G. (1980), Groves (1974, 316–20); in Brazil, Jaguaribe (1956), Wahrlich (1957, 240, 247), Siegel (1966), Graham (1968); and in Uruguay, Taylor (1960, 103, 178–79, 222).

3. Question from a survey conducted by Júlio Barbosa et al., "Political Behavior and Attitudes in a Brazilian City, 1965–66," made available by the Inter-University Consortium for Political and Social Research (ICPSR 7613), University of Michigan, $N = 645$. This question was asked in agree-disagree format, so acquiescence may have inflated somewhat the proportion who agreed.

4. This question is also from the Barbosa survey.

government without corruption," nearly four times the number who chose the next most popular alternative, "a government that gets things done."[5]

Bureaucratic competence had also become a public issue in Argentina. Based on surveys she conducted in the 1960s, Jeane Kirkpatrick (1971, 184) finds the level of consensus over the need to "end corruption and inefficiency in government" higher than for any other issue except the need to reduce unemployment.[6] In an earlier survey, when Argentines were asked, "Do you believe that today in this country one can get or cover up anything if one has money or influence?" 93 percent answered yes and only 1.7 percent answered no. When asked to make a choice between the two options, "Let them [political leaders] steal and get things done" or "Don't let them steal and not get things done," 54 percent preferred an end to corruption even if it reduced efficacy, while 36 percent thought it better to "let them steal."[7]

Survey evidence thus indicates the existence of a widespread latent interest in administrative reform. Most people believed they would benefit from reforms that improved the quality of state intervention in the economy and the quality of government services to the public.

Nevertheless, during democratic periods, when widespread political participation should have made it possible to make effective demands for an end to corruption, governments in Latin American countries rarely passed reform laws. Quite the contrary. The preferences that actually found expression in law strongly opposed administrative reform.

IMPEDIMENTS TO REFORM

Some individuals who occupy official positions, have political connections, or have the money to pay bribes derive benefits from corrupt and inefficient bureaucracies. Traditionally in Latin America, the friends, relatives, and political allies of politicians and officials have found in bureaucratic jobs "an excellent refuge from which to make a last-ditch stand for their right to a quiet, incompetent existence" (Hirschman 1958, 154). These individuals benefit from the bureaucratic status quo and naturally oppose changes.

5. Question from a survey conducted by the United States Information Agency in March 1964, "World Survey II: Attitudes Toward Domestic and Foreign Affairs" (ICPSR 7048), $N = 466$.

6. Survey conducted October–December 1965, $N = 2014$.

7. Questions from a survey conducted by José Miguens, "Voting Attitudes—Argentina," 1963 (ICPSR 7038), $N = 1383$.

The group that would have to bear the costs of reform includes the administrators and politicians who under traditional arrangements have the power to decide who will be hired to fill government posts. These officials have the choice of hiring the people who will contribute most to the officials' personal welfare (usually members of their own families); hiring the people who will contribute most to consolidating political support for themselves or their parties; or hiring the people who will contribute most to administrative effectiveness (probably the most technically qualified applicants). For the administrator or politician involved, choosing the applicant most likely to contribute to improving the administration often involves a certain and immediate loss of either personal or political benefits. They are therefore unlikely to favor reform unless other benefits—to be considered below—outweigh these costs.

Most people in developing countries, however, have no hope of either securing or being able to dispense government jobs or other largesse. They would benefit from an increase in the honesty and competence of the officials making policy decisions. But the achievement of bureaucratic reform entails difficulties, not only because certain interests oppose it, but also because, for the majority who would reap the benefits of reform, it is a public good.

The defining feature of a public good is that, once the good becomes available, no member of the relevant group can be easily excluded from enjoying it.[8] The benefits of bureaucratic reform are largely public in the sense that virtually everyone in society would benefit from a more honest and competent administration. Reforms are costly to some, just as installing anti-smog devices is costly to factory owners, but the effects of reform, like cleaner air, benefit all.

Since individuals cannot be excluded from enjoying public goods such as bureaucratic reform, whether or not they helped organize movements to achieve them, ordinary citizens have no incentive to take the risks and expend the resources needed to organize. Efforts to achieve reforms thus entail collective action problems in that most members of a given society would be better off if all cooperated to bring them about, but cooperation would require sacrifices which it would not be rational for individuals to make.

8. Some definitions of public goods include jointness of supply (consumption of the good by one user does not affect its availability to others). The definition used here is less restrictive but sufficient for the logic of collective action to hold. It is the inability to exclude that creates the possibility of free riding and thus the collective action problem. See Taylor (1987, 6), Barry and Hardin (1982, 181–5), and Head (1982, 186–94) for discussions of the various meanings of public goods and citations to additional literature.

In addition, the cost to individuals of cooperating is certain and must be borne in the present; benefits are uncertain and will accrue in the future. As a result, individuals attempt to free ride, that is, to share the benefit without contributing to its achievement, and consequently organizations to demand reform tend not to form.

Those who would be hurt by reform face no similar impediments to organizing to press their interests. The costs of reform are private and must be borne disproportionately by a set of individuals who are already well-organized in parties and unions. Changes in recruitment and promotion that would convert a personalistic, patronage-based system into a merit-based system threaten existing employees and reduce the patronage resources controlled by political activists. Consequently, civil servants' unions, politicians, and party activists have often opposed such changes.

Because so many of the policy changes that contribute to reforming the state involve collective action problems, in most instances[9] we cannot expect to see them brought about by spontaneous mass action or, as is shown below, by the automatic representation of interests in democratic governments.

THE POSSIBILITY THAT COOPERATION MIGHT EVOLVE

So far, I have implicitly treated administrative reform as a one-shot prisoner's dilemma.[10] If this were an accurate description, one could predict that reform would never occur. In reality, of course, a struggle that goes on for many years is analogous to an iterated game with no known end point.

The outcome of open-ended, iterated prisoner's dilemma games is not logically determined, and therefore analysts have argued that under many circumstances cooperation to achieve benefits for all will evolve

9. Occasionally a small privileged group may exist who can benefit so much from the provision of a public good that they will be willing to bear the cost of supplying the good for everyone. On privileged groups, see Olson (1965, 48–50).

10. Hardin (1982, especially pp. 16–30) shows that collective action problems are prisoner's dilemma games. Taylor and Ward (1982) note that some collective action problems involving lumpy public goods such as bureaucratic reform can be modeled as *assurance games* or *chicken games* rather than *prisoner's dilemma games*, but their argument does not apply to the situations discussed here. In chicken games, mutual defection is worse than the sucker's payoff; such is clearly not the case here, since an individual would be worse off if he or she expended resources trying to bring about a reform that failed because few others contributed than if he or she were one of the many who refrained from contributing. In assurance games, mutual cooperation brings more benefits than free riding; again, this is clearly not the case in this instance.

spontaneously among interacting individuals.[11] In a very influential argument, for example, Robert Axelrod (1984, 73–87) notes that soldiers opposing each other across the trenches during World War I often developed live-and-let-live conventions; they did not shoot at enemy soldiers walking around within rifle range between battles, despite officers' efforts. This strategy produced a marginal improvement in the quality of life for soldiers on both sides. If cooperation can evolve in such a hostile environment, it seems that it should also evolve in many other situations. Members of latent interest groups, such as the one favoring administrative reform, might then be expected to organize over time to make demands on political leaders, and long-term cooperative relationships could be expected to develop between responsive political leaders and members of the group. In this way, spontaneous cooperation could bring about reform. I turn now to a consideration of whether such cooperation can be expected to emerge in the real world circumstances of developing countries.

THE EFFECTS OF UNCERTAINTY ON
THE PROBABILITY OF COOPERATION

Expected payoffs, that is, the benefits people expect to receive as a result of their actions, depend on their assessments of how *likely* particular outcomes are, as well as how much they expect to benefit from particular outcomes if they occur. Real world games thus differ from those with fixed, known payoffs, such as the ones used in many experiments (e.g., Rapoport and Chammah 1965) and Axelrod's simulations. Individuals in developing countries have reason to feel especially uncertain about the likelihood of actually receiving future benefits. Based on past experiences, they may have good reason to expect the distribution of benefits to be arbitrary, unpredictable, or unfair. The government that wields the enhanced state instruments can be expected to change within a short span of time, and there is no guarantee that future governments will

11. Open-ended iterated games among individuals who can recognize one another and remember past behavior differ from single games in that the repetitions provide players with the opportunity to develop strategies that compensate for the inability to make binding agreements. These strategies depend on the ability to reward each other in subsequent games for cooperating in earlier ones, and to assess the probability, based on past behavior, that the other will cooperate in the future. Since the payoff for mutual cooperation is higher than the payoff for mutual defection, the possibility of rewarding or punishing past behavior in future plays may make it rational to try to establish reciprocal cooperation. Hardin (1982, 155–230) refers to the spontaneous emergence of cooperation as "contracts by convention."

honor commitments made by the present government. Consequently, gains expected to accrue in the future are heavily discounted.

In Third World settings, the discount on future gains may also be augmented by uncertainty about the future more generally. Cooperative strategies are unlikely to arise when the future seems very unpredictable, as it does in many Third World countries. Uncertainty reduces the expected payoff for cooperation relative to the payoffs associated with other choices and thus reduces the incentive to cooperate.

Uncertainty will affect the expected gain from many selective incentives, as well as the individual's expectation of gain from the collective good itself. And, since uncertainty lowers the ratio of benefit to cost, it will also decrease the probability that what Mancur Olson (1965) calls a privileged group will find it rational to provide the good for the whole group. In short, although cooperative strategies have been shown to be rational in some circumstances for iterated prisoner's dilemma games, cooperative solutions to the collective action problems associated with administrative reform in developing countries seem unlikely to emerge spontaneously since they involve large numbers of people and high levels of uncertainty about the probability of actually receiving promised benefits.

COOPERATION WITHIN SMALL GROUPS AS AN IMPEDIMENT TO WIDER COOPERATION

Though cooperation may have difficulty emerging in large latent interest groups for the reasons discussed above, it can emerge in smaller groups in which frequent interaction and the development of norms of reciprocity reduce uncertainty. As is shown below, however, cooperation within such small groups is as likely to hinder as to advance the achievement of collective goods such as administrative competence that would benefit the entire group.

Axelrod (1984) shows that cooperative strategies based on reciprocity[12] can be rational for clusters of individuals, even if most of their interactions are with outsiders who do not cooperate, and that cooperative strategies, once established within a group, can defend themselves against individuals using exploitative strategies. These findings seem to offer hope that cooperative solutions to collective action problems will develop spontaneously as cooperation spreads from the cooperating clus-

12. Axelrod defines cooperative strategies based on reciprocity as strategies that never defect first but that respond to the other's defection with immediate defection to punish the other's attempt at exploitation, followed by "forgiveness" to induce further cooperation.

ter to the larger society. Axelrod's optimistic conclusions gain plausibility from the existence of cooperating clusters based on reciprocity—in the form of clientele networks, informal groups for the exchange of labor, conventions of reciprocity within extended families or villages, and so on—in all human societies. But an examination of the interaction between small cooperating groups and larger latent groups shows that cooperative strategies that have evolved within small groups may just as easily impede the achievement of collective goods as contribute toward achieving them.

Individuals in an extended family, neighborhood, village, agency, or party may learn to cooperate so as to maximize the long-term advantages for the group rather than their own short-term individual advantages.[13] When cooperative strategies emerge within groups small and permanent enough to prevent free riding, they can be expected to persist and to prosper. Members of clusters of reciprocal cooperators do better than individuals who are not members of such clusters. Politicians enmeshed in patron-client relationships, for example, are usually more electorally successful than those who are not, and their clients are better off than similar individuals who have no patron.[14]

Limits on human ability to remember past transactions, however, restrict the size of groups within which conventions of reciprocity can develop. The group must either be small enough so that individuals can recognize all other members and remember past transactions, or members of the group must be identifiable by some easily recognized characteristic (for example, belonging to the same village or political clique), and mechanisms for enforcing norms of reciprocity within the group must have developed to the point where any member encountering any other can assume with reasonable certainty that he or she will cooperate.

As time goes on, even in simulations, reciprocal strategies become dual strategies. That is, individuals cooperate with the other cooperators

13. Cf. Hardin (1982, 155–87) on contracts by convention. It is important to bear in mind that the emergence of a particular cooperative strategy does not imply that it is the only, or the best, such strategy. "Indeed, that one convention has arisen means that numerous others have not. Hence, it may be that of a set of possible conventions—all preferable to no convention, but some of them preferable to others—a less beneficial one will arise, blocking a more beneficial one" (Hardin 1982, 190).

14. Reciprocal cooperators do not by any means do better in every encounter, but in simulations involving many encounters with many other players, their total scores are higher than those following less cooperative strategies (Axelrod 1984, 50–69). This is so because, on the one hand, they achieve high scores when interacting with other cooperators and, on the other, reciprocity limits the amount they can be exploited by the uncooperative. As long as reciprocal cooperators have at least some of their interactions with other cooperators (members of the cluster), cooperative strategies remain rational.

in their cluster, and they refuse to cooperate in all but the first interaction with outsiders. In the real world, recognition that another individual is, or is not, a member of the cooperating cluster—family, tribe, village— substitutes for the extensive mental bookkeeping that would be required to remember the outcome of one's last interaction with each other individual. Instead of cooperating in the first interaction with any new acquaintance and then remembering what he or she did in order to reciprocate next time, individuals follow a simple rule of thumb: cooperate with members of the cluster and refuse to cooperate when dealing with outsiders. This shortcut solidifies the dual strategy, making it quite unlikely that cooperation within a cluster will spread.

Not only do norms of cooperation that have evolved within small groups usually fail to spread to the larger society, but the small groups often hinder the achievement of public goods that would benefit larger groups or society as a whole.

Benefits such as praise and esteem and costs such as malicious gossip and ostracism can enforce norms of cooperation within small groups and thus substitute for the need to remember each transaction in order to reciprocate appropriately. Such psychic incentives and more tangible group sanctions alter individual payoffs in ways that make cooperation rational within the small group even in single games (Hardin 1982, 191–205).

In consequence, group norms may persist long after the environment has changed and altered objective payoffs in ways that make the cooperative strategy that evolved earlier far less objectively successful. Group membership may so shape the incentives facing members that any deviation, including cooperation in some larger, more impersonal group to achieve collective goods, becomes extremely painful.

The most politically relevant cooperating clusters in developing countries are political clientele networks. Typically such clientele networks include politicians, their supporters of high and low degree, and bureaucrats. The supporters staff the political machines that keep the politicians in office. In return, they receive benefits in the form of legislation and, often more important, the politician's help in obtaining services and favors from the bureaucracy.[15] Bureaucrats provide the services requested because they owe their jobs to politicians. The benefits

---

15. Cf. Fiorina and Noll (1978) for a similar image of the relationship between supporters and legislators.

of cooperating in clientele networks thus depend on access to state resources.

Where the state intervenes heavily in the economy, as it has in virtually all developing countries, many of the benefits that cement cooperation within clientele networks are products of state intervention. State intervention creates gaps between supply and demand and, consequently, opportunities for officials to profit from their role in allocating scarce goods. These profits, along with resources such as jobs and contracts drawn directly from the state itself, are the goods that make cooperation within clientele networks rational for supporters. Once such a mutually beneficial arrangement has developed, members of the cooperating cluster can be expected to oppose any reforms that would reduce the supply of benefits available, even if they recognize that the reforms would improve economic performance for the nation as a whole.

If, for example, a government has previously sought to reduce balance of payments deficits by placing quantitative restrictions on certain imports, it has reduced the supply of these imported goods. Assuming that demand does not change, the price of the goods that do enter the country rises, and increased profit opportunities are created for those few lucky enough to be allowed to import the goods. Licenses to import restricted goods thus become very valuable. Potential importers will be willing to pay large sums to acquire them (Krueger 1980).

In some settings, only members of the same clientele group as the official in charge of allocating licenses will have any opportunity to buy them. In other settings, potential importers might be able to buy their way into a network by offering sufficiently large payments for licenses. In either case, the profit from the sale of the license will be distributed in some fashion between the individual official and the official's bureaucratic superiors, political patrons, and party coffers, with the amounts that end up being used for electoral purposes as opposed to consumption by officials depending primarily on the extent of party discipline and the seasonal press of electoral needs. Whatever the final distribution of profits, all those who benefit from it—favored importers, bureaucrats, politicians, and lower level party activists who depend on such contributions to grease the wheels of political machines—will have reason to oppose lifting quantitative restrictions on imports, even if they understand fully the welfare losses quantitative restrictions cause relative to other means of equilibrating the trade balance.

A change in the method of dealing with balance of payment deficits would be a public good if it resulted in greater economic efficiency, but the many who would benefit from the change tend to be unorganized and thus would have to bear the costs of organizing to express their interest, while the few who benefit from the status quo can easily express their interests through the politically powerful members of the clientele network. When the political-economic system is honeycombed by such policy-created profit opportunities and the political clientele networks that have evolved to take advantage of them, policy changes that would provide benefits to larger but less organized groups become politically difficult. In this way, the existence of cooperating clusters may impede the development of cooperation within larger latent interest groups to achieve collective goods. For societies facing the collective action problems associated with bureaucratic reform, the persistence of cooperative strategies that have evolved informally within small permanent groups can be a major obstacle to the emergence of cooperative strategies in the larger context.

Each individual in the real world faces a large number of analytically distinguishable "games," each with different sets of incentives. Some of these games involve repeated plays within a small group; others involve large groups. The choice of a particular alternative or strategy in one game often removes or changes the costs of alternatives from the feasible set in other games (Tsebelis 1990).

Analyses of collective action problems usually rest implicitly on a comparison between what individuals can gain by acting anomically and what they can gain by cooperating within a collectivity specified by the analyst. In the real world, however, anomie is rare; collective action problems frequently involve not inducing people to cooperate per se, but inducing them to cooperate in a new and risky game at the expense of an old and predictable one.

It is for this reason that solutions to large-scale collective action problems frequently involve insulating those whose behavior is crucial to achieving collective goals from primordial groups and clientele networks. Within these small groups, conventions of cooperation have evolved that are antithetical to the achievement of large-scale collective aims. And the costs members of such small groups can impose on each other are often sufficient to prevent individual members from abandoning the small group in order to cooperate in a larger, more impersonal one.[16]

In short, cooperative solutions to collective action problems involving very large numbers of people cannot be expected to evolve incrementally. To the extent that cooperative strategies do evolve in smaller groups, they may be more likely to impede than to help achieving collective goods for the larger group. Consequently, the kind of mass movement that would more or less force politicians to respond to constituents' wishes cannot be expected to develop spontaneously.

So far, this chapter has depicted the struggle for administrative reform as a collective action problem in which the pursuit of individual interests would result in suboptimal provision of the reforms that would be expected to contribute to enhanced state capacity to intervene in the economy and to provide government services. It has been argued that the pursuit of individual interests can impede the achievement of goals that would, if achieved, improve the quality of life for most of the people who currently stand in the way of reaching them.

There are two parts to this argument. First, for most ordinary people in developing countries, achieving increased administrative competence and honesty is a collective action problem. Consequently, their interest in reform remains latent; it does not spontaneously develop into politically compelling demands.

Second, the disincentives to spontaneous innovations in collective action are even more formidable than most rational choice literature suggests. New cooperative solutions compete not with what individuals can achieve through their own unaided efforts, but rather with what they achieve by cooperating in small, informal clusters. In order to cooperate to achieve a collective good for some large, impersonal group, individuals must often forgo the benefits produced by cooperation in small, informal networks. And, in addition, they must bear the costs their past allies will impose on them as punishment for desertion.

How then do such changes come about? More generally, given the logic of collective action, how can the provision of public goods be explained?

16. See Price (1975) for a discussion of the costs to bureaucrats of ignoring their responsibilities to family and village members.

POLITICAL ENTREPRENEURS

Welfare economists expect states to provide public goods. The crucial link between welfare economists' notion that the state should provide public goods and political scientists' questions about which public goods will in fact be provided is the political entrepreneur. Political entrepreneurs are individuals who, because of their connection with a government or some other organization, such as a party or union, can further their own individual interests by "selling" public goods to some group of individuals in exchange for their support.

Political entrepreneurs supply public goods in the expectation that they individually will receive some reward for doing so (Salisbury 1969; Frohlich, Oppenheimer, and Young 1971). The kind of public goods that can profitably be "sold" depends on institutional arrangements as well as the distribution of political influence in society. Thus, legislators, whose career interests depend on the vote, will supply collective goods to those groups that electoral laws allow to reward them with votes and that are large enough to affect electoral outcomes, but not to others. They may, for example, vote for minimum wage laws in the expectation of gaining support from working-class beneficiaries of the law.

Legislators in some developing countries have shown much more reluctance, however, to vote for land reform, even though it could potentially result in the grateful support of an even larger number of citizens. Their reluctance can be accounted for in part by electoral laws, especially literacy requirements and procedures to undermine the secret ballot, that reduce the importance of the peasant vote (Lapp 1993). The failure to pass land reforms is often attributed to the overrepresentation of landlords in the legislature, but this is just another symptom of the systematic underrepresentation of peasant interests caused by electoral laws. Once suffrage is extended and political mobilization in the countryside legalized, land reforms pass quickly (as, for example, in Chile during the Frei and Allende administrations, after many years of frustration, or Venezuela under the Acción Democrática government).

Incentives also determine the behavior of political leaders in nondemocratic settings. Revolutionary leaders ideologically committed to collectivization often distribute individual plots of land in the expectation that ownership will induce peasants to help defend territory controlled by the revolutionary movement. Once the revolution has succeeded, however, and active peasant support is no longer needed to fight opposing armies, these same leaders carry out collectivization despite peasants' marked lack of enthusiasm for it. The political survival of party cadres after the revolution depends on implementation of directives from central party leadership, whereas during the phase of revolutionary struggle it depends on attracting peasant support (Jowitt 1975). Consequently, party cadres will supply public goods such as land reform[17] to followers when their own success depends on followers' support, but follow the directives of leaders—in opposition to followers' interests—when their careers depend on doing this.

As is apparent in the examples above, the individual interests of potential political entrepreneurs are shaped by the institutions in which they are embedded. Legislators' interests center on reelection; their strategies for pursuing reelection will depend on the party system and electoral laws that affect them. The career success of party cadres in stable Leninist systems depended on their success in implementing goals set by top leaders. Whether potential entrepreneurs will actually find it in their interest to supply particular public goods or not thus depends on the political context within which they act.

In contrast to the discussion above, in which both the motivation of the potential political entrepreneur and the resources for providing a public good come from an organization outside the latent interest group, most solutions to collective action problems proposed by scholars fall into one of two broad categories. The first category depends on one or more members of the latent interest group having individual reasons to pay the cost of securing the public good. This can occur because a privileged group exists, because selective incentives induce members to cooperate who would not find it rational to do so otherwise (Olson 1965), or because particular features of the public good make the effort to acquire it an assurance or chicken game rather than a prisoner's dilemma (Taylor 1987, 34–59).

The second category depends on changes in assumptions about the preferences of members of the group. Frohlich, Oppenheimer, and Young (1971) contend, for example, that individuals will cooperate if they are assured that others will, which implies a change in utility functions such that individuals no longer prefer to free ride but only want to be protected from others who might do so. Alternatively, if one assumes that

---

17. A land reform law or decree that affects all members of a target group of beneficiaries regardless of political allegiance is a public good for the target group. In practice, it is often easy to use loyalty criteria to exclude potential beneficiaries, in which case land reform ceases to be a public good. At the implementation stage, land reforms are often transformed into private goods to be exchanged for support both by governing democratic parties (a charge often leveled at Acción Democrática) and by revolutionary movements.

individuals have both self-regarding and group-regarding elements in their utility functions (Margolis 1982), it will be rational for individuals to contribute to the achievement of public goods if they expect their contribution to make a difference in the probability of successfully attaining them. These changes in assumptions about preferences obviously change the nature of the game, and thus eliminate the collective action problem.

In all these arguments, the solution to collective action problems arises from within the latent interest group (that is, the group that would benefit from the public good). The role of political entrepreneurs is to provide selective incentives or monitoring to prevent free riding within the latent group. If the solution requires government action, such action occurs in response to strong pressure from the group.

In contrast to other arguments about the role of political entrepreneurs, the one posed here emphasizes that collective action problems often owe their solutions to individuals who do not share the interests of members of the latent group. Instead, their membership in some outside organization (for example, party or legislature) makes it rational for them to supply public goods to others, whether or not the others have organized or expressed any demand for the particular public good. Just as a private entrepreneur may profitably sell a new product for which no prior demand existed, a political entrepreneur may profit from providing a public good for which the public has expressed no demand.

POLITICAL ENTREPRENEURS IN DEMOCRATIC POLITICS

It might seem that in democracies with universal suffrage, free competition among parties, and the secret ballot, political entrepreneurship would become routinized and the supply of public goods unproblematic. After all, the standard expectation about the outcome of competitive elections if voters are rational and politicians maximize the vote is that outcomes will reflect the policy preferences of the median voter in the constituency of the median legislator (Downs 1957; Black 1958; Buchanan and Tullock 1962). Less precisely, policies are expected to reflect the preferences of average citizens.

Challenges to the median voter result arise from three directions of relevance for this study. The first involves institutional variation. The arguments leading to the expectation of policies reflecting median voter interests were developed to explain political behavior in political situations that offer voters a choice between two options. They therefore seem to offer a plausible stylized description of outcomes in two-party systems such as the United States. When, however, more than two parties contest elections and/or districts elect multiple candidates, as occurs in most Latin American legislative elections, concern with winning will not necessarily lead candidates to cluster at the median. Instead, they can often do better by moving away from the median, that is, by failing to reflect the median constituent's desires (Cox 1990). These results lead to the expectation that public (as well as private) goods will be provided for target groups that do not include the median voter. Recent formal literature, in other words, leads to the expectation that legislative outcomes in countries with institutional structures like those in Latin America might well diverge from the outcomes desired by most voters.

Second, even in two-party systems, Morris Fiorina and Roger Noll (1978) show that, given a system of taxation in which individuals' taxes do not reflect the value they place on government services, and a dual role for legislators as (1) policymakers and (2) mediators between bureaucracy and constituents in need of service, legislators will not necessarily reflect median voter interests. Instead, they will supply more constituency services than would be optimal from a social welfare point of view and fewer or smaller amounts of public goods. This conclusion has special salience for Latin America, where the legislator's role as mediator between bureaucracy and constituents in need of service is especially important.

A third challenge to standard expectations arises from consideration of the principal-agent problem between political leaders and citizens. All theories that link politicians' behavior to constituents' interests assume constituents have sufficient information to choose the candidate who will best serve their interests or, at the very least, to punish by withholding votes in the next election those who have failed to serve their interests. But many citizens, especially in developing countries where levels of education are low and few read newspapers, have almost no ability to monitor the policy-relevant activities of politicians.

Their only indicators of whether politicians are carrying out promised policies are the availability of particular benefits and the overall performance of the economy. These indicators are seriously flawed, since politicians can often provide particular benefits without carrying out the general policies preferred and because overall economic performance reflects many factors over which politicians have no control.

In short, citizens do not have the necessary information to judge whether politicians are carrying out their promises and therefore cannot make credible threats to punish at the next election those who do not. This information asymmetry has the expected effect of reducing the citizenry's ability to select the candidates most likely to provide—as opposed to simply promising—the public policies they prefer. Citizens' limited ability to monitor permits politicians considerable autonomy when it comes to deciding which policies to support (cf. Kalt and Zupan 1984, 1990).

Principal-agent problems are caused by an interaction between information asymmetries and conflict of interest between principal and agent (Moe 1984). In theory, democracy eliminates the conflict of interest between principal and agent. The best way for politicians to pursue their own interest in political survival should be to give constituents the policies they want. In practice, however, politicians face multiple constituencies and therefore cannot be expected to represent completely the interests of any one. Of special salience for the issue of bureaucratic reform is what Harold Demsetz (1990) calls the internal constituency, that is, party activists, to distinguish it from the external constituency made up of voters. These two constituencies differ from each other with regard to both interests and resources.

Party activists may have policy preferences different from those of the average voter. But, for the purpose of the argument being made here, it is the resources needed to pay party workers for their efforts that are important. Because citizens cannot adequately monitor politicians' policy performance, electoral machines become essential to the successful mobilization of the vote. They distribute the individual benefits and favors that affect many people's electoral decisions (cf. Shepsle and Weingast 1981; Cain, Ferejohn, and Fiorina 1987). Individual benefits include things like coupons that entitle pregnant women to free milk or school children to free lunches, and help getting pensions, loans, and many other government services to which the client has a legal claim but no access without political help.

To reach large numbers of voters with individual benefits, politicians need extensive political machines staffed by party activists and workers. Politicians' ability to deliver individual benefits depends on the extent to which members of their parties occupy positions in the bureaucracy, the importance of partisan loyalty in bureaucratic recruitment and promotion, and the size of the state bureaucracy.

In order to maintain their electoral machines, politicians need to be able to "pay" their local party leaders, ward heelers, precinct workers, and campaign contributors with jobs, contracts, licenses, and other favors. What kinds of payments are common or even possible depends on political traditions, legal constraints, and the amount of state intervention in the economy, among other things. Where state intervention has customarily been high, politicians depend heavily on the distribution of state largesse to cement party loyalties.

Because of the need to "pay" party workers, politicians may fail to reflect voters' interests even if politicians themselves and party activists have no independent policy preferences at all and care only about reelection. They may have good reason to spend the resources they control in the distribution of individual benefits to important supporters rather than the pursuit of public goods to benefit external constituents. Because of the difficulty of assessing day-to-day policy implementation as compared with the ease of determining whether one has received particular benefits, and because particular benefits go mainly to party activists and contributors who influence other people's votes, politicians' interest in reelection gives them an interest in responding to the demands of this limited clientele even when it means undermining the goals of the aggregate principal, the citizenry.

In other words, although a democratic political system should ideally provide politicians with good reasons for supplying public goods desired by citizens whose votes they need to stay in office, in reality the combination of the information asymmetry and the influence asymmetry between members of internal and external constituencies gives politicians an incentive to respond to the particular interests of some politically useful citizens rather than to the general interests of the public as a whole.

CIRCUMSTANCES IN WHICH REFORMS OCCUR

In short, democracy cannot be expected to routinize the provision of public goods, especially not those necessary to build bureaucratic competence and hence state capacity. Instead, the achievement of these goods will depend on the specific incentives that face political leaders in different political systems. From these, one can predict when particular kinds of public goods will be enacted and when they will fail. Administrative competence is an especially costly form of collective good to most politicians because, as detailed above, politicians in unreformed systems rely on access to state resources to build their support organizations, and administrative reform threatens such access. Effective reforms establish merit as the criterion for employment, price competition as the criterion for awarding contracts, and impersonal rules for determining who receives government benefits—thus depriving politicians of important resources.

Politicians who might otherwise consider offering reforms as a strategy for attracting support will not be able to afford the cost in lost political resources as long as they compete with others able to use such resources in the struggle for votes. This is the politician's dilemma. A politician might in some circumstances, however, be willing to give up this resource if everyone else were also willing. Succeeding chapters explore the circumstances in which this might happen.

THREE

Insulation and the Struggle for Reform in Brazil, 1930–1964

There is nothing more difficult to carry out, nor more
doubtful of success, nor more dangerous to handle, than to
initiate a new order of things. For the reformer has enemies
in all those who profit by the old order, and only lukewarm
defenders in all those who would profit by the new.
— *Machiavelli,* The Prince

Chapter 2 made a series of general arguments about the obstacles that impede bureaucratic reform and other collective goods in developing countries. This chapter follows the course of reform efforts over several decades within one developing country, Brazil. Events in the Brazilian case, as will become apparent, are consistent with expectations generated by arguments in chapter 2. Despite substantial popular support for increasing the honesty and competence of the government bureaucracy, no movement to support reform developed. Moreover, potential political entrepreneurs failed to mobilize the latent interest in reform.

The purpose of this chapter is to give the reader a feel for the actors, issues, and interests involved in the struggle over reform; to provide, in other words, some of the concrete historical details that will add flesh and plausibility to later, more abstract arguments. The concrete case study allows an examination of how specific historical circumstances affected the incentives that confronted potential political entrepreneurs and thus shaped their behavior.

In Brazil between 1930 and 1964, elected presidents faced crosscutting incentives: they needed more competent administration in order to carry out campaign promises, but they also needed to reward supporters. Most reacted to these conflicting needs with a compartmentalization strategy that aimed to improve performance in a small, economically crucial sector of the bureaucracy, while using the rest of the appointments at their disposal in the traditional exchange of jobs for support.[1] During the authoritarian interlude from 1937 to 1945, in contrast, the president did not need to consider the electoral needs of party allies and so could give greater emphasis to reform. At the other extreme, when a democratic president faced imminent military intervention, he had to use all his appointment resources in the effort to shore up support. Throughout the period, most legislators in the Brazilian multiparty system found reform too politically costly to support.

BRAZILIAN BUREAUCRACY IN 1930

Consciousness of a need to reform the bureaucracy in order to increase the government's ability to intervene effectively in the economy began to spread rapidly among educated Brazilians in about 1930. By then, state capacity in Brazil had fallen to a low point. The federal bureaucracy, which under the monarchy had been considered quite effective, had deteriorated badly during the republican period when national office was passed to and fro between regional political machines. The previous forty or so years of federalism had left the central government poor and enfeebled. It did not control the powerful state militias, and observers were not at all certain that the national army could defeat them in battle if called upon to do so. The government had only a limited capacity to tax, and had been borrowing abroad for some time to cover the resulting shortfall. The Depression reduced state capacity still further, since taxes on trade were the main source of revenue, and trade plummeted during the Depression.

Getúlio Vargas, who seized power in 1930, undertook many reforms aimed at increasing state capacity. His centralization of the political system and experiments with corporatist institutions have been treated at length elsewhere (e.g., Skidmore 1976; Schwartzman 1975). This chapter focuses on the struggle to increase an aspect of state capacity that has received less attention, namely, bureaucratic competence.

In 1930 virtually everyone who had any experience with the Brazilian bureaucracy viewed it as incompetent. The government was, for example, unable to determine how much money it owed to foreign lenders

1. Several of the central ideas in this chapter, including the idea of a compartmentalization strategy, initially emerged in conversations with my colleague during graduate school, Edson Nunes. I am deeply grateful to Edson for sharing his observations and insight with me.

because officials could not find copies of more than half of the loan agreements that had been signed.[2] The purchase of supplies for the government was handled through friends, relatives, and cronies, as was recruitment to bureaucratic jobs. In fact, in 1935, after five years of trying to systematize buying supplies and impose price as the criterion for choosing suppliers, the Vargas government had succeeded in routinizing the purchase of office supplies, primarily paper and printed forms for government use, but nothing else (Siegel 1966, 37–40).

The bureaucracy's main function was not the provision of public service but the provision of private services. It provided jobs and profit opportunities for individuals with the right political contacts, and it defended the only well-organized special interest that existed at the time, the coffee growers. It was basically a distributor of largesse to the politically well-connected. As Hélio Jaguaribe (1958, 22–23) observed: "Public employment does not in reality aim at rendering any public service, but rather at subsidizing clienteles . . . in exchange for electoral support. [As a result, the public administration] is converted into a pyramid of positions where innocuous papers are circulated and where the only activity carried out is tax collection to provide sustenance for bureaucrats." Bureaucrats at the time had no way of protecting themselves from demands for favors that would now be considered illegitimate or corrupt, and possessed, in fact, no set of values or ideology on the basis of which to define the claims of friends and family members as illegitimate.

Some key parts of the Brazilian bureaucracy have improved dramatically since the 1930s. This chapter focuses on the series of slow and faltering steps taken toward improving bureaucratic performance in the years between Vargas's initial accession to power and the military coup in 1964. The chapter describes the struggle to increase the honesty, competence, and efficiency of the state agencies charged with fostering economic development in Brazil.

INSULATION AND BUREAUCRATIC PERFORMANCE

In every developing country tensions exist between the development and other programmatic goals selected by citizens through their votes for particular candidates and parties, and pressures that would, if acceded

---

2. Getúlio Vargas, "A reorganização financeira dos Estados e Municípios e o esquema das dívidas externas," speech delivered August 15, 1934, reprinted in Vargas (1938, 266).

to, dissipate the human and material resources needed to attain those goals. State-led development, like any other form of development, implies fundamental changes in the distribution of resources, and the agents of such change inevitably meet resistance from those who benefit in various ways from the status quo. In order to perform their task effectively, government bureaucrats acting as the agents of change, even if competent and committed, require some form of *insulation* from the pressures they face.[3] In the early stages of the process, bureaucratic agencies are often too weak to provide their own insulation. They need to be shielded from claims on their resources made by powerful individuals or groups in society.

A bureaucratic agency may be thought of as a machine that uses human and material inputs to accomplish tasks. The machine's ability to get things done can be undermined in three ways. Its material inputs can be inadequate, that is, it can lack funds. Its human inputs can be inadequate, that is, it can lack sufficient expertise. Or, finally, its human inputs, having free will, can opt to pursue their own personal goals to the detriment of the agency's.

In any political system, whether democratic or authoritarian, pressures exist to divert inputs needed by bureaucratic agencies and thus to undermine state capacity. Political leaders, under unremitting pressure to maintain political support, face a constant temptation to exchange jobs in the bureaucracy and funds needed by agencies for support. Political leaders can also reap political benefits from their control of bureaucratic decisions. They can, for example, exchange contracts and subsidies for support from politically powerful individuals and groups. They thus have an incentive to persuade bureaucrats to use agency resources to pursue goals other than those officially approved.

Because temptations to expend resources in the quest for political support exist, the insulation of bureaucratic agencies from the exchange relationships that pervade the political arena contributes to maintaining adequate inputs in all three problematic areas: human resources, material resources, and resource allocation.

The competence of bureaucratic personnel depends on two factors: the availability of trained people in the society from which to recruit and a recruitment process that selects among potential employees on the basis of merit rather than partisan or personal loyalty. Political

---

3. The initial insight from which this section has developed comes from Kenneth Jowitt (especially 1971, 7–69).

activists accustomed to distributing jobs in return for political support and employees who got their jobs that way, and whose status is threatened by the change to a merit-based system, can prevent the upgrading of human inputs even where an adequate pool of competence and expertise exists, as it does in the larger countries of Latin America. Insulating the agency from that traditional exchange of favors for political support may be necessary in order to improve the quality of agency personnel.

The adequacy of the material resources available to bureaucrats for carrying out their tasks may depend on the insulation of the funding process. One of the problems agencies face is that funds originally earmarked for their use tend to disappear. Members of Congress may use funds for pet projects from which they derive electoral benefits, or officials in the finance ministry may informally reallocate funds to serve more pressing political needs. The separation of the funding process from the traditional political game may be necessary in order to prevent funds allocated for development projects from being used for other purposes.

Insulation of agencies from political exchange relationships also contributes to creating appropriate incentives for agency personnel. Bureaucrats control resources in the form of decisions about who gets projects, licenses, cheap credit and other subsidies, special exceptions, and government contracts, which can be turned into political currency. If bureaucrats form part of the political exchange network, their own success will be linked to that of particular politicians, and, as a result, they will have compelling reasons to make decisions that maximize support for their patrons rather than furthering agency goals.

This situation could be thought of as a type of principal-agent problem, with the citizenry as principal and politicians and bureaucrats as agents. The citizenry, through its choice of a president, chooses a set of policies. Implementing these policies requires that politicians agree to devote adequate material and human resources to their accomplishment and that bureaucrats use these resources in ways that contribute to accomplishing policy goals. Two potential agency problems thus exist: that between citizens and politicians and that between politicians and bureaucrats.

The principal-agent problem between citizens and politicians is discussed in chapter 2. The agency problem between politicians and bureaucrats is somewhat similar. Politicians often cannot really tell whether bureaucrats are efficiently and diligently pursuing policy goals. They

can, however, tell whether they are distributing the private benefits that
politicians request for their clients because clients will report dissatis-
faction. In other words, they can monitor performance of one kind
much better than they can another. Politicians can therefore sanction
poor performance in one area but not the other, which leads bureaucrats—who need to retain the favor of politicians—to devote attention
to performing the services upon which they will be judged.

Conflicts of interest also exist between politicians and bureaucrats,
but they may actually be less important in developing countries than in
more advanced ones because the lack of institutionalization of bureaucratic agencies and the incomplete coverage of civil service reduces job
security and gives politicians more influence over the incentives facing
bureaucrats. As in other settings, bureaucrats may prefer leisure to work
and may wish to use their positions to help family members and friends.
Bribes may induce in them a preference for helping other individuals.
But where jobs depend on political favor, bureaucrats concerned about
career success must also respond to politicians' wishes. Some shirking
and some informal distribution of government resources always occurs.
How much, though, depends on their costs and benefits to bureaucrats,
many of which are determined by political patrons.

In Third World settings where new bureaucratic agencies are constantly being created and old agencies marginalized and starved of resources, and in which high-level bureaucrats often migrate rapidly from
agency to agency (Schneider 1991), agency-specific resources such as
"slack" play a lesser role in motivating bureaucrats than in more institutionalized settings. Instead, the goals of ambitious bureaucrats center
on personal career success and building a loyal entourage that migrates
with them. They will try to build their personal reputations for depend-
ability, loyalty, and getting done the things that are easy to assess—that
is, specific projects and the distribution of favors. They will expend less
energy building the bureaucratic entities that temporarily house them.
They will not be able to count as much on the political and legal support
of their agencies in struggles against the whims of politicians as bureaucrats in more institutionalized settings can. All in all, bureaucrats in
developing countries will tend to be more vulnerable to costs and benefits imposed by politicians since they often lack institutional protection.

The inability of most bureaucrats to resist politicians' desires means
that if an agency problem exists between citizens and politicians, an
agency problem will exist between citizens and bureaucrats. Even if
bureaucrats want to implement public policies supported by the citi-

zenry, they may find it costly to do so if politicians reward other behavior. Citizens on their own have almost no way to reward or punish bureaucrats.

Procedures such as meritocratic recruitment and promotion rules that insulate bureaucrats from some of the pressures otherwise brought to bear on them can reduce agency problems between the aggregate citizenry and their political and bureaucratic agents. By reducing bureaucrats' incentives to comply with the requests of individual politicians, such reforms permit bureaucrats to be more responsive to the aggregate policy choices of the citizenry.

Thus insulation, as used here, does not imply a lack of responsiveness either to popular demands expressed through the democratic process or to interest groups. On the contrary, the argument here is that bureaucrats need protection from politicians' efforts to transform state resources into particularistic benefits for supporters *in order to respond* effectively to popular demands.

Insulation can result in greater responsiveness because it changes the costs and benefits of different activities to bureaucrats. It reduces the benefits available for permitting the partisan allocation of agency resources, and increases the career benefits to be gained from pursuing agency goals set by popular demand via the election of a president who advocated a particular set of policies during the campaign. If institutions develop that insulate bureaucrats from political exchange, their incentives change, sometimes radically. Their orientation turns inward toward the agency, its goals, and the values of colleagues and superiors within the agency. And, most critically, the route to personal advancement becomes the successful performance of the formal functions of the agency. Agencies composed of officials intent on personal advancement through the achievement of agency goals conduce, in the aggregate, toward greater state capacity.

This is not to say that insulation solves all bureaucratic problems or leads to optimal performance. Bureaucracies will still have reasons to inflate their budgets and tolerate inefficiency. Agency heads will still find it in their interest to accumulate slack resources. The fluidity of bureaucratic structure and the career paths of high-level bureaucrats, as noted above however, mitigate these impulses somewhat. Turnover among top bureaucrats is rapid in most agencies in Latin America. Bureaucrats cannot take slack or the budget allocation with them when they move to new agencies, so these resources are less useful to them for building their own careers than they would be if careers were built largely within single agencies. The fluidity characteristic of most Latin American bureaucracies limits some of the pathologies associated with government bureaucracy in the U.S., but at the same time reduces the ability of agencies to insulate themselves from partisan distributive pressures.

Insulation does not mean that government bureaucrats must be surrounded by stone walls and moats. Rather, an insulated agency is like a cell surrounded by its semipermeable membrane. Information and resources flow through the membrane from the environment into the agency and vice versa, but the agency, like the cell, is able to maintain its organizational integrity and stick to its own goals. It can enter into coalitions and cooperative relationships, but it is able to limit the capacity of outside actors to define its tasks or to "capture" it. It is not that no one does favors for friends in insulated agencies, but only that the favors are not so pervasive that the formal functions of the agency cease to be performed. In short, insulated agencies interact with their environments, but they are not overwhelmed by them.

Insulation, as discussed here, bears some resemblance to what J. D. Thompson (1967) calls "buffering." Buffering is an organization's attempt to manage the supply of human and material inputs necessary to its technical task so that they will be available in the quantities required. Thompson sees buffering as a way of dealing with scarcity or uncertain supply. Insulation, in contrast, is a way of preventing the tasks of an organization from being subverted.

The two concepts imply alternative ways of understanding and dealing with the scarcity of inputs. An organization that cannot function without highly trained personnel, for example, may seek to buffer itself by setting up a training program. Alternatively, the organization might insulate itself by establishing rules to prevent untrained personnel from being appointed. In this example, buffering and insulation would have the same aim: each would try to ensure that personnel were adequately trained. The difference between them lies in what is perceived to be the cause of the tendency toward hiring untrained personnel. The notion of buffering assumes that the problem is technical—a shortage of training—and can be solved technically. The notion of insulation assumes that the problem is political—a conflict over whether the resources of the agency should be used to hire individuals capable of pursuing agency goals or individuals who can help consolidate political support. Thus the solution must also be political.

Insulation is especially needed during the early stages of agency life. Once the central cadre of an organization has developed within which the rewards to individuals depend on performance in accordance with professional criteria, this cadre will seek control over the resources on which the organization depends. These resources include hiring, budget allocations, and the incentives facing other personnel, all of which influence whether the agency can perform adequately. Over time, an agency ideology and sense of mission tend to develop among personnel, as do informal boundaries between themselves and the environment that insulate them from pressures the agency deems inappropriate. But, given the pervasiveness of particularistic and partisan pressures and the impermanence of high-level agency personnel in developing countries, the attempts of agencies to insulate themselves can be overwhelmed. Agencies therefore need shielding from the outside during the time it takes to build up their own internal resources and capacities.

The history of the evolution of insulated agencies in the Brazilian bureaucracy illustrates the argument above. Since 1930, Brazilian presidents committed to the achievement of rapid economic progress through state intervention, and supported in their commitment by most of the citizenry, have perceived administrative reform as a necessary concomitant to furthering their goals. Between 1930 and 1964, they supported a succession of efforts to create effective bureaucratic entities in Brazil. Several of the efforts were successful in the short run. During periods of effectiveness, key agencies were insulated from partisan pressures. Procedures to secure agency resources did not become institutionalized, however, and ultimately their insulation deteriorated as a result of opposition from more traditional political actors who found the reforms politically costly. The rest of this chapter describes these efforts.

THE FIRST INNOVATION STRATEGY: CIVIL SERVICE REFORM

In response to the disasters of the Depression, President Vargas and his supporters urged state action to speed economic development and make Brazil's economy less vulnerable to such external shocks. But, at the same time that developmentalist ideas were becoming widespread, it was also becoming apparent that the federal bureaucracy would be incapable of carrying out plans for modernizing the country. It simply lacked the necessary competence.

Vargas set up commissions to study the problem and suggest reforms. Since reformers considered the lack of expertise and the absence of efficiency values among personnel to be the principal shortcomings of the bureaucracy, they suggested various proposals for meritocratic entrance and promotion requirements (e.g., Vieira 1938, 9–12). Each of these proposals advocated reducing, but not eliminating, the role of patronage in recruitment and promotion. Everyone agreed that total elimination of patronage would be impossible. Each attempted reform, however, was blocked by the Finance Ministry and/or Congress. Politicians were accustomed to using bureaucratic jobs as a political resource, and a majority of them could not be persuaded to give up a significant part of that resource (Siegel 1966, 40–55).

This impasse lasted as long as the government remained quasi-democratic and political competitors remained able to defend their political resources. In 1937, however, Vargas dissolved the legislature and set up a corporatist authoritarian regime, the Estado Novo (New State). Among many other administrative reforms, he established the Departamento Administrativo de Serviço Público (DASP, Administrative Department of Public Service), an administrative agency in charge of the civil service.[4] Its purpose was to upgrade and systematize a sector of the public bureaucracy and to oversee the purchase of materiel for government use. When no longer forced to consider the interests of other political actors, Vargas could pursue his own interest in a more effective administrative machine.

The unsuccessful reform attempts between 1930 and 1937 had convinced administrative reformers that more stringent methods were needed. Reform laws and decrees promulgated without enforcement mechanisms had proved ineffective. Avoidance of responsibility, corruption, and inefficiency had continued to be endemic in the bureaucracy, in spite of regulations designed to eliminate them. As Urbano Berquó (1938, 7) stated:

> Those who remain opposed [to civil service reform], either because they suppose that their ambitions will be thwarted, or because they perceive in this reform a threat to the self-indulgence that goes with positions obtained through means other than merit, have lost no opportunity for carrying out a stealthy and tenacious defeatist campaign against the [new] system.

People with "intelligence [and] good intentions alone were not enough to transform a bureaucracy, which existed mainly for the purpose of providing jobs, into an instrument of the modern state" (Siegel 1966, 76). Reformers realized that institutional changes would be required to

---

4. Established July 30, 1938, by Decree-Law 579.

turn their intentions into reality, since bureaucrats had demonstrated a resistance to internalizing efficiency values.

Hence, the DASP was set up as a superministry, accountable directly to the president, with branches in the other ministries to ensure their compliance. The first priority of the DASP was upgrading personnel. The "revolution" of 1930 that brought Vargas to power had not changed the perception of public employment as a sinecure. Only the clientele to be rewarded had changed. Reacting to this environment, the reformers established rigid controls over placement, transfer, promotion, leave, and disciplinary measures. The DASP either okayed or subsequently audited every single government personnel action. The regulations were "enforced so thoroughly and painstakingly that it became a nightmare for many in administration" (Wahrlich 1955, 11).

The most important concrete reform carried out by the DASP was the introduction of entrance exams for the civil service.[5] The DASP broadly classified civil servants into three categories: permanent functionaries; interim appointees, whose tenure was supposedly limited to one year; and "extranumeraries," lower status public employees only partially covered by the provisions of civil service law. Entrance exams were required only of permanent functionaries, that is, about a quarter of all public employees. Even the most zealous reformers realized that merit could not be made the only criterion for gaining public employment. Like other political leaders, Vargas needed to use some appointments to pay political debts and attract support. Reformers made an attempt, however, to turn the permanent functionary category into an elite civil service, limiting mobility between it and lower status categories and granting permanent functionaries higher salaries and more security than were granted to other public employees.

The DASP succeeded in its efforts to upgrade bureaucratic performance, whereas earlier efforts had failed. With the legislature closed, the usual incentives to exchange bureaucratic resources for political support operated within a much smaller circle of politicians. Vargas and his allies certainly exchanged favors for support, but Vargas clearly perceived his own need for an effective administrative apparatus and, as a result, reserved sufficient resources for the DASP.

The DASP faced considerable resistance from the rest of the bureaucracy but had the support of Vargas to ensure its survival. In terms of

5. The law authorizing entrance exams, Law 284, was passed in October 1936 but did not begin to be effectively implemented until the DASP was created.

the argument posed above, Vargas and the authoritarian institutions of the Estado Novo insulated the DASP from efforts to divert its resources or subvert its purposes. Vargas, in other words, created an effective agent in the DASP by insulating it from the pressures that would otherwise have created a conflict of interest between employees of the DASP and himself.

Protected as it was, the DASP was able to upgrade its human resources and develop the subcultural norms and incentives, in the form of promotions and status within the organization, that would serve to keep the personal goals of employees consistent with the pursuit of agency goals. It attracted a cadre of competent and committed people to leadership positions. Its staff was relatively well trained and had an enormous esprit de corps and sense of purpose. One of its most important functions was training new recruits. In addition to technical training, it emphasized socialization to norms of efficiency and public service. It accomplished quite a remarkable assembling and training of elite personnel who combined competence with commitment to efficient and honest public administration. Its lasting contribution was the people it trained, who have been drawn upon ever since by both the public and the private sector in Brazil (Siegel 1966, 77–78).

The DASP became Vargas's most important administrative agent because it was more efficient than the rest of the bureaucracy. It was given more and more functions, including, eventually, responsibility for drawing up the budget, much to the annoyance of the Ministry of Finance. The DASP functioned at the state level as well as the federal. *Daspinhos*, "little DASPs," were set up to oversee the operations of state administrative bureaucracies (Graham 1968, 27–28).

The DASP made enemies inside and outside the bureaucracy, at both the federal and local level. It was a threat to traditional status and perquisites within the bureaucracy. It was also an effective instrument of an authoritarian government and thus generated opposition on ideological as well as instrumental grounds.

The antipathy of much of the traditional political elite to the DASP has been attributed to its authoritarian work style and its rigid attachment to rules and procedures, both very much at odds with Brazilian behavioral norms and political culture. A more consultative work style, however, would have resulted in the agency's being penetrated by the very forces whose influence it sought to overcome. Beatriz Wahrlich (1964, 33–34), one of the early reformers, maintains that the DASP's authoritarian methods were perfectly understandable and even justifiable given the state of affairs it proposed to change. It is difficult to make the transition from a system of nepotism to a system of merit smoothly. . . . [T]he DASP's objective was a radical change in attitudes toward public functions. [In the pre-existing system] the group in power considered itself entitled to the right to distribute public posts on the basis of political debts and obligations to friends and family.

While Vargas held office, he protected the DASP from its bureaucratic enemies, and the authoritarian system eliminated many potential threats from other politicians. But if the DASP was fairly well insulated, its insulation depended on the support of a single individual rather than on laws and institutionalized procedures. It ended abruptly when Vargas was ousted. The DASP was one of the first casualties of the return to democracy in 1945.

José Linhares, the interim president between Vargas's fall and new elections, stripped the DASP of many of its functions and reduced its status.[6] Those functions of the DASP that had most irritated traditional bureaucrats were eliminated. These included control over departmental personnel decisions, research functions dealing with control of personnel, and auditing public buildings (Siegel 1963, 27). Civil service exams were canceled. Instead, positions were filled by interim appointments, which included several hundred of Linhares's friends and relatives. Much of the DASP leadership resigned in protest (Siegel 1963, 6).

Although the DASP continued to exist and occasionally played a role in succeeding administrations, it could no longer initiate major reforms. Its leadership cadre dispersed. Civil service appointments were, to a considerable extent, returned to the realm of patronage via the device of extranumerary and interim appointments rather than "regular" appointments by exam.

Furthermore, Congress, which reconvened in 1946, passed a series of laws that tended to blur the distinction between the elite functionary category and the rest of the civil service. The 1946 constitution (written by the legislature sitting as a constituent assembly) conferred functionary status on all extranumerary appointees with five or more years of seniority and tenure on interim appointees with five years' seniority. Law 488 of November 1948 equalized the pay of functionaries and extranumeraries. Law 522-A of December 1948 gave tenure to interim appointees (Láfer 1970, 100; Graham 1968, 140–43). In passing these

6. The DASP's status and functions were reduced by Decree-Law 8323-A of December 7, 1945. Decree 20489, January 24, 1946, implemented the new law in detail.

laws, Congress showed its sensitivity to traditional patronage concerns as well as its responsiveness to the demands of organized civil servants for improved benefits.

In addition to lowering the general level of competence in the public bureaucracy,[7] the increase in patronage appointments also created a larger and larger number of people with government jobs, a very strong union, and disproportionate access to legislators. This group expressed vehement opposition to civil service reform because it threatened their jobs. The larger and more vocal this group became, the harder legislators found it to ignore their demands. During the 1950s and early 1960s, numerous proposals for reform came before the legislature. The press and the public expressed support for reform. Nevertheless, with one exception to be discussed below, all major reforms failed to pass.

Legislators customarily used jobs in the bureaucracy as one of the principal ways of rewarding the political activists who formed the cogs and wheels of their political machines. Moreover, they needed to have loyalists in many bureaucratic agencies in order to deliver constituency services to supporters. Reforms that would have reduced legislators' appointment prerogatives and cut them off from special bureaucratic help for constituents would have shut down the power source of traditional political machines. Reforms, in other words, would have cost legislators political resources and, not surprisingly, they refused to vote for them.

During the democratic period, presidents as well as legislators succumbed to some extent to the pressure for public jobs. Although they were constitutionally prohibited from seeking immediate reelection and hence did not need to exchange jobs for support in the upcoming election, they needed to build their political machines in preparation for becoming candidates again after a term out of office. In addition, to maintain the support of coalition partners and achieve passage of their programs in the legislature, presidents often had to respond to their supporters' need for patronage to distribute. The first elected president, Eurico Dutra (1946–51), filled vacancies with interim and extranumerary appointments rather than hiring through exams.

Vargas, during his second administration (1951–54), continued his

7. Based on data supplied by ninety-six heads of departments in charge of 55,072 public employees, Astério Dardeau Vieira (1967) concluded that those who had attained their positions as a result of competitive exams performed their jobs better than those who had not.

commitment to state-led developmentalism. As part of the effort to implement developmentalist programs, he instituted a number of reforms aimed at rebuilding the elite civil service on the basis of competence. But he also continued to use extranumerary and interim appointments to reward supporters. During his administration, entrance exams were held again, and the DASP resumed auditing appointments, which entailed dismissing some employees deemed to have been inappropriately hired and requiring others to prove their qualifications by taking an exam. These decisions affected some five thousand public employees.

At the same time that he worked to rebuild the elite core of the civil service, however, Vargas continued making patronage appointments in the extranumerary category.[8] Vargas tried to insulate a segment of the bureaucracy from patronage because he recognized his own interest in a competent administrative apparatus, but he continued to use the rest of the bureaucracy in the traditional manner as a reservoir of favors to be distributed.

João Café Filho, who succeeded to the presidency after Vargas's suicide, belonged to the Partido Social Progressista (PSP, Social Progressive Party) and had achieved the vice presidential slot through a preelection deal between Vargas and the populist leader of his own party, Adhemar de Barros. He had no hope of achieving the presidency again, and he was, in consequence, largely unmoved by pressures to distribute jobs. He published an open letter to job seekers at the beginning of his administration informing them that the government would be unable to provide any more jobs since it was incapable of paying any more salaries. He also publicly supported admission to the civil service through competitive examinations. He remained in office only a short time, however, and had little long-term effect on public administration.

The next president, Juscelino Kubitschek, came to power promising fifty years' progress in five. More than any other president until that time, he led the drive for industrialization. This commitment to state-led development gave him a strong interest in increasing the competence of state personnel. At the same time, however, Kubitschek faced intense patronage pressures because of his initially weak political base. His narrow election victory was only possible because of an alliance between his own party, the Partido Social Democrático (PSD, Social Democratic

---

8. This and succeeding paragraphs dealing with the extent of patronage during successive democratic governments are based on Graham (1968, 140–58), unless other sources are cited.

party) and the Partido Trabalhista Brasileiro (PTB, Brazilian Labor party).
To maintain PTB support, he had to make patronage appointments
available to party activists.

To deal with these conflicting needs, Kubitschek, following the practice begun by Vargas, compartmentalized the bureaucracy. He made use
of the DASP, increasing its power and status, and used his discretionary
powers to recruit the ablest technocrats in the country for some agencies.
Meanwhile partisan considerations determined appointments in others.
He is credited with making seven thousand patronage appointments
during his first year in office (Amaral 1966, 17–19; Siegel 1963, 7),
notwithstanding his public support for the merit system. Most of these
appointments were made by the head of the PTB, João Goulart, in the
Ministries of Labor and Agriculture and their subsidiary autonomous
agencies, especially the social security institutes. Since civil service exams
were not held as legally prescribed, interim appointees were able to
retain their jobs year after year.

According to Wahrlich (1964, 37), Kubitschek's positive attitude toward the DASP

> [collided] head-on with the "spoils system" that prevailed in some sectors of
> government.
>   It is well-known that administrative posts at all levels of two ministries
> and the autarchies under the jurisdiction of those ministries were handed
> over to one political party [the PTB] which selected the candidates for pres-
> idential choice.

Through most of his term, Kubitschek struggled to defend his patronage
powers. Near the end of his term in late 1960, however, Kubitschek
became concerned about the growing power of the PTB (Maram 1992)
and engineered the passage of a law aimed at reforming the social
security institutes by limiting future appointments in the social security
institutes to those who had passed an entrance exam. The majority of
legislators supported this law, unlike other proposed reforms, because
its cost fell mainly on the PTB. The PTB controlled the distribution of
virtually all jobs in the social security institutes. Thus, whereas universal
reforms would have been costly to all parties, reform of these institutes
cost the PTB much of its patronage, but conferred benefits on the other
parties since it reduced the PTB's ability to compete for votes.

By the time this reform passed, the financial disorder in the social
security institutes had become a national scandal. Reformers greeted
this attempt to limit patronage in the Institutes with relief. The new law

also had the less obvious consequence of protecting Kubitschek's appointees from being replaced by the next president. What's more, Kubitschek made at least 4,436 and possibly as many as 15,000 new appointments before the law went into effect one month before he left office (Graham 1968, 151).

At the end of the Kubitschek administration, Congress also passed a law eliminating the distinction between permanent functionaries and extranumerary personnel.[9] This law in effect blanketed in many of Kubitschek's patronage appointments, thus securing their jobs in case of the expected victory of a reformist in the upcoming presidential election.

Kubitschek's successor, Jânio Quadros, appeared to be seriously interested in administrative reform. He was an independent politician known for effective administration while mayor of São Paulo and governor of the state of São Paulo. Elected on the União Democrática Nacional (UDN, National Democratic Union) ticket, few of his own supporters had found comfortable berths in the federal bureaucracy, and thus he had little to lose from bureaucratic housecleaning. In fact, his investigations into financial scandals and irregular appointments in the bureaucracy served to discredit his political opponents who had monopolized appointments for several decades.

Although President Quadros had nothing to lose and much to gain from reforms and the exposure of past abuses, his vice president, João Goulart,[10] and most members of Congress could not say the same. The president failed to get cooperation from the rest of the political leadership for his proposed reforms. He resigned, declaring Brazil ungovernable, after seven months.

Once Vice President Goulart assumed the presidency, irregular appointments increased. Goulart's political base was extremely weak. His party, the PTB, had never controlled more than about 20 percent of the seats in the national legislature. The military and much of Congress opposed allowing him to take power. Consequently, he searched for support with special desperation. In an effort to solidify his political position, Goulart even attempted to foist cronies and clients onto sectors of the bureaucracy that had customarily been immune from political

9. Law 3780, July 12, 1960, Articles 22 and 26, Brazil (1960), *Coleção das Leis*, Vol. 5, pp. 10–11.

10. At that time, Brazilian electoral law allowed voters to split their tickets between president and vice president. Goulart, the PTB candidate for vice president, defeated the UDN candidate and was reelected, even though his PSD running mate was defeated.

appointments, such as Petrobrás (the state oil monopoly), the Banco Nacional de Desenvolvimento Econômico (BNDE, National Development Bank), and the Bank of Brazil. In the words of Wanderley Guilherme dos Santos (1979, 217–18), "State administration at large under Goulart . . . was increasingly transformed into a deck of disposable cards for exclusive use in the political influence game. . . . The more Goulart tried, and failed, in his reshuffling moves aimed at accumulating political support, the more he inflated the game by bringing new State resources into its permissible range." More serious yet, Goulart's weakness led him to allow supporters and allies to usurp control over patronage appointments. Vargas and Kubitschek had defended presidential patronage and used it as an effective tool for achieving their political ends. Goulart was less successful at concentrating patronage on the achievement of his own political goals. He was only sporadically able to prevent PTB functionaries, legislators, and heads of bureaucratic agencies from rewarding their own clients with government jobs. The severity of this problem became clear when Goulart, having succumbed to the demands of civil servants to the extent of increasing their salaries between 56 percent and 136 percent (thus increasing the projected federal budget by 90 billion cruzeiros) and granting all interim employees tenure (Nascimento 1966, 37–87), attempted to freeze public hiring for a year in order to contain the rising cost of public employment. Thousands of patronage appointments were made by Goulart's PTB allies in the social security institutes the day before he signed the decree. Goulart attempted to dismiss the new employees, but pressure against the dismissals overwhelmed him. In the end, about six thousand people retained jobs in the Institutes (Amaral 1966, 3–36).

The Goulart administration is considered in greater detail below. For now, the period can be summed up as follows: Irregular appointments increased and were perceived by the public as increasing. The president struggled, often unsuccessfully, with his political allies to maintain his own control over patronage. Goulart's hold on office was so tenuous that he was forced to use his power over appointments primarily to shore up his disintegrating political position.

By 1964 the effort to improve bureaucratic performance through civil service reform, though it had achieved some success in particular areas, had failed as a grand strategy. Throughout the democratic period, elite reformers committed to modernization and economic development had sought bureaucratic reform. Their efforts, however, were regularly defeated by a legislature accustomed to using jobs to reward supporters and responsive to pressure from organized civil servants and by presidents who, though they might maintain competence in a portion of the bureaucracy, also used appointments on a large scale as a means of consolidating political support. With the return of democracy, the electoral benefits of exchanging resources needed to ensure agency capacity in return for political support were simply too essential to political survival to be forgone.

THE SECOND INNOVATION STRATEGY: "POCKETS OF EFFICIENCY"

By the mid-1950s, well before the severe deterioration of competence under Goulart, modernizers disillusioned with the progress of civil service reform began advocating an alternative means of achieving bureaucratic competence. Jaguaribe (1956, 11–12) noted that there were only two possibilities if interventionist development plans were to be carried out: overall administrative reform, or the creation of what he called "nuclei," competent, effective agencies within the administration but separate from the traditional bureaucracy.

Since reformers had been unable to muster sufficient support in Congress to pass universal reforms (Láfer 1970, 103–8), presidents had begun the ad hoc creation of insulated agencies outside the traditional bureaucracy, charged with specific, usually developmental, tasks and accountable to the executive. Brazilians dubbed these agencies *bolsões de eficiência*, "pockets of efficiency." They included some public enterprises, some *autarquias* (literally "autarchies"—bureaucratic agencies organizationally separate from the federal bureaucracy, whose staffs were hired and fired at executive discretion), and executive groups (*grupos executivos*), whose task was to oversee and coordinate specific sectoral development projects. Though diverse in form and goals, all these agencies shared the key characteristic of insulation from the legislature and traditional bureaucracy (Nunes 1984). They were responsible for implementing some of Brazil's most impressive pre-1964 economic achievements.

One of the most important of these agencies was the BNDE (National Development Bank).[11] It was established in 1952, during Vargas's second presidency, with the mission of providing credit for national develop-

11. The bank's name has been changed to Banco Nacional de Desenvolvimento Econômico e Social, BNDES, but at the time being discussed, it was still called the BNDE so I have used that name.

ment. It was set up as a new agency, outside the federal bureaucracy, in an effort to decrease the ability of politicians to use development funds for partisan purposes (Pinto 1969, 29–35). The original staff of the BNDE included a number of former Daspians.

The BNDE was separate from the traditional bureaucracy, and it eventually had a first-class staff with a strong sense of mission, but it was dependent on the president and did not control the resources it was supposed to be able to disburse. Its activities were kept quite limited by Vargas and during the first half of the Café Filho presidency. The BNDE was directed by a board of directors and an administrative council, all members of which were appointed by the president. Vargas appointed political cronies to head the bank, and under both administrations, the Finance Ministry failed to disburse about a third of the funds that had been allocated for bank use (Pinto 1969, 48). Between 1952 and 1954, the BNDE provided less than 10 percent of federal investments (Willis 1986, 185–230; Pinto 1969, 41–48; BNDE 1955, 24).

Prevented from carrying out its intended functions, the BNDE staff turned its attention to collecting information about the economy and turned itself into the most important source of economic expertise in Brazil. Lacking effective protection, it could do little else. The BNDE during this period illustrates the points made earlier about organizations' tendencies to build their own capacities, and also about the limitations on the extent to which they are able to do so without presidential support.

The performance of the BNDE improved dramatically after Café Filho appointed Glycón de Paiva and Roberto Campos to leadership positions in 1955. These appointments, in contrast to previous ones, were based on merit more than political criteria. Beginning with this change in leadership, the bank's role changed. It established rigorous procedures to ensure recruitment and promotion based on merit.[12] The number of loans granted increased markedly. Moreover, compared with its earlier tolerance for the use of bank funds to consolidate political support, the bank began to assert, though it could still not always enforce, a loan policy based exclusively on economic criteria. It refused, for example, to grant loans for several projects involving insolvent government-owned railroads on the grounds that they were incapable of repaying them (BNDE 1955, 101). The bank's annual report for 1955

12. See Wahrlich (1957) for an extended description of the recruitment and promotion procedures established by the BNDE.

states that "the Bank has tried to prevent its financial cooperation from turning into a mere government subsidy. We are trying to keep the organization operating as a Bank" (BNDE 1955, 102).

The bank also proposed changing its policy concerning loans to local governments to finance public utilities. These loans in the past had been used primarily to consolidate support for the government in power. The economic criteria determining their distribution had been quite relaxed. The BNDE asked Congress to make the rules governing loans to local governments much more stringent (Pinto 1969, 44).

When Kubitschek became president, he turned to the BNDE to spearhead his cherished national development program. Kubitschek appointed the ablest people he could find to leadership roles in the bank and allowed the bank to borrow expert personnel from other bureaucratic agencies (Láfer 1970, 149–50). Probably most important, though, through adroit political maneuvering, he created autonomous sources of the funds for development projects to be administered by the bank.

Prior to that time, the funds for development projects had tended to evaporate between plan and implementation. First, there was a problem with getting Congress to allocate the money every year. Then, the Ministry of Finance routinely disbursed only a portion of the funds that had been allocated, using the rest to cover the deficits of other parts of the government. As a result, bureaucratic agencies spent much of their time and energy in the struggle for political influence that would translate into leverage with the Ministry of Finance (Pinto 1969, 37, 40; Willis 1986, 59–71, 205–9, 260–77).

Kubitschek's solution was to set up or reorganize funds for specific purposes based on a series of surtaxes—on fuels, petroleum imports, railway fares, electricity, maritime freight, and so on. These funds amounted to 22 percent of total federal receipts in 1957 (Delfim Netto et al. 1965, 128). The surtaxes were collected and deposited directly with the BNDE. They were never included in the federal budget, and thus, after their initial approval by Congress, there was no chance that funds would be taken away the next year or disappear between allocation and disbursal.[13] Once the funds were set up, Congress had no further discretion over their use.

Kubitschek secured the resources for the BNDE itself in a similar way. The domestic portion of the investment to start the BNDE had come from a forced loan equal to a 15 percent surtax on the income tax

13. See Láfer (1970, 116–21) for details about the various funds.

of individuals and corporations above a certain income, collected between 1952 and 1956 (Law 1474, September 26, 1951). Kubitschek
persuaded Congress to extend the collection of this surtax for an additional ten years in order to finance his development project (Law 2973,
November 26, 1956). In addition, Law 2973 guaranteed that portions
of the surtax previously withheld by the Treasury would be repaid to
the BNDE at the rate of at least one billion cruzeiros per year (Láfer
1970, 124–25; Willis 1986, 260–77).

Under Kubitschek's administration, the BNDE came into its own,
playing a central role in planning and implementing Kubitschek's Programa de Metas, his Target Plan for economic development. BNDE staff
members did much of the initial planning for the Programa de Metas
during Kubitschek's presidential campaign. Once the plan was underway, the bank did more than provide investments and the matching
funds required by foreign lenders. It also performed an important quality
control function. Its control over funds allowed the BNDE to enforce
efficiency criteria and consistency with plan goals as conditions for
receiving successive increments of loans. The ability to enforce performance standards was especially important when projects were being
carried out by public enterprises or bureaucratic agencies (Láfer 1970,
128–30).

The BNDE was strongly committed to what bank employees refer to
as "global rationality." They distinguish global rationality from both
political rationality—the use of resources to buy political support—and
short-term economic rationality, that is, short-term profit maximization.
Global rationality refers to long-term growth maximization.[14] And indeed, between 1955 and 1959, Brazil took advantage of a favorable
international economic climate to nearly double its industrial output
and lay a foundation for future growth.

Kubitschek created another kind of insulated agency, the *grupo executivo,* by presidential decree, "which rid them of Congressional interference" (Benevides 1976, 229). These groups had the task of implementing the goals for particular sectors of the economy designated by
the overall plan. They were separate from the federal bureaucracy. In
fact, they were officially charged with circumventing the bureaucracy.

Before the establishment of the *grupos executivos,* an industrial project would have taken many months to meander through bureaucratic

14. Based on interviews with former BNDE employees, conducted in Rio de Janeiro,
1982 and 1983.

channels in one agency after another. A proposal for a new industrial plant had to be analyzed by the Foreign Trade Section of the Bank of Brazil to determine whether similar products were already being produced domestically; then the Ministry of War assessed the implications of the project for national security; finally, the Foreign Exchange Section of the Bank of Brazil ascertained whether foreign exchange was available for importing needed machinery, fuel, or raw materials. The process took a long time. Projects were not examined as a whole. Instead, different agencies assessed different aspects of each project, using different criteria to judge them. As a result, several agencies had veto power over each project (Motta 1968). Some of the main functions of the *grupos executivos* were to coordinate, speed up, and avoid, where possible, the passage of projects through the bureaucratic morass. The *grupos executivos* included representatives of all the agencies in the executive branch whose decisions affected a project, and their decisions were binding on represented agencies.

The *grupos executivos* were insulated from congressional intervention in that neither their resources nor their personnel were subject to congressional manipulation. Appointments depended entirely on executive discretion. Kubitschek's arrangements for circumventing the congressional budgetary process were described above. According to Maria Victória Benevides (1976, 230), "The principal advantage of the *grupos executivos* was their autonomy with regard to budget and personnel recruitment . . . which guaranteed them a degree of operational flexibility that would have been impossible if clientelistic interests whether party-based or not—had been taken into consideration."

Besides the BNDE and the *grupos executivos,* several other agencies existed in which expertise and commitment to development were being nurtured prior to 1960. They included Petrobrás, the state oil monopoly; Superintendência de Moeda e Crédito (SUMOC), the monetary authority; Itamaraty, the Ministry of Foreign Affairs; Fundação Getúlio Vargas, an institute set up to train administrative personnel and collect economic data; Carteira de Comércio Exterior do Banco do Brasil (CACEX), the Foreign Trade Department of the Bank of Brazil; and Carteira de Câmbio do Banco do Brasil, the Foreign Exchange Department of the Bank of Brazil. All these agencies had in common autonomy from the traditional political game (Santos 1979, 214–17), as well as meritocratic recruitment.

Though part of the traditional federal bureaucracy, Itamaraty, the Ministry of Foreign Affairs, had a long tradition of recruitment through highly competitive exams and ran its own rigorous elite training school for career diplomats (Barros 1978, 225–28). Since horizontal entry into the diplomatic service was virtually impossible, decision-making positions in the Foreign Ministry were never included in the spoils system.

The Bank of Brazil instituted its own system of meritocratic appointments even before the DASP began to operate. Although local branches of the Bank of Brazil and the loan programs they sponsored provided important resources to members of Congress and other local politicians (Nunes 1984, 139–40), departments of the bank that dealt with foreign trade were insulated from political pressures.

SUMOC was created at the end of the dictatorship, when technocrats expected the imminent return of democracy, in a self-conscious effort to insulate monetary policy from congressional intervention (Lago 1965). Initially it was staffed by functionaries borrowed from the Bank of Brazil (Láfer 1970, 151–52).

The Fundação Getúlio Vargas was proposed and, to a considerable extent, staffed and run by Daspians. These agencies "provided strategic places within the government where [technocrats] could develop their careers and their influence on policy" (Leff 1968, 147).

Several of these agencies engaged in direct or indirect cooperation with foreign experts or agencies. Foreign influence and the conditions insisted upon by foreign banks tended to insulate from domestic politics projects in which foreigners were involved. Furthermore, many of the individuals who filled leadership positions in these agencies had been trained abroad and/or had worked on cooperative projects with North American experts in working groups such as the Comissão Mista Brasil–EUA (Brazilian–U.S. Joint Commission) and the Abbink Mission (Benevides 1976, 225).[15] They tended, as a result of socialization to international professional norms, to be somewhat insulated personally from traditional Brazilian attitudes toward clientelism (cf. O'Donnell 1973, 79–89).

Most of the agencies that played an important role in formulating and carrying out the Programa de Metas had existed prior to Kubitschek's election. Kubitschek's contribution lay in creating the *grupos executivos* to coordinate the activities of the several agencies involved

15. The purpose of both these missions was to suggest solutions to Brazil's economic problems. See Malán (1977, 431–43) for a list of the members of the Comissão Mista and the Abbink Mission. See also Dreifuss (1981, 73–92) for documentation of the connection between many of Brazil's most important technocrats and multinational corporations.

TABLE I

THE EFFECT OF INSULATION ON THE
COMPLETION OF GOALS IN THE TARGET PLAN

	Average Achieved (%)
Targets Dependent Only on Special Funding and Exchange Provisions	91
Targets Involving Production Within Insulated Agencies or Enterprises, along with Special Funding, Exchange, and Tariff Provisions	102
Targets Involving Special Funding and Subsidies Distributed by Traditional Uninsulated Agencies	60[a]
Targets Administered by Insulated Agencies Involving Production in the Private Sector, Special Funding, and Subsidies	58[b]

SOURCE: Tables 18–21, Appendix A.
[a] Wheat excluded from calculation of average.
[b] Coal excluded from calculation of average.

in each project; assuring secure ongoing financing for projects by setting up funds over which Congress and the Ministry of Finance had little discretion; and concentrating the ablest personnel available in the relevant agencies. In effect, he insulated the agencies from the forces in Brazilian government and society that would have made carrying out their tasks impossible, and, by doing so, created a series of effective agents for achieving developmental goals.

To assess how effective the insulated agencies were, one can compare their performance in carrying out the goals of the Programa de Metas with that of the traditional federal bureaucracy. Kubitschek's Target Plan focused on thirty targets or goals for overcoming specific bottlenecks in the economy that had been identified by foreign and Brazilian economists. The targets included such things as increasing installed electrical capacity, petroleum refining capacity, the number of miles of paved roads, the production of wheat, and so on. The achievement of different targets required the cooperation of different government agencies as well as different private actors, depending on the nature of the target itself. In table 1, all the targets that can be quantitatively assessed are categorized according to the agencies and actors involved in their achievement. (Detailed tables showing all the targets and information about how the figures in the tables were calculated can be found in appendix A.)

The first category in table 1 includes the targets in which achievement depended only on imports. Since sufficient imports were made possible by assured access to foreign exchange, preferential exchange rates, and funding by the BNDE, all under the direct control of insulated agencies, it is not surprising that most goals were achieved. Only the railroads experienced any difficulty achieving these targets (see table 18, appendix A). The state-owned railroads were part of the traditional bureaucracy, and their long-standing financial difficulties impeded funding some of their imports (Lessa 1964, 165).

Targets that involved actual production within insulated agencies or state enterprises, as well as funding handled by the BNDE and special exchange and tariff provisions overseen by SUMOC are included in the second category of table 1. These are targets that involved actual production, not just imports, and thus required considerably more technical and managerial expertise. The targets in this category include increases in installed electrical capacity, petroleum production, refining capacity, and production of chemical fertilizers, steel, alkalis, and synthetic rubber. On average, the insulated agencies and state enterprises had achieved 102 percent of their targets by the year after the target date.[16] The only conspicuous failure was iron exports, which were affected by the world market for iron ore. By 1962, iron ore exports had risen to 91 percent of the target, which suggests that Brazil had successfully expanded its capacity to export, even if market factors sometimes prevented exporting at full capacity (see table 19, appendix A).

Targets that involved special funding (usually provided by the BNDE) and subsidies distributed by traditional, uninsulated agencies are included in the third category of table 1. Targets in this group are extremely modest compared to targets in others. Planners recognized limits to what could be achieved in areas under the jurisdiction of the traditional bureaucracy. Even with modest goals, achievement of targets by uninsulated agencies was conspicuously lower than achievement by insulated agencies (see table 20, appendix A). The average percentage of the target achieved by the year after the targeted date was 48 percent, or, if wheat is excluded, 60 percent.[17]

---

16. Calculated by averaging the percent of each target achieved by the year after the target date. Where particular targets included more than one goal, they were averaged and that average was used to represent the target as a whole.

17. Calculated as described above. Wheat production should probably be excluded

Targets that involved administration by insulated agencies but production within the private sector, included in the fourth category of table 1, were characterized by high variance in levels of achievement caused by market forces. This high variance accounts for the relatively low average achievement. Coal production declined in spite of special funding and subsidies because the shift to diesel engines made possible by imports of railroad cars and track carried out under another target reduced the demand for coal. Credit and subsidies were made available for the construction of refrigerated warehouses and cold storage facilities, but potential investors did not take advantage of them. Targeted increases in the production of nonferrous metals proved to be impossible because ores had not been discovered. Cement producers, in contrast, took full advantage of the subsidies available and the boom in construction during the Kubitschek administration to achieve their full target. And, with the domestic market protected, the new auto industry also registered very impressive growth (see table 21, appendix A).

In short, although insulated agencies could not perform miracles—they could not produce minerals where ores had not been found or export products for which there was no market—they did, on average, perform markedly better than uninsulated federal agencies. The insulated agencies were able to play the role they did because, with Kubitschek's protection, they controlled their own recruitment and their funding was not subject to legislative or ministerial diversion.

THE RELATIONSHIP BETWEEN INSULATION AND "STATE" AUTONOMY

While he protected the insulated agencies and guaranteed their material and human resources, Kubitschek managed the rest of the political system in the traditional way, which reduced potential challenges to his developmentalist goals and his way of pursuing them. His skillful use of patronage in sectors of the bureaucracy not vital to the economy increased his autonomy with regard to macroeconomic decisions, as well as guaranteeing the cooperation of those rewarded with jobs and favors.

---

because the Wheat Accord signed during the Kubitschek administration reduced the price of imported wheat and thus reduced the incentives for the domestic production of wheat. The Wheat Accord was signed, however, in part because efforts to raise domestic wheat production had ended in dismal failure.

Chapter 1 argued that state policy-making autonomy has little importance if the state lacks the capacity to implement its decisions. This chapter has argued that the insulation of crucial government agencies contributes to such capacity. A closer examination of the Kubitschek period in Brazil permits a more nuanced understanding of the relationship between insulation and "coalitional" autonomy, that is, policy-making autonomy from powerful interest groups.

Kubitschek is usually portrayed as a populist pursuing the interests of an urban coalition of the working class, middle class, and manufacturers, but, in reality, his electoral support came largely from conservative rural interests. In spite of an election campaign emphasizing rapid industrialization that should have appealed to a broad urban coalition, Kubitschek won the 1955 presidential election with only 36 percent of the vote, most of it turned out by the old-fashioned rural political machinery of the conservative PSD. Although his alliance with the PTB (Brazilian Labor Party) undoubtedly brought in some working-class votes, Kubitschek received only one-eighth of the vote in São Paulo, the most industrialized state, and thus the state in which his campaign promises and the policies he ultimately pursued should have had most appeal.

Thus, at the time he was elected, the broad coalition that eventually supported Kubitschek still remained to be created. Policies fostering industrialization obviously played a role in building this coalition and so, less obviously, did Kubitschek's strategy of dealing with the bureaucracy. Although the industrialization drive conferred immediate benefits on some manufacturers and other urban dwellers, and medium-run benefits on the urban sector more generally, several specific policies were initially opposed by groups concerned about their own short-term interests. The wholesale distribution of patronage appointments to party activists of the PTB, along with a successful campaign to shape public opinion, prevented these potential sources of opposition from coalescing into a political force capable of pressing its demands.

The extension of traditional clientelist relationships to new participants via the appointment of numerous PTB activists to government jobs reinforced the customary Brazilian practice of seeking individual improvement through personal connections with the politically powerful. With many of its potential leaders co-opted, the working class did not mobilize itself to demand policy changes (for example, more attention to income distribution or increasing employment). Instead, political action tended to follow the pattern already established by higher status participants in the political system. It tended to be individualistic and focused at the implementation stage of policy making—to be dominated by petitions for exceptions, requests to be included in government programs, demands for government jobs. As a result, the president had a great deal of autonomy in the formulation of policy.[18]

In addition to the autonomy he enjoyed in the absence of the effective articulation of opposing interests, Kubitschek was very successful at building and maintaining generalized public support for his policies.[19] He and his supporters carried on an effective public relations campaign through speeches and in the press (Maram 1992). They were able to mobilize a very broad consensus in support for their vision of development and their strategy for achieving it.

The favorable public attitude toward foreign investment in manufacturing during the Kubitschek presidency illustrates this manipulation of public opinion. Hostility toward foreign investment can be traced back to the 1920s in Brazil. It reached a high point in the public controversy that led to the nationalization of the oil industry in 1952. In addition to the widely shared antipathy toward foreign investment in general, the most powerful domestic industrialists in Brazil opposed allowing foreign manufacturers into Brazil on the more mundane grounds that they feared foreign competition.[20] Nevertheless, during the Kubitschek administration, public opinion came to favor foreign investment in manufacturing. On April 6, 1958, the *New York Herald Tribune* published a poll showing that only 14 percent of Brazilians surveyed believed foreign investment to be "bad" for the country. This was the lowest percentage in any of the twelve countries included in the survey.[21]

In 1955, less than a year before Kubitschek's election, SUMOC Instruction 113 had initiated a new policy designed to attract foreign manufacturing investment into priority sectors of the Brazilian economy. It contained attractive provisions concerning both initial investment and profit remission. The initial policy change embodied in Instruction 113 was possible, even though opposed by public opinion, because SUMOC decisions did not require legislative approval and because it corresponded to the policy preferences of President Café Filho, as well as his

18. See Leff (1968, 118–31) for a similar argument.
19. Cf. Eric Nordlinger (1981, 99–117), who notes that the ability to shift societal preferences so that they conform to the preferences of governmental actors is one of the capacities that grants autonomy to the democratic state.
20. The first issue of *Desenvolvimento & Conjuntura*, the organ of the Confederação Nacional da Indústria, dated July 1958, warns against the denationalization of Brazilian industry as a result of SUMOC Instruction 113.
21. Cited in Leff (1968).

conservative minister of finance, Eugênio Gudin, and most of the government economic elite at the time. As noted in the discussion of civil service reform, Café Filho became vice president because of an electoral deal and unexpectedly ascended to the presidency after Vargas's suicide in 1954. He had no serious future political aspirations, and thus his policy choices were relatively unconstrained by concern for public opinion or reelection. In fact, near the end of his time in office, Café Filho told an interviewer that "his government had made no attempt to be popular."[22]

Café Filho and Gudin continued in office less than a year after Instruction 113 was issued, but the policy continued in effect until 1962, long after the original conjuncture of events that made it possible had passed. The Kubitschek administration's propaganda campaign meanwhile subtly changed the image of foreign investment in Brazil.

Kubitschek and his advisors did not believe that the goals of the Programa de Metas could be achieved without foreign participation. Under Kubitschek's leadership, foreign investment in manufacturing came to be perceived as legitimate in that it contributed to national economic development. It was seen as a means of increasing needed imports, especially of capital goods and technology, without having to expend foreign exchange. This view of foreign investment in manufacturing, espoused by Kubitschek and his economic advisors, did not begin to be challenged in the press or by elite opinion until near the end of the Kubitschek presidency—though opposition to all foreign investment had once again become widespread within a couple of years after Kubitschek left office, as illustrated by the very popular law limiting profit remissions passed during the Goulart administration. Nor was the policy of encouraging foreign investment in manufacturing effectively challenged by domestic industrialists, even though many saw their interests as threatened. Most opposition by industrialists took the form of personal efforts to influence SUMOC and members of the executive. The belief that foreign investment would contribute to development had become so pervasive within elite opinion that industrialists felt that they were expressing egoistic, personal claims in opposition to the overriding national interest in development (Leff 1968, 59–66). Even in an area in which Kubitschek's policy contrasted with customary views, and with the interests of powerful economic actors, no alternative policy was articulated in a way that could mobilize widespread support.

22. *O Estado de São Paulo,* September 6, 1955, cited in Skidmore (1976, 148).

This shift in Brazilian public opinion is usually interpreted as a rational response to the balance of payments problem. This explanation, however, fails to account for the lack of attention given to other possible, and at least equally rational, responses to the crises. Policies to increase exports, for example, were never seriously considered. The challenge of recurrent balance of payments crises, in other words, led informed Brazilians to consider alternatives to traditional policies but did not determine which would be chosen. That choice was made within a narrow circle of Kubitschek advisors and then disseminated to the public.

In the Kubitschek period, then, the president and his advisors were relatively unconstrained with regard to the pursuit of their economic policy preferences. They successfully mobilized a consensus around a particular development strategy that rendered opposition by industrialists suspect and morally difficult to defend. By permitting the numerically largest portion of the bureaucracy to continue operating in its usual clientelist way, they reinforced customary personalist political activities and reduced the probability that serious class or interest group-based challenges to policies would arise. At the same time, though, Kubitschek insulated the agencies crucial to the implementation of his development goals from those same clientelist pressures in order to ensure their competence and to secure steady and adequate investment for economic projects.

In short, an effective public relations campaign combined with a judicious mixture of meritocratic and partisan staffing of the bureaucracy resulted in Kubitschek's "coalitional" autonomy from some potential interest group pressures, although Kubitschek made no effort to insulate his government from interest groups per se. In fact, formal consultation with interest groups was built into agencies such as the *grupos executivos*. He did, however, successfully undermine these groups' ability to press for policies (such as a labor intensive rather than capital intensive development strategy) that his team saw as serious obstacles to the achievement of development goals.

Kubitschek's solution to the problem of insulating economic decisions in a democratic system had some built-in disadvantages, as was becoming apparent even before he left office. First, the addition of these new insulated agencies with enormous development budgets to the already large traditional bureaucracy was expensive. Many would argue that the large budget deficit bequeathed by Kubitschek to his successors was the underlying cause of the economic and political crises of the early sixties. Second, depending as they did on Kubitschek's personal support, the insulated agencies—though shielded from other partisan pressures—were unable to resist grandiose and expensive presidential schemes such as the new capital in Brasília. And finally, Kubitschek's solution, because it depended on his personal endeavors, could not survive his departure from office.

THE DISINTEGRATION OF THE
SECOND INNOVATION STRATEGY

João Goulart did not, and perhaps could not, function as a political entrepreneur in the way that Kubitschek had. He had fewer resources with which to influence the incentives facing other political actors.[23] Economic difficulties forced him to make hard choices among uses for resources rather than being able to maximize both support and the achievement of economic goals at the same time, as Kubitschek had. Furthermore, with much less political support—a large fraction of the military and upper class opposed even allowing him to take office—his need to "buy" support was greater and more urgent than Kubitschek's had been. It also seems clear that Goulart, who had risen to prominence as a consequence of his masterful use of patronage to build the PTB, did not clearly perceive the economic costs of a bureaucracy staffed by partisan appointments.

The disintegration of the Kubitschek amalgam of clientelism and meritocracy contributed to the economic and political chaos that led to the military coup in 1964. Many things went wrong during the Goulart presidency. I do not want to minimize the importance of ideological opposition to Goulart or the economic consequences of weaknesses inherent in import substitution as an economic development strategy (Fishlow 1971; Hirschman 1968). An additional cause, however, of both the economic chaos and elite opposition to Goulart was his attempt to return previously insulated sectors of the bureaucracy to the realm of clientelism and cronyism (Santos 1979, 217–18).

Undermining the insulation of agencies and enterprises central to national economic performance had negative consequences for the already deteriorating economy. Perhaps even more important, it galvanized support for the military coup among some of the most important

---

23. Mark Schneider and Paul Teske (1992) show that greater availability of resources makes the emergence of political entrepreneurship more likely.

economists in the country and among other elites committed to development.[24]

The section on civil service reform showed that efforts at universalistic reform as a means of creating competent bureaucratic agencies were defeated by actors whose short-term political goals undermined their longer-term interest in economic development. This section will show that the alternative approach to increasing bureaucratic competence, the *bolsões de eficiência*, was also vulnerable to political intervention and subversion.

The agencies most visibly affected by Goulart's attempt to consolidate political support through appointments to previously insulated sectors of the bureaucracy included the BNDE, Petrobrás, and the one social security institute noted for competence, the Instituto Aposentadoria e Pensões dos Industriários (IAPI, the Social Security Institute for Industrial Workers). The kind of political interference differed in each of these cases, but the consequences were the same: first, a fall in performance, as competence in the agency declined and political decision criteria superseded economic decision criteria; and, second, an attempt by members of the agency who had become committed to achieving its stated goals during the earlier period of insulation to defend its boundaries, carry out its allotted tasks, and rally public support against political incursions. As noted above, members of organizations make efforts to secure the resources they need and to maintain organizational integrity and boundaries. These efforts sometimes led to successful outcomes, but were insufficient to protect the coherence of economic decision making under Goulart.

At the BNDE, political intervention took the form of appointing administrators who were inexperienced and accessible to political pressures. At the beginning of his term, Goulart appointed Leocádio de Almeida Antunes, a PTB deputy and crony with no experience in finance or economics, concurrently to the two most important leadership positions in the BNDE, president and superintendent. The performance of the BNDE deteriorated during his time in office, as did its reputation for integrity. Loans promised to major state-owned manufacturing enterprises were delayed, causing them serious financial embarrassment. The bank's ability to resist pressure to grant loans to the politically well connected declined. It authorized a loan, for example, to an agricultural

24. See, for example, Roberto Campos (1975, 35), who complained that Congress had been turned into an "engine of inflation" before the 1964 coup due to its "hypersensitivity to . . . pressures."

cooperative in Rio Grande do Sul that failed to meet eligibility requirements in response to pressure from Governor Leonel Brizola, Goulart's brother-in-law. Antunes cast the deciding votes in favor of the loan. The technical staff of the BNDE fought Antunes, but they could not maintain professional standards without support from the president (Pinto 1969, 56–57).

In 1963 Goulart attempted to repay a political debt to his close friend Lomanto Junior, governor of Bahia, by allowing him to name the next president of the BNDE. During his campaign for governor, Lomanto had attacked the BNDE for channeling too few resources to Bahia, and he had promised to secure more funds if elected. Lomanto's choice for president of the BNDE was his brother-in-law, Lelivaldo de Brito, a man with no training or experience in economics. In this case the bank, threatened with having an incompetent foisted onto it who was, in addition, publicly committed to undercutting the economic criteria used to evaluate loan requests in order to benefit his region, was able to mobilize opposition to the appointment in Congress and in the press. Bank employees carried out a successful publicity and lobbying campaign against the Brito nomination, and the president was eventually persuaded to nominate a qualified candidate. This is one of the first instances in which a government economic decision-making agency, after a period of being protected by the president, succeeded in defending its own boundaries against political interventions.

Goulart's intervention at Petrobrás initially took the form of increasing the decision-making power of the Oil Workers' Union. As the political situation became more chaotic, Goulart lost control over the unions and over the management of Petrobrás more generally. As a result, a coalition made up of union leaders, managers, and some technicians was able to achieve control over decision making in the enterprise. This coalition's concerns centered on the welfare of its members and allies inside and outside the enterprise, not the economic performance of Petrobrás. The management of Petrobrás became increasingly disorganized, and production fell. Petrobrás had four presidents during Goulart's term, only one of whom lasted more than six months (Carvalho 1976, 166). It lost technical and managerial personnel who were dissatisfied with low pay and frustrated by the general mismanagement. In the words of Getúlio Carvalho (1976, 150): "[T]he institutional objectives of the enterprise were damaged and seriously distorted as a result of the search for political support among the unions. There was an excessive emphasis on the "reflexive" objectives of the organization [that is, the interests of managers and employees], disregarding the functional objectives [that is, maximizing output or efficiency], since the central concern of the dominant coalition appears to have revolved around possible benefits for its members, relegating to second place the economic goals of the state enterprise."

As a result, many technicians at Petrobrás became more and more demoralized and frustrated. Scandals and corruption reported in the press led to a public outcry against the union and Goulart. Most important, mismanagement of Petrobrás increased the hostility of the military, which had a longtime national security concern with petroleum supply, toward Goulart.

The final example of political intervention and consequent subversion of agency performance involves IAPI (the Social Security Institute for Industrial Workers). In 1960, IAPI was the only social security institute with a reputation for competence and honesty. It was a haven and breeding place for social security reformers committed to efficiency and influenced by international norms. It was the only institute that consistently recruited personnel through competitive exams (Malloy 1979, 79–105).

Under Goulart, over a thousand and perhaps as many as three thousand political appointments were made at IAPI.[25] Its efficiency declined. Massive increases in hiring, coupled with the government's failure both to release the funds legally committed to the social security agencies and to enforce the collection of the portion of funds owed to the system by employers, had pushed all the institutes close to bankruptcy. The morale of the IAPI technocrats disintegrated. Hostility among the technocrats toward Goulart and the PTB was so intense that some began to meet privately to plot resistance. Many supported or at least acquiesced in the military coup (Malloy 1979, 119–22).

These three agencies had been known for competence and professionalism before Goulart took office. All three had been shielded by presidents from partisan pressures during periods of their existence. But none was able to protect itself from political intervention when presidential support was withdrawn, though all tried, and the BNDE had some success. In all three, performance and morale declined when their insulation from individuals and groups bent on using their resources for partisan purposes deteriorated. In all three, some individuals, demoral-

25. Malloy (1979, 183), based on interviews with former administrators at IAPI. *Jornal do Brasil* (June 16, 1962, p. 8; June 23, 1962, p. 8; June 26, 1962, p. 4) reported that over three thousand irregular appointments had been made.

ized and frustrated by their inability to function effectively because of the agencies' inability to maintain their organizational integrity, responded by supporting the military coup.[26]

CONCLUSION

The picaresque story told in this chapter can be summarized as follows. Since 1930, development-oriented elites in Brazil, supported by public opinion, have attempted to increase state capacity by establishing competent bureaucratic agencies capable of contributing to economic growth. Throughout the period, however, tension has persisted between reform attempts aimed at increasing bureaucratic capacity, on the one hand, and pressures for the distribution of jobs and other benefits, on the other. Where agencies have been successfully insulated from those pressures, even temporarily, their effectiveness has improved. For example, the performance of the insulated agencies, the BNDE and the *grupos executivos,* in carrying out the goals of Kubitschek's Programa de Metas contrasts sharply with the performance of the uninsulated federal agencies.

Economic policy-making agencies have needed to be protected by the president from partisan and particularistic incursions in order to sustain their ability to perform, however. They have not been systematically able to defend their own boundaries and secure the resources they need.

This chapter, in other words, has described the increase in capacity of a sector of the Brazilian state bureaucracy. And it has noted some of the characteristics a bureaucratic agency needs in order to act competently: meritocratic recruitment to ensure the competence of personnel; sources of funding protected from the depredations of rivals within government; and an incentive structure for bureaucrats that makes achieving their personal career goals consistent with achieving agency goals. It has also described the day-to-day pressures from which a government agency needs to be insulated if it is to perform effectively and reasonably efficiently.

These more capable agencies also displayed a certain amount of autonomy from dominant economic groups. The most important private sector beneficiaries of the Kubitschek development project were domestic and foreign entrepreneurs who seized the opportunity to build new

26. O'Donnell (1973, especially 79–89) also notes the frustration of "incumbents of technocratic roles," though he does not discuss the possibility that an earlier period of insulation, when they had a justified feeling of accomplishment, might have contributed to their expectations. He attributes their frustration to foreign professional socialization.

industries in Brazil, not members of the traditionally most powerful manufacturing sectors. The Kubitschek administration's ability to mold rather than respond to public opinion might also be considered evidence of autonomy. One cannot really speak of an autonomous "state" during the period under discussion, however, since even the relative autonomy of certain agencies during certain periods depended on the protection and support of a particular president. When that support disappeared, agency autonomy and capacity disintegrated.

This case study suggests four conclusions of broader theoretical significance.

1. *Bureaucratic agencies perform more effectively when they are insulated from personalistic and partisan demands.*

The insulation of bureaucrats in key agencies from clientelism helps to secure the resources and maintain the incentive structure needed if the agencies are to perform effectively and reasonably efficiently as agents of presidents attempting to carry out campaign promises. Thus insulation, as used in this book, does not imply failure to respond to popular demands. Quite the opposite.

The characteristic feature of the temporarily successful reforms initiated by both Vargas and Kubitschek is that segments of the bureaucracy deemed central to promoting economic development were effectively insulated from the pervasive exchange of favors for partisan support. As a result, their human resources—competence, expertise, efficiency, morale, honesty—were preserved, and their material resources safeguarded. The agencies thus protected became famous in Brazil for professionalism and competence, an indication that incentives within these agencies did indeed operate to reward performance.

2. *Political leaders act as political entrepreneurs helping to bring about reforms only when it serves their own interests—as determined by political institutions and circumstances—to do so. Differences in political institutions through their impact on the incentives facing political leaders thus affect the likelihood of changes that would contribute to increases in state capacity.*

Because politicians customarily exchange the resources and outputs of bureaucratic agencies for political support, the insulation of such agencies is costly to them. Political leaders can be expected to promote reforms designed to increase bureaucratic honesty and competence only when the benefits to them individually of doing so outweigh these costs.

Their individual interests depend on the political institutions within which they operate.

In Brazil between 1930 and 1964, all elected officials confronted incentives in the electoral game that undermined their commitment to administrative reform, even though most of the public favored reform. No candidate in competition with other candidates who were exchanging favors for support could afford to eschew such exchanges. During the dictatorship (1937–45), in contrast, the political cost of reforms decreased, and civil service reform was initiated.

Within a particular structure of political institutions, different roles determine the incentives faced by the individuals who occupy the roles. The cost to elected officials of embracing administrative reform varies depending on the office held. Since elected presidents in Brazil could not succeed themselves, they were concerned with accomplishing programmatic goals and with their own long-term popularity and political power, which would affect their election prospects in the more distant future, rather than immediate reelection. Their concern with the implementation of policies provided reason for supporting reforms aimed at improving some of the bureaucratic instruments at their disposal.

For individual members of Congress, in contrast, electoral concerns had to take precedence over programmatic goals. Reform, because it reduces legislators' discretion over the distribution of benefits, reduces the individual legislator's ability to deliver benefits personally and to claim credit for them.[27] Even though many legislators believed that administrative reform would contribute to more effective economic policy making, the electoral costs of embracing it dissuaded them from voting for it.

Presidents have had more reason to be concerned with national economic performance than legislators and thus more reason to favor administrative reform. At the same time, however, they have faced strong pressure from members of their parties—who care deeply about the next election—to continue distributing jobs. In response to these conflicting incentives, presidents have tended to attempt some amalgam of reform and patronage.

Institutional roles can be thought of as creating a probability distribution over a range of possible outcomes, but the case study shows that other factors in the political environment also affect outcomes. Two

27. On legislators' general preference for the distribution of particularistic goods, see Fiorina (1977), Jacobson and Kernell (1983), and Arnold (1979).

presidents, Getúlio Vargas and Juscelino Kubitschek, made significant contributions to increasing bureaucratic competence, although they also used patronage appointments to consolidate political support at the same time. They differed from other Brazilian presidents in that they controlled unusual amounts of resources. These resources made it possible to change the incentives facing the other officials whose cooperation was necessary to achieve improved administrative performance.

These resources took a number of forms: both men had great personal political skill in manipulating supporters and opponents alike; in Vargas's first administration, unusual political power because of the abolition of Congress; in Kubitschek's administration, unusual amounts of capital because of favorable occurrences in the international economy. Such resources took on special weight in Brazil because Brazilian presidents lack some of the institutional resources—such as party discipline and a stable party system—that contribute to the ability of presidents in other Latin American countries to initiate reforms.[28]

3. *Reforms that depend on the support of individual leaders are fragile; they tend to disintegrate at the end of the leader's term in office.*

Many of the innovations initiated by Vargas and Kubitschek did not survive them. Vargas's first effort to institutionalize his reforms failed when the return to competitive politics reestablished the connection between patronage appointments and winning elections.

Kubitschek chose to *dar um jeito,* that is, to find a devious way around the obstacles created by the traditional electoral game, rather than confronting the much more difficult task of trying to initiate radical institutional reforms against strong congressional opposition. Kubitschek's innovations deteriorated after he left office and the resource environment changed.

João Goulart controlled few political and economic resources. The military threatened his survival from the beginning, and he had virtually nothing to exchange for much needed political support except jobs and favors. Consequently, he tried to further his political interests by trading the resources even of previously insulated agencies for support, which led to the disintegration of Kubitschek's amalgam of reform and patronage.

4. *The kind of autonomy that actually contributes to better economic performance is not autonomy from interest groups but instead auton-*

28. See chapter 6 for a more general explanation of why some presidents have more success building state capacity than others.

omy from politically motivated pressures to distribute the resources needed for effective policy making and implementation.

In developing countries, the individuals most capable of undermining state efforts to initiate change are not members of powerful economic groups or unionized workers intent on pursuing their own economic interests. Rather, they are politicians, party activists, and bureaucrats intent on "spending" scarce state resources to "buy" political support.

FOUR

Legislators and the Supply of Public Goods

A Brazilian Example and a Model

The "real world" is a sloppy actuality.
— *Koster*, The Dissertation

The purpose of literature, and every other art, is to translate us from the so-called "real" world into others more carefully organized.
— *Koster*, The Prince

Political entrepreneurs are individuals who can themselves profit in some way from providing others with collective goods. In competitive political systems, officials, party activists, and candidates are potential political entrepreneurs since they may be able to further their own political interests by exchanging collective goods for votes. Politicians can thus be expected to try to appeal to latent interests, to help latent interest groups organize to secure their wants, or to exert themselves to provide public goods in exchange for support.

Most of the literature on politicians as political entrepreneurs implicitly assumes the U.S. political system as the background for interactions between politicians and potential supporters. This assumption, in effect, holds the institutional setting constant and focuses attention on changes in latent interests as causes of changes in politicians' interest in the provision of public goods. When, however, one compares across institutional settings (as is done in the next two chapters), it becomes clear that institutional factors such as electoral rules and party procedures have as much influence on politicians' decisions about whether to supply particular public goods as do latent interests. The example below of a Brazilian party that attempted to appeal to the latent interest in bureaucratic reform will demonstrate how a strategy that appealed to voters' policy preferences was nevertheless rendered futile by the formal and informal rules governing the electoral system.

A BRAZILIAN PARTY'S EFFORT TO INITIATE REFORM

From its inception, one major Brazilian political party, the União Democrática Nacional (UDN, National Democratic Union), made an explicit appeal to the constituency for competence and honesty in government. The UDN was organized as a reform party in opposition to other more traditional machine parties. It drew its most vocal support from the educated middle class in the more economically advanced parts of the country (Benevides 1981, 209–18; Cardoso 1978). In its official rhetoric, it strongly favored "clean" politics, administrative reform, and a general commitment to introducing impersonal norms into public life. Party platforms called for emphasizing "the struggle against the forces of administrative corruption and the compromise of the moral bases of public life that for many years had dominated."[1]

Party leaders harangued against demagoguery, opportunism, and *negociatas* (shady deals made by politicians). The UDN played a major role in publicizing political scandals and corruption.[2] It supported electoral reform aimed at preventing fraud, laws that would force presidential candidates to disclose their financial circumstances, and civil service reform. The party condemned union corruption and *peleguismo* (the co-optation of union leaders by the government). The symbol of the one successful UDN presidential candidate was the broom, with which Jânio Quadros proposed to sweep government clean of many years' encrustation of dirt and corruption (Benevides 1981, 266–77).

In spite of their sincere concern for government honesty and competence,[3] party leaders felt great pressure to play the traditional political game. Pragmatic party leaders argued that "the UDN is tired of glorious defeats; now we need to make a deal in order to get into the Government

1. Cited in Magalhães Pinto (1960) "Relatório Político do Presidente Magalhães Pinto," manuscript.
2. Carlos Lacerda (1978) was one of the most vehement and vituperative campaigners against corruption.
3. This sincerity is the reason that the UDN's inability to live up to its ideals is so well documented. Conflict between idealists and pragmatists within the party was intense, and a substantial number of denunciations of the UDN's deterioration have been published, as well as defenses of deals and opportunism as the only way to achieve power. Afonso Arinos (1953, 1965a, and 1965b) was among the most important spokesmen for the idealist position. See also Afonso Arinos Filho (1976) for a description of corruption involving the UDN in Guanabara.

and attend to the needs of our comrades."[4] The founder of the UDN in the state of Rio de Janeiro told an interviewer: "At that time [1958] . . . being a member of the UDN meant not having your daughter chosen as teacher, it meant not having the road that led to your farm maintained. It was really a tremendous persecution to be a member of the UDN."[5]

Throughout the 1950s and early 1960s, the UDN continued its rhetorical campaign against corruption and inefficiency. In day-to-day politics, however, especially local politics, they faced the politician's dilemma. The exigencies of electoral needs often overwhelmed other commitments. The UDN frequently entered into coalitions with those parties most deeply enmeshed in the traditional web of patronage. UDN candidates, competing with other candidates offering jobs and favors in return for political support, often perceived such exchanges as the only way of having a chance to be elected. Constituents, who saw favors going to the supporters of other parties put pressure on UDN politicians for their "fair" share.

In spite of the existence of widespread support for reform, the UDN was never able to turn that support into electoral currency. It was forced to rely instead on the same practices as other parties. In its day-to-day activities, it became increasingly hard to distinguish the UDN from other parties. The demands of a competitive system in which other parties used favors, jobs, and deals to gain support led many UDN politicians to do the same. While an important faction of the national leadership carried on their public campaign against corruption, numerous party members were distributing favors, making deals, and sometimes winning elections (Nunes 1984).

Some within the UDN argued that this strategy should be embraced wholeheartedly since it was the only way to achieve power.[6] They never succeeded in converting the party as a whole, however, and the UDN remained the least successful of Brazil's three major postwar parties until the military coup in 1964. It is a measure of the importance of the values of probity, rectitude, and personal disinterestedness to many

4. Interview with Deputy Saramago Pinheiro, founder of the UDN in the state of Rio de Janeiro, conducted by Márcia Silveira, November 11, 1979. He attributed this argument for compromise in the 1958 gubernatorial election to Prado Kelly, another prominent Udenista.

5. Saramago Pinheiro, from the same interview cited above.

6. Carlos Lacerda (1961), for example, though also a crusader against corruption, urged the party to use political strategies to reach political ends and to refuse "the honor of glorious defeats."

members of the UDN that they remained committed to their ideals. Even the idealists, however, realized that this strategy involved a trade-off. "To win elections was not important; what was important was to defend the moral and political principles that had impelled the founding of the UDN."[7]

UDN politicians and candidates had to operate in a system in which a refusal to make deals and trade favors placed them at an electoral disadvantage. Not all of them valued being elected over adherence to principles, and these members helped limit the UDN's electoral success. Those who did value being elected, either as an end in itself or as a means to other ends, found it necessary to distribute jobs and favors and to make deals just as other politicians did.

The party attempted to enact civil service reforms in Congress that would have prevented everyone from using government jobs as political resources. As a minority party in Congress, however, they were unable to do so. Having failed repeatedly to make it impossible for everyone to use jobs as a reward for political support, individual Udenistas could not afford to be the only ones who disdained patronage.

Politicians from the UDN did attempt to provide the public good of administrative reform to members of the general public with a latent interest in honest government. But the effort proved futile. Politicians from other parties refused to cooperate. To understand why the attempt failed, we need to go back to the logic of the argument about political entrepreneurs.

THE INTERESTS OF POLITICIANS

Whether latent interests will be satisfied by political entrepreneurs depends crucially on the incentives the potential entrepreneurs themselves confront. If the individual aspirations for power, status, wealth, or even political change of activists and politicians can be furthered by behavior that impedes rather than contributes to the satisfaction of a latent interest in public goods, the latent interest will not be satisfied. A formalization of the incentives faced by Brazilian politicians making a choice about whether to use their limited resources to bring about bureaucratic reform shows that the failure to satisfy the latent interest in better administration could have been predicted.

7. Arrobas Martins, reporting the attitude of "several great old leaders of the UDN," cited in Benevides (1981, 272–73).

The interests of politicians in Brazil resemble the interests of politicians in any other country. They want to be elected,[8] and they prefer some policies over others. Without doing them too great an injustice, one can assume that, for most politicians most of the time, the quest for office takes precedence over policy preferences. For some, the desire for office and its perquisites is truly more important than their commitment to particular policies. Others may only want to be elected in order to enact preferred policies, but if they fail to get elected, they lose their chance to influence policy outcomes. Thus, even for the public spirited, the preference for election will be strong since only election grants the possibility of achieving other preferences (Mayhew 1974). This is not to deny that, for some politicians, ideological commitments outweigh the desire to be elected. The electoral process tends to weed them out, however; they are elected less frequently than individuals who play the political game more conventionally. This selection process also contributes to the predominance of electoral motives among those who hold office.

As a useful simplification, then, suppose that politicians compete with each other in a constant-sum electoral game, that is, a game in which any advantage to one comes at the expense of others, and that the desire to win this game overrides other goals.

In addition to the desire to be elected, which every politician shares, virtually all Brazilian politicians want to see their country develop economically. They differ about how to achieve development, but the preference for development is almost universal among the politically active in Brazil. This preference might be caused by politicians' personal preference for the comforts of living in a more advanced economy, by their interest in the electoral advantage that accrues to incumbents during prosperous times, or by an altruistic element in some of their utility functions (Margolis 1982).

In all the decisions they make, politicians naturally consider the effect of the decision on the likelihood of reelection and on the growth rate. Politicians make decisions that will benefit some and burden others:

---

8. Presidents may appear to be an exception to the assertion that politicians care most about reelection since, in most Latin American countries, they cannot be immediately reelected. They can, however, serve again after one or two terms have elapsed. Some do so (e.g., Fernando Belaúnde, Carlos Andrés Pérez, and Juan Perón), and more hope to but are prevented from doing so either by military intervention (e.g., Eduardo Frei and Juscelino Kubitschek) or by ambitious competitors within their own parties (e.g., Carlos Lleras Restrepo and Rafael Caldera). The incentives presidents face as they confront the issue of administrative competence are detailed in chapter 6.

they determine who gets transfer payments such as social security and how much they get; they set tax rates and create tax loopholes; they make the rules about awarding contracts for everything from the procurement of paper clips to the building of new capitals; they make the rules that determine who gets government jobs and how much they are paid; they decide which communities get roads, schools, clinics, and potable water. All these decisions obviously affect who will vote for them and how well the economy will perform.

In addition to these formal powers, politicians in Brazil and much of the rest of the world have informal control over other resources as well, in part because of the formal rules they have made about the distribution of the goods and opportunities listed above. Brazilian politicians have traditionally had individual discretion over the distribution of some number of contracts, loopholes and other exceptions, jobs, and miscellaneous individual benefits such as loans and scholarships. These more informal decisions also affect who votes for them and how well the economy does.

In each decision to grant discretionary benefits to one individual rather than another, the politician faces a potential conflict between expending the resource to increase his probability of being elected and expending it to further programmatic goals. If he can do both—if, for example, the ablest of several competing contractors also happens to be an important political supporter—the politician's choice will be easy. Such happy coincidences occur infrequently, however.

When politicians, who are always in competition with other politicians, must choose between conflicting uses for their finite resources, their situation can be depicted schematically, as in the payoff matrices below. In these games, all politicians want to be elected more than they want anything else, though all prefer better economic performance to worse as long as it does not prejudice their immediate election chances. All control fixed numbers of appointments that they can distribute either to the applicants they think will add most to government economic performance or to the applicants they think will help most to elect them. The same person is unlikely to be best at both.

All politicians have clientelistic exchange relationships with *cabos eleitorais,* ("electoral corporals"), intermediaries who promise blocs of votes in return for various kinds of rewards, including bureaucratic jobs. *Cabos eleitorais* serve informally as party workers, ward heelers, precinct captains, and so on. They negotiate individual deals with candidates for shares of state resources, some of which they distribute to their

FIGURE 1

THE PATRON — CLIENT RELATIONSHIP AS
AN ITERATED PRISONER'S DILEMMA

		Client	
		Cooperate	Defect
Politician	Cooperate	Support $- C_j$, Job $- C_s$	$- C_j$, Job
	Defect	Support, $- C_s$	0, 0

Where

C_j = the cost to the politician of providing the job or other favor

C_s = the cost to the client of providing political support

Support $>$ Support $- C_j > 0 > - C_j$, and Job $>$ Job $- C_s > 0 > - C_s$

own clienteles in exchange for their continued support and some of which they use to increase their personal wealth and power.

Each politician thus simultaneously engages in two overlapping games:[9] a competitive electoral game with other politicians and an ongoing exchange relationship with supporters. These games overlap in the sense that the same resource, in this case jobs, determines the payoffs in both games.

THE PATRON-CLIENT GAME

The patron-client relationship in which the politician exchanges jobs or other favors for political support is an iterated prisoner's dilemma, as shown in figure 1. The upper left cell shows the payoffs to the patron and client when both fulfill their reciprocal responsibilities; the politician benefits from the client's efforts to elect him, but has to expend some resources to arrange for the client's job, and the client benefits from the job, but has to use her time and energy to help elect the politician. The upper right cell shows what would happen if the politician provided the client with a job, but the client failed to carry out her responsibilities as part of the politician's electoral machine. If the client could get away with it, she would be better off in the upper right cell. The lower left cell shows what the payoffs would be if the client provided the expected services, but the politician reneged on his promise of a job.

9. What I refer to as overlapping games are a subset of what George Tsebelis (1990) labels nested games in multiple arenas.

The politician would prefer to end up in this cell, if he could get away with it. The lower right cell shows the payoffs if neither cooperates; neither benefits and both are worse off than they would have been if both had cooperated.

The politician would like to increase his support without having to pay the cost of providing the favor, and the client would like to get the favor without going to the trouble of rallying support for the politician. If the election were a single isolated situation, neither would cooperate, and patron-client networks would fail to develop. But these and similar situations recur indefinitely, defection is visible, and punishment fairly certain. If the politician does not reward his supporters, they will not work for him next time he runs for election. If the client does not carry out her responsibilities, she can lose her bureaucratic job. In ongoing reciprocal relationships such as this, an individual who defects can always expect to be excluded from future benefits.

Even if the candidate fails to be elected, the client can expect her actions to be rewarded or punished. Political machines reinforce the exchange relationship between politicians and clients, ensuring that the client will be rewarded for her services regardless of whether the individual politician wins. In other cases, the candidate, having higher status and better political connections than the client, can individually reward her, though the reward will be greater if the candidate wins. Consequently, cooperation between the politician and the client routinely develops.

HOW PATRONAGE AFFECTS THE ELECTORAL GAME

The evolution of cooperative strategies in patron-client games affects the achievement of the politician's other goals because they increase the probability of being elected but may decrease the probability of achieving programmatic goals. Assuming that politicians' utilities are linear with the probability of winning the election, the payoff matrix for the electoral game politicians play with each other is shown in figure 2.

The top left cell of the matrix shows the candidates' probabilities of winning when neither distributes favors; these are just the baseline probabilities v_1 and v_2. In the lower left cell, Politician 1 uses patronage, gaining an electoral advantage of x_1 from it; his opponent, who does not use patronage, then suffers a decline in her probability of winning of $-x_1$ (since the total vote percentages must always add up to one). The upper right cell shows the reverse situation. The lower right cell

FIGURE 2

THE EFFECT OF PATRONAGE ON THE
PROBABILITY OF ELECTION

		Politician 2	
		Merit	Patronage
Politician 1	Merit	v_1, v_2	$v_1 - x_2, v_2 + x_2$
	Patronage	$v_1 + x_1, v_2 - x_1$	$v_1 + x_1 - x_2, v_2 + x_2 - x_1$

Where

v_i = the probability that Politician i will be elected if no jobs are distributed for political purposes. Probability v rises and falls exogenously with normal political tides.

$\Sigma\, v_i = 1$

x_i = the amount by which Politician i can increase his chances of election (at his opponents' expense), by rewarding more political activists with government jobs. (It is assumed here that, on average, each individual who works to maintain the candidate's political machine, get out the vote, etc., in the expectation of receiving a job will increase the candidate's probability of being elected by some positive, though possibly quite small, amount.)

x_i not necessarily $= x_j$

illustrates the pre-reform milieu in which both candidates rely on patronage.

If the abstractions in the above matrix are replaced by numbers, as in figure 3, its implications become more obvious. The matrix in figure 3 shows the average situation for Brazilian congressional candidates during the 1950s. As an approximation of the probability of winning when both parties rely on patronage, I have used the average vote for each party (rounded off) between 1945 and 1962.[10] The numbers in the patronage-patronage cell, the cell that reflects the real world, approximate the average vote for the UDN and for the loose PSD-PTB coalition. With all candidates relying on patronage—as they did—the probability that a UDN candidate would be elected averaged in the vicinity of 25 percent. In this matrix, the proportions in the cells do not sum to one because small parties have been excluded.

The amounts by which the probability of winning could be affected

10. If null votes and votes for coalition candidates are excluded from calculations (the identity of coalition partners cannot be determined from the available source), the average vote for the PSD in legislative elections was 35.8 percent; for the PTB, 22.9 percent; and for the UDN, 24.1 percent. Calculated from data in Ruddle and Gillette (1972).

FIGURE 3

THE ELECTORAL GAME IN BRAZIL, 1946–1964

		Politician from PSD/PTB	
		Merit	Patronage
Politician from UDN	Merit	.35, .50	.20, .65
	Patronage	.40, .45	.25, .60

SOURCE: Calculated from data in Ruddle and Gillette (1972).

by patronage were chosen to correspond to the assumption that a party's access to patronage depends on present and past electoral strength. The exact amounts by which patronage affects the probability that each party would win were chosen arbitrarily—15 percent for the PSD and PTB together and five percent for the UDN—but they reflect the distribution of electoral strength and the historic ties of the PSD and PTB to the bureaucracy. I have used numbers here, even though we can never know what the exact numbers are, in order to make the matrix more comprehensible. Changes in the numbers used would not affect the results as long as their order remained the same.

As the matrix shows, for the party disadvantaged by the distribution of patronage resources, in this case the UDN, the electoral game is like a prisoner's dilemma. In a single game, it is rational to use patronage, but individuals would be better off in the merit-merit cell than in the patronage-patronage cell where the choice of patronage lands them. Thus the party would find it rational to introduce the merit system— which would force everyone to forgo patronage—since the party plays an iterated game.

Individual members of the party, however, for whom elections are single shots, can maximize their chances of being elected by relying on patronage. Elections are not usually iterated games for individual candidates. Most candidates who lose an election will not be able to play next time, and most candidates who win will face different competitors next round. Consequently, candidates of the UDN could be expected to rely on clientelistic exchange during election campaigns—as most of them did. In other words, the matrix predicts the actual behavior of most members of the UDN; the party advocated reform and tried to pass legislation to reduce the patronage resources available to everyone, but individual candidates continued to use patronage during election campaigns.

Members of the PSD and PTB faced a different set of incentives, as the matrix indicates. Even if the game were repeated indefinitely, they would have no reason to vote for reform. Members of the PSD and PTB would be better off using patronage no matter what the UDN did and no matter how many times the game was repeated. And this is what, in fact, they did. They opposed legislation to limit patronage, and they continued to rely on it as an electoral resource.

HOW DEMAND FOR REFORM AFFECTS
THE ELECTORAL GAME

Although the electoral game above seems to fit the Brazilian case, it is not the whole story. Politicians under some circumstances do value reform, either because they expect it to result in more effective government delivery of services or because they expect it to increase the probability of being elected by responding to the public demand for reform. The electoral value to a politician of voting for reform will generally be small but positive. It will be small because politicians cast many votes on many issues, some of which are more important to constituents. Even among those voters who care about reform and know how legislators vote, many other considerations will help determine candidate preference.

So even if a vote for reform could be expected to result in a small electoral gain, politicians would only find it rational to vote for reform under special circumstances. If reform were to pass, politicians would have to decrease their reliance on patronage. At the extreme, reform would force them to move from the patronage-patronage cell in the matrix in figure 2 to the merit-merit cell. In this case, a vote for reform would only be rational if the expected gain from the vote were greater than the difference between the amount the legislator expected to gain from patronage and the amount he or she expected to lose as a result of the patronage appointments of opponents. For the larger party or coalition, the patronage advantage would virtually always outweigh the small electoral benefit of a reform vote.

Where popular demand for reform exists, giving legislators a reason to vote for it even though that reason rarely outweighs reasons to vote against, the incentives facing legislators as they decide how to vote are schematized in figure 4 below. The lower right cell is the same as in figure 2 above. Members of both parties vote against reform, so neither

FIGURE 4

THE EFFECT OF VOTING FOR REFORM
ON THE PROBABILITY OF REELECTION

		Legislator from Majority Party or Coalition	
		For Reform	Against Reform
Legislator from Minority Party	For Reform	v_1, v_2	$v_1 + x_1 - x_2 + e, v_2 + x_2 - x_1 - e$
	Against Reform	$v_1 - e, v_2 + e$	$v_1 + x_1 - x_2, v_2 + x_2 - x_1$

Where

v_i and x_i are defined as in figure 2 above; $v_2 > v_1$ (i.e., the vote for the majority party is greater than the vote for the minority party); and $x_2 > x_1$ (i.e., the majority party controls more patronage than the minority party).

e is the small amount of electoral advantage a legislator can expect for voting for reform. (At the limit, if all or none vote for reform, e would go to zero. If members of smaller parties or some members of the parties represented in the matrix failed to join the bandwagon, however, $e > 0$.)

can claim credit for supporting it and neither is hurt by the other claiming credit. The reform fails since neither large party voted for it, and candidates from both parties continue to trade jobs for support during election campaigns. The upper left cell shows the situation when both parties vote for reform. Since both voted for it, the electoral advantage from voting for reform cancels out. The reform passes, and neither party can rely on patronage during future campaigns. The lower left cell shows the payoffs that would result if the majority party[11] voted in favor of reform and the minority party voted against. The reform passes so neither party can use patronage in future campaigns, and the majority party reaps a small electoral advantage, e, from voting for reform, at the expense of the minority party. The upper right cell shows what happens when the majority party votes against reform and the minority votes in favor. The reform fails to pass so both parties continue to distribute patronage. The minority party gains a small amount of credit at the majority's expense by voting for reform.

Whether legislators will vote for reform when they face the incentives schematized in figure 4 depends on the relative magnitudes of x_1 and x_2.

11. Speaking of majority parties in the Latin American context involves a degree of simplification. In fact, legislative majorities are often coalitions. This should not, however, affect the logic of the argument.

If $(x_2 - x_1) > e$, that is, if x_2 is any significant amount larger than x_1, the majority party will vote against reform and it will fail. If, however, x_1 and x_2 are approximately equal, that is, if the two parties have approximately equal access to patronage resources, the majority party will vote for reform, and it will pass. The minority party, as long as e has any positive value at all, will always prefer reform.

To reiterate in nontechnical language, in an election all candidates can be expected to rely on patronage, as shown in figure 2. But where patronage is *equally distributed* among the two or more largest parties, and politicians can gain even a small amount from a vote for reform, members of all the larger parties have reason to vote for it in the legislature. In this situation, patronage conveys no relative advantage, but voting for reform may improve electoral chances. Consequently, political interest dictates the passage of reform.

If patronage is unequally distributed, members of parties disadvantaged by the distribution of patronage resources would be better off if the merit system were imposed on everyone. Thus, smaller parties (if not allied to the largest party) always have a reason to support reform in the legislature. Giving up the use of patronage would make them better off as long as everyone else also gave it up. As many observers have noted, the reform issue generally appeals to the "outs" in politics. By themselves, however, smaller parties will not be able to pass legislation.

Members of parties with greater access to patronage, in contrast, have no incentive to vote for reform in the legislature and no reason to eschew patronage during the electoral campaign either. They can always improve their chances of being elected by relying on patronage, no matter what members of other parties do.

Members of the majority party who have more access to patronage, then, could be expected to opt for reform *only* if they thought other gains from voting for reform would outweigh the certain costs that the loss of patronage would entail. Such a situation could occur if public outrage over bureaucratic incompetence and graft had become so vehement that politicians might fear that they would lose more votes by opposing reform than by reducing their ability to distribute patronage.

Descriptions of the reform movement in the United States suggest that public outrage over the assassination of President Garfield by a disappointed office seeker played just such a catalytic role in bringing about reform (Van Riper 1958, 88–94). Even in this case, however, "so deaf to the voice of public opinion and so blind to the signs of the times were the men who composed the Forty-Sixth Congress" (Hall 1884,

454) that the legislature only voted to pass the reform after the election of 1882.

This election, more than a year after Garfield's death, gave Democrats a majority in the House, and thus marked the end of the Republicans' post–Civil War dominance over patronage. The Republican-dominated Congress, which had greeted the project of reform with "ribald sneers" in August 1882, passed the Pendleton Act by an overwhelming majority in December. "Men who could not laugh loud enough at the ridiculous whim of transacting the public business on business principles, now tumbled over each other in their breathless haste to make that whim the national policy."[12]

As the U.S. example shows, even when opinion runs high, legislators and party leaders can usually afford to ignore the public's desire for reform because reform is only one of many issues that affect voters' choices, and it is rarely, perhaps never, the most important issue to most voters.

For advantaged parties, the dominant strategy will always be to stick with patronage, unless the payoff for voting for reform is remarkably high and the future quite certain. How large the payoff for voting for reform and how certain the future have to be depend on how unequal the original distribution of patronage resources was.

Factors that affect the distribution of patronage will be discussed at greater length in the next chapter, but for now, suffice it to say that parties will have greater access to patronage if they (1) control the presidency, (2) have more seats in the legislature than other parties, (3) have controlled the presidency or held more seats in the legislature in the past (because bureaucratic appointees tend to retain their positions after their parties have lost support and to continue using them to benefit members of the clientele network), or (4) were originally established as electoral vehicles for incumbent presidents.

In Brazil from 1946 to 1964, the loose PSD-PTB coalition enjoyed most of these conditions most of the time. Except for seven months, the presidency was held by either the PSD, the PTB, or a coalition including both parties.[13] The PSD was the largest party in Congress throughout

---

12. George William Curtis (1883), address delivered at Newport, Rhode Island to the annual meeting of the National Civil Service Reform League, cited in Hall (1884, 462).

13. Vargas was nominated by the PTB and Partido Social Progressista (PSP, Social Progressive party), but not the PSD. He attracted many PSD votes, however, governed with a cabinet drawn mainly from the PSD, and could count on PSD support in the

the period. And both the PSD and the PTB were originally created out of the Vargas political machine at the end of the dictatorship, which gave them special access to state resources and patronage from the beginning (Nunes and Geddes 1987). Given this very unequal distribution of patronage resources, the game theoretic argument above would predict the failure of reform efforts, as happened in Brazil.

Attention to the incentives confronting potential political entrepreneurs, then, suggests that such reforms are unlikely to occur in Third World countries, with their unpredictable economies and frequent military interventions, except when the largest parties share equal access to patronage. Evidence from the Brazilian case study is consistent with that prediction. The next chapter will consider evidence from other cases.

CONCLUSION

This chapter has approached explaining the impediments to state reforms from the standpoint of the individuals who must make the countless decisions that would promote or impede change. These individuals may face choices between actions that serve their immediate personal interests and actions that would improve the long-run welfare of everyone in their societies. Since they are naturally alert to their own self-interest, individuals make more choices that contribute to general welfare when these choices also contribute to their individual welfare than when the choices require sacrifice.

In general, as the chapter indicates, political entrepreneurs cannot be counted on to mobilize latent interests in collective goods such as administrative capacity, since the individual interests of potential entrepreneurs themselves may not be furthered by doing so. Solutions to collective action problems depend on political entrepreneurs who themselves face a set of incentives that makes it rational for them to respond to some latent interest groups. The argument in this chapter notes, however, that often the incentives that confront individual members of the political elite who might serve as entrepreneurs militate against their doing so.

As the attempts at administrative reform in Brazil show, even if a

---

legislature. It therefore seems legitimate to include his government in the PSD-PTB coalition category.

latent interest group exists and a party sees the potential of the latent interest and tries to use it, the interest will not be satisfied if the individual interests of political leaders can be better served in other ways. This will often be the case with regard to latent interests in administrative reform because the same resources needed to increase state capacity can instead be used by politicians to increase their chances of reelection.

FIVE

A Test of the Game Theoretic Model

When Legislators Initiate Reforms

Game theory does often have the advantage of being naked
so that, unlike those of some less explicit theories,
its limitations are likely to be noticeable.
　　　　　　　—*Schelling,* Choice and Consequence

The game theoretic argument detailed in chapter 4 leads to a prediction
that spoils will be outlawed in democracies when two conditions are
met: (1) the benefits of patronage are approximately evenly distributed
among parties; and (2) legislators have some additional incentive to
eschew patronage, such as widespread pressure for reform from
constituents.

The payoff matrices in the previous chapter showed the incentives
facing members of different parties in systems with two major parties
or coalitions. The same logic holds for systems with three or more parties
large enough to have a real chance of being elected and consequently
large enough for other parties to take seriously as competitors.

This chapter tests the model developed in chapter 4 on the South
American countries that have enjoyed fifteen or more years of continuous competitive democracy since 1930.[1] Reforms have occurred in some
of these countries, but not others. The choice of this set of cases holds
roughly constant several variables often mentioned as possible causes
of honesty and competence in government: culture, colonial institutional
structure, and level of economic development. At the same time, it

---

1. Although bureaucratic incompetence and corruption also plague authoritarian regimes, this chapter examines only democracies because the incentives that determine
whether political leaders will initiate reform depend on institutional features of the political system. Consequently, one would need a different model to explain reform in authoritarian institutional settings.

preserves sufficient variation in contemporary political institutions and reform outcomes to allow the testing of hypotheses.

Before turning to the evidence, two factors of importance when the analysis is extended beyond Brazil need to be discussed: the role of party leaders and differences in electoral rules. When looking only at Brazil between 1946 and 1964, there was no need to consider variations in electoral rules, but, as is shown below, differences among countries in electoral procedures shape the interests of politicians and thus affect the likelihood of reform. Party leaders play a greater role in countries with more institutionalized and disciplined parties than they do in Brazil. In countries with disciplined parties, the interests of party leaders have important effects on reform outcomes and thus need to be taken into consideration.

THE INTERESTS OF PARTY LEADERS

Some of the costs and benefits associated with administrative reform depend on idiosyncratic characteristics of individual political leaders (for example, the psychological benefits they might gain from the altruistic act of providing reform) or specific conjunctures of events. These idiosyncratic and conjunctural factors may be unmeasurable or at least unpredictable, and thus not very useful for producing general explanations. Though recognizing the possible importance of individual values and historical conjunctures in explaining particular reforms, the argument here will focus on other more systematic factors that shape the incentives of politicians and that can, as a result, be used to build a general explanation.

Two groups of political actors play an important role in the struggle over reform: elected politicians and party leaders, who often hold no elected office. Throughout this study it has been assumed that these individuals want, above all, to further their political careers. Given this first-order preference, their strategic second-order preferences regarding policies will vary, depending on the specific possibilities available to them. The interests of politicians were detailed in chapter 4.

Party leaders further their careers by increasing the electoral success of their parties and by achieving higher positions within their parties. Many of their goals will thus coincide with those of politicians in their parties, since both politicians and party leaders benefit from policies that give their party electoral advantages. Many individuals, of course, combine these two roles. Nevertheless, it seems analytically useful to separate them. In certain respects, the interests of party leaders diverge from those of elected politicians.

Party leaders benefit from policies that advance the interests of the party as a collectivity over the long run, whereas, in some situations, individual candidates may be injured by such policies. Party leaders, for example, favor rules that enforce party discipline, but in some circumstances individual legislators may be able to improve their electoral chances by breaking ranks. Situations may thus arise in which party leaders have interests that are not shared by the average legislator. Party leaders must then deploy the incentives at their disposal to influence legislators' votes.

Meritocratic hiring rules and other reforms that introduce impersonal criteria for the allocation of government resources reduce party leaders' discretion over the distribution of the jobs and favors that fuel political machines and thus influence the vote, just as they do politicians'.[2] Like politicians, party leaders cannot afford for the party unilaterally to cease distributing patronage, but some might be willing if they could be assured that other parties also would do so.

In Latin America, the distribution network for most government services involves party links with national (or, in Brazil, state) legislators and bureaucrats. Local patronage is much more firmly tied to the center than it is in the United States because municipalities have historically had little political autonomy and very limited powers to tax.[3] Consequently, local leaders rely on the central (or state) government for virtually all important services. This centralization of decisions and resources means that election outcomes at the local level often depend on the success of local candidates in obtaining favors through the intervention of national legislators. In return for such intervention, local leaders are expected to turn out the local vote for the legislator when the time comes.[4]

2. For concrete descriptions of the exchange of jobs and other favors for support, see the following: in Brazil, Singer (1965), Bastos and Walker (1971), Greenfield (1972), Maram (1992), and almost any Brazilian newspaper published in 1992; in Uruguay, Biles (1972); in Chile, Valenzuela (1977); in Colombia, Leal Buitraga (1984), Kline (1988), and Martz (1992); in Venezuela, Coppedge (1988), and Capriles et al. (1989).

3. Municipalities have gained power since the late 1980s in several countries as a result of legal changes during redemocratization or liberalization of previously centralized democratic regimes.

4. Brazil has always been a partial exception to the generalization made here. Municipalities in Brazil have been weak (though less so since the improvement in their fiscal base provided by the 1988 constitution), but state governments have been very powerful. Local political bosses often depend on state patronage as much as national, and state party machines have played an important role in Brazilian national politics. On the process

Reformers in the United States at one time thought that a greater centralization of the political system would destroy political machines by cutting them off from their lifeblood of local patronage (Schatt-schneider 1942). Latin America's experience with constitutionally pre-scribed centralism shows that centralism does weaken the resource base of local bosses. The scarcity of resources available at the local level, however, leads not to the withering away of political machines, but rather to the development of national (or, in Brazil, state) political machines. These machines have been no less tenacious than the local machines against which North American reformers railed. The reason for the longevity of patronage-based machines is that, regardless of their effect on the general welfare, they help politicians in the struggle against other politicians.

The influence of party leaders in the struggle over reform depends on how much these leaders affect candidates' electoral chances. Virtually all Latin American countries elect legislators using systems of propor-tional representation. The factors that contribute to the probability that candidates will win elections depend on how candidate lists are selected and whether lists are closed (that is, placement on lists is determined by party leaders) or open (that is, determined by voters). In open-list sys-tems, the vote for candidates depends on the popularity of their positions on issues, voters' party loyalty, candidates' personal charisma, and con-stituency services, patronage, and favors, much as it does in the weak party, single-member district system of the United States. In closed-list systems, the candidate's probability of winning depends primarily on his or her position on the party list. Factors such as charisma, individual issue position, and constituency service affect the candidate's probability of winning by influencing party leaders' decisions about placement on the list more than by influencing the vote directly.

In systems of closed-list proportional representation, voters vote for a party or faction. The number of candidates elected from each party or faction depends on the proportion of the vote received by the party or faction as a whole, with individual candidates selected in descending order from the list.[5] Thus, candidates at the top of the list have a much

---

through which local demands are linked to national legislators in the countries studied here, see the following: for Chile, Valenzuela (1977); for Brazil, Leal (1949) and Hagopian (forthcoming); for Venezuela, Powell (1971); for Colombia, Miranda and González (1976), Leal Buitraga (1984), and Kline (1988); for Uruguay, Biles (1972, 1978).

5. For the details of proportional representation systems in Latin America, see Institute for Comparative Study of Political Systems (no date).

greater chance of being elected than those near the bottom. So, if a deputy thought that a vote against reform might be punished when the next list was drawn up, he or she would have a strong incentive to vote for it. Where, for reasons to be discussed below, leaders of the major parties have reached an agreement to support reform and made its enactment a matter of party discipline, individual members have had an additional incentive to vote for reform.

This incentive probably would not equal the advantage to be gained by distributing patronage (since placement on the list would depend on votes on many bills as well as on other considerations). But, even if quite small, it would be sufficient to make it rational for a legislator to agree to forgo some patronage *if* he or she could be sure others would also forgo the same amount. In effect, this additional incentive, even if very small, could affect a legislator's decision about voting for reform.

In systems in which party leaders' control over the list determines who is elected, they exercise great power over the votes of politicians who have to be concerned about future reelection. In systems such as Brazil's, in which party leaders have less control over who runs for office, or Colombia's during the later National Front, in which central party leaders lost control of the lists, they exercise little influence.[6] Where party leaders determine election chances, the calculations of legislators considering a vote for reform will focus on the vote's expected effect on the judgment of party leaders.

I turn now to an examination of how evidence from five Latin American countries squares with the arguments above and in chapter 4.

THE EFFECT OF THE DISTRIBUTION OF PATRONAGE ON REFORM

The countries examined in this chapter are Chile, Uruguay, Colombia, and Venezuela, in addition to Brazil. The model used assumes that politicians are motivated primarily by the desire to remain in office. (Costa Rica was excluded from the universe of cases because legislators cannot be immediately reelected there.) I limited the universe to those countries with fifteen or more years of consecutive democratic experience since 1930 because it seemed that a very unstable or unpredictable

6. Control of the list is obviously not the only way party leaders can influence legislators and impose party discipline. Both Britain, with a single-member district system, and Chile, with an open-list system, are usually judged to have strong, disciplined parties. Control of the list does, however, give party leaders a powerful weapon. In its absence, some alternative basis of influence must be developed if parties are to maintain discipline.

political environment might affect politicians' assessments of feasible alternatives and their costs.

The 1930 cutoff point was chosen because pressure to improve administrative competence began to mount when the Depression led governments to try novel interventions in their economies. At that time, it became obvious to some observers that incompetent administration had national welfare consequences, and they began to advocate reform. Prior to that time, demand for reform was insufficient in most countries to give legislators any incentive to supply it.

The test of the argument below focuses mainly on the introduction of merit-based hiring for civil servants. This element of reform was selected for emphasis because the many administrative reform packages that have been proposed during recent decades nearly always include it; rules for merit-based hiring, unlike other kinds of reform, vary only moderately from country to country; and the results of laws requiring recruitment by exam are relatively easy to assess. Meritocratic recruitment may not be the most important aspect of administrative reform, but it is always at least moderately important, and it is the easiest element of reform to "measure" accurately.

This chapter is narrowly focused to make possible an empirical test of the proposed model. A theory that explains this element of reform, however, should be generalizable to any other reform that involves a loss of electoral resources to the politicians who must initiate it. The kind of model used here should be useful, for example, in explaining why so many governments were slow to return money-losing public enterprises to the private sector, and why it seemed for so long to be so much easier to increase state intervention in the economy than to decrease it. Intervention in the economy always creates opportunities for the distribution of jobs, contracts, and profit opportunities of various kinds to political supporters. Thus it is not surprising that political leaders show reluctance to give up these resources, even when economic advisers strongly urge them to do so (cf. Bates 1988, 46–53). A focus on the incentives that face political leaders in specific historical and institutional settings should generate predictions about when they might agree to give up some of the political resources derived from control of parts of the economy—as well as when they would cooperate to achieve administrative reform.

Of the five countries examined, three—Colombia, Venezuela, and Uruguay—passed initial civil service reforms during more-or-less democratic periods.[7] Brazil's initial reform occurred during the Vargas dictatorship in the late 1930s. Most attempts to further extend the reform during the democratic period failed. No comprehensive civil service reform passed in Chile during its long period of democracy prior to 1973. This section examines the circumstances under which reforms occurred in Uruguay, Venezuela, and Colombia to see if they are consistent with the predictions of the model noted above. It then discusses Brazil and Chile as contrasting cases.

In the real world, there is no way to measure amounts of patronage or how much influence on the vote it has. In the case studies that follow, I deal with this measurement problem by relying on two plausible assumptions.

1.   All else being equal, the distribution of jobs and favors increases the probability of being elected. (Otherwise, politicians would not expend so much of their energy on providing such services.)

2.   The amount of patronage to which a candidate has access for distribution depends on his or her party's control of elective and administrative offices at the national level. Such control is a function of the party's present and past electoral success. (Generally, a waning party that has lost many of the seats it formerly held in the legislature will still be able to call upon loyalists in the bureaucracy for a number of years.)

These assumptions permit an approximate rank ordering of each party's access to patronage, which is a level of measurement sufficient for the simple model used here. They imply that if parties control roughly equal numbers of seats in the legislature and alternate in the presidency over a period of years, each party will have access to about the same amount of patronage. If, in contrast, one party dominates the presidency and the legislature, one can assume that it also dominates patronage opportunities.

---

7. Categorization of Uruguay as a democracy at the time of the reform is somewhat dubious. The elected president had staged a coup and replaced the elected legislature. Still, two factions continued to function as the most important political competitors. Since party competition continued during this period of modified democracy, Uruguay was retained in the small sample of democracies. See Taylor (1952) for details about the coup and its aftermath.

COLOMBIA

Competition between the Liberal and Conservative parties for control of government and the spoils associated with control has structured all of Colombia's modern history. Fernando Guillén Martínez characterizes Colombian history as: "a mass of public employees arms in hand faces a mass of armed aspirants to public office" (Kline 1988, 19). Until 1958, transfers of power from one party to the other were usually accompanied by large-scale turnovers of personnel and by widespread partisan violence (Solaún 1980). According to Robert Dix (1967, 148), "The parties have treated government as an objective to be seized and, once won, as a bastion in which to entrench themselves like armies of occupation, subsisting on the bureaucratic booty of battle."

Public welfare suffered from the inefficiency of a bureaucracy composed of patronage appointments as well as from periodic outbreaks of violence. As early as the 1920s, critics identified the parties' excessive reliance on patronage as one of the pathologies of Colombian life. Reforms have been undertaken, however, only during two time periods, both of which correspond to periods of approximate equality between the two parties.

Colombia's first experiments with merit-oriented administrative reforms occurred during the presidency of Enrique Olaya Herrera (1930–34). The Olaya administration marked the first electoral victory of the Liberal party in the twentieth century. Olaya won only because the Conservatives split their vote between two candidates, and the reformist Liberals' hold on government during the first half of his administration was fairly tenuous, as shown in table 2. Several administrative reforms were passed at this time, the most important of which aimed at improving the performance of the Ministry of Public Works and other agencies responsible for the construction and maintenance of railroads and highways (Hartwig 1983, 105–7).

By 1934, the Liberals had consolidated their electoral dominance, and Alfonso López Pumarejo (1934–38) won the presidency easily. He continued many of the reformist economic policies of Olaya, but permitted the reassertion of partisan considerations in hiring. The early merit-based reforms of the Olaya administration quietly disappeared during the period of Liberal hegemony from 1934 to 1946 (Hartwig 1983, 106–11). As table 2 shows, no other period of approximate parity[8] occurred in Colombia until the National Front.

8. "Approximate parity" cannot be defined exactly because, as shown in chapter 4,

TABLE 2

DISTRIBUTION OF PARTISAN STRENGTH IN THE
COLOMBIAN CHAMBER OF DEPUTIES, 1931–1953[a]

Date of Election	Party	
	Liberal (% vote)	Conservative (% vote)
1931	51.1	48.9
1933	62.4	37.4
1935	100.0	abstained
1937	100.0	abstained
1939	64.4	35.1
1941	63.8	35.7
1943	64.4	33.8
1945	63.0	33.6
1947	54.7	44.4
1949	53.5	46.1
1951	abstained	98.6
1953	abstained	99.7

SOURCES: 1931–33, calculated from Eastman (1982, 639); 1935–53, Hartlyn (1988, 150).

[a] No Congressional elections were held between 1953 and the beginning of the National Front in 1958.

Colombia's next attempt to establish merit as the basis for recruitment to the civil service occurred in 1958. At that time, each of the major parties controlled exactly half of the legislature and half of the available administrative appointments.

This division resulted from a pact, the National Front, between the Liberal and Conservative parties, that established parity between the two traditional rivals in the national legislature, in departmental (that is, state) legislatures, in municipal councils, and in administrative appointments. This pact, designed to end a decade of repression and partisan violence in which more than two hundred thousand people had

how equal the parties need to be to make a vote for reform rational for legislators depends on the strength of popular demand for reform. For practical purposes in this chapter, however, I have considered parties "approximately equal" if the difference between them in terms of the percentage of legislative seats controlled was less than 3 percent.

been killed, was initially supposed to remain in effect for sixteen years, though some elements of the pact survived longer. Each party would receive 50 percent of the seats in legislatures and councils regardless of the vote. The presidency would rotate between the two parties. A career civil service was proposed as a means of removing key administrative jobs from partisan control, and other administrative jobs were to be distributed equally between supporters of the two parties. In short, the pact established an equal sharing of power and patronage regardless of electoral outcome for sixteen years (Dix 1980; Berry, Hellman, and Solaún 1980; Hartlyn 1988).

The pact called for the creation of a merit-based career civil service, but presidential and legislative action were required to initiate it (Groves 1974; Morcillo 1975). Individual legislators facing this decision about whether to forgo a portion of customary patronage would have to consider the electoral costs and benefits associated with patronage.

Two factors contributed to make a vote for reform more attractive than it might otherwise have been. The first was the interest of all politicians in reestablishing a democratic system, which depended on ending partisan violence. Administrative reform was expected to contribute to ending the violence by providing a fair means of distributing jobs and also by contributing to growth-producing economic policies.

Party leaders in both parties had committed themselves to a set of agreements, including complicated parity arrangements as well as civil service reform, as a way of reducing the violence and reestablishing a competitive political system. In other words, party elites had managed to forge an enforceable cooperative solution to the prisoner's dilemma of unrestrained party competition. The career interests of high-level party leaders in reestablishing a competitive electoral system explain their support for the pact. Party leaders in Colombia could then influence legislators' decisions with special effectiveness because of the closed-list proportional representation system.[9]

Evidence from the Colombian case is thus completely consistent with the model. Reform occurred when access to patronage was distributed equally. Once party elites had bound themselves (Elster 1979) to behave strategically in order to end civil strife and return to democracy, party discipline enforced by the closed-list system provided legislators with the additional incentive needed to make a vote for reform rational.

9. Kline (1976) shows high levels of party discipline in Colombia on issues of special interest to party leadership.

URUGUAY

In Uruguay, the career civil service was first mandated by the 1934 constitution. This constitution legalized a pact between two factions of the traditional dominant parties, the Terrista faction of the Colorado party and the Herrerista faction of the National, or Blanco, party.

In the Uruguayan party system (until recently limited to two parties), multiple factions within parties have independent legal status and run their own lists of candidates in elections. The total votes received by all the factions within a party are summed to arrive at the total vote for the party. Seats within each party are distributed to factions on the basis of proportional representation. Thus, there are no electoral disincentives to running multiple lists of candidates.

Prior to the 1934 reform, Gabriel Terra had been elected president as the head of his faction on the Colorado party ticket. In the face of severe economic distress caused by the Depression and an apparently insurmountable policy immobilism caused by Uruguay's collegial executive and powerful but factionalized legislature, Terra staged a coup d'etat from within in 1933. Luis Alberto Herrera, caudillo of the most important Blanco party faction at the time, collaborated with Terra, and the two faction leaders entered into a pact to share government offices, excluding other factions of both parties (Taylor 1960, 23–29).

The sitting legislature was dismissed. Terra and Herrera chose a deliberative assembly of ninety-nine members, made up of approximately equal numbers of Colorado supporters of Terra and Blanco supporters of Herrera, to act as a provisional legislature. This assembly in turn elected a constituent assembly made up of Terra and Herrera supporters.

The resulting constitution institutionalized the pact by mandating minority representation in the president's Council of Ministers for the largest faction of the opposition party and the equal division of Senate seats between the most voted lists of the two most voted parties. This division of the Senate assured these two factions equal control of appointments of all important administrative positions, the boards of directors of state enterprises, supreme court justices, and members of the accounts tribunal (Taylor 1960, 171). These high-level appointees controlled lower-level appointments. At the same time, the pact excluded other factions from access to spoils. In effect, it transformed what had been a de facto multiparty system into a two-party system with approximately equal access to patronage for both parties.

Traditionally, the Colorado party had attracted more electoral support and controlled more patronage than had the Blancos. As a result of the pact between Terra and Herrera, however, competing factions of both parties were excluded from government, and parity between the two factions in the Senate and in high administrative positions became the law of the land. Usually, more popular parties have access to more patronage, but in this instance the pact resulted in an equal division in spite of electoral inequality. In this setting, the constituent assembly was also able to agree to establish a career civil service, which would remove some appointments from the discretion of party activists. As in Colombia, the closed-list proportional representation system provided faction leaders with incentives they could deploy to affect the votes of members of the constituent assembly.

VENEZUELA

Venezuela's first merit-based career civil service law also passed during a period of temporary equality between parties. At the beginning of the democratic period in Venezuela, administrative reform seemed to be supported by everyone. Excessive corruption had helped discredit the former dictator, Marcos Pérez Jiménez, and administrative reform was widely seen as needed both to reduce corruption and to enable the state to use oil revenues effectively to foster industrialization and increase social welfare. President Rómulo Betancourt (1959–64) expressed strong support for reform, foreign experts were hired to help formulate a reform and train Venezuelans to implement it, and a reform agency attached to the presidency was created (Brewer-Carías 1975a, 452–59, and 1975b; Stewart 1978, 30–43).

The agency completed its draft plan for civil service reform in 1960, and the president submitted it to Congress, where he had a coalition majority. Since party discipline in Venezuela is strong, in part because of party leaders' control of electoral lists, prospects for reform should have been good. Nevertheless, the civil service reform bill was never reported out of committee (Groves 1967).

It continued, moreover, to languish in Congress throughout the Betancourt presidency and through that of his successor, Raúl Leoni (1964–69). Venezuelan observers note that, despite flamboyant public statements supporting reform, neither president really pushed the bill (Brewer-Carías 1975a, 454–57). Throughout this period, Acción Democrática (AD, Democratic Action) controlled the presidency and a

TABLE 3

DISTRIBUTION OF SEATS AMONG THE
LARGER PARTIES IN THE VENEZUELAN
CHAMBER OF DEPUTIES, 1946–1988[a]

	Party		
Election Date	AD (%)	COPEI (%)	URD[b] (%)
1946	85.6	11.9	
1958	54.9	14.3	25.6
1963	36.3	22.3	16.2
1968	29.6	27.7	9.4
1973	51.0	32.0	2.5
1978	43.2	43.2	1.5
1983	57.4	31.3	1.5
1988	48.3	33.3	

SOURCES: 1946–83, McDonald and Ruhl (1989, 139); 1988, Wilkie and Ochoa (1989, 249).
[a] A military dictator governed Venezuela from 1948 to 1958.
[b] URD: Unión Republicana Democrática (Democratic Republican Union).

strong plurality in Congress, as shown in table 3. They had much more to lose from giving up patronage than had the other parties.

In 1968, Rafael Caldera of the Comité de Organización Política Electoral Independiente (COPEI, Social Christian party) was elected president with 28.9 percent of the vote, as compared with the AD-led coalition vote of 28.1 percent (Ruddle and Gilette 1972, 101). In the legislature, seats were split between the two largest parties, with 29.6 percent for AD and 27.7 percent for COPEI. The civil service reform was brought forward for consideration in Congress again, revised to make it congruent with recent constitutional and institutional changes, and passed in 1970 with support from both AD and COPEI (Brewer-Carías 1975a, 475–79; Stewart 1978, 39–40). Again, reform passed when access to patronage had become approximately equal.

CHILE

In its long history of democratic government, Chile never passed a comprehensive civil service reform. It had no civil service commission and no uniform system of recruitment and promotion (Valenzuela 1984, 256; López 1972). It did have some requirements for entry, such as completion of the tenth grade, but even these were sometimes violated in practice.[10] Each agency controlled its own system of recruitment. As a result, some agencies were highly professionalized and others extremely politicized (Ascher 1975, 57–86; Urzúa and García 1971, 175–78).

As table 4 shows, the larger Chilean parties won approximately equal numbers of seats in the Chamber of Deputies in 1949 and came fairly close on two other occasions, 1937 and 1945. All else being equal, one would expect reforms to have occurred. But all else was not equal. Two characteristics of the Chilean political system created obstacles to reform: the fragmented party system that resulted in the need for coalition government and open-list proportional representation.

The Chilean party system was more fragmented than those of the other countries examined (except Brazil after 1985). With the single exception of Christian Democrat Eduardo Frei, Chilean presidents always relied on coalitions for support since their parties never had sufficient seats in Congress to pass legislation. These coalitions affected the chance that reforms would pass in two ways. First, they dichotomized parties into blocs of insiders and outsiders. The governing coalition formed a dominant bloc allied with the president that enjoyed disproportionate access to spoils, and consequently opposed reform.

During each of the legislative terms in which the larger parties approached parity in the Chamber of Deputies, the president's coalition excluded one of the major parties, thus giving members of included parties a stake in the status quo that helped them at the expense of members of the excluded party. During the term of the legislature elected in 1937, President Arturo Alessandri governed for the first year and a half with a coalition of Conservatives, Liberals, and small parties that excluded the Radicals. During the latter part of the 1937 legislative term, President Pedro Aguirre Cerda governed with a coalition made up of Radicals, Socialists, Communists, and other small parties, excluding Liberals and Conservatives. During the term of the legislature elected in 1945, President Juan Rios governed for the first year or so with a coalition of Radicals, Liberals, and small parties, excluding the Conservatives (Caviedes 1979). After September 1946, President Gabriel Gon-

---

10. Petras (1969, 350) shows that substantial numbers of low- and middle-level public employees had not completed secondary school.

TABLE 4

DISTRIBUTION OF SEATS AMONG THE
LARGER PARTIES IN THE CHILEAN
CHAMBER OF DEPUTIES, 1932–1973[a]

Election Date	Party						
	PC	PL	PR	PS[b]	PDC[c]	PAL	PCCh
1932	23.9	12.7	23.9				
1937	23.8	23.8	19.7	12.9			
1941	21.8	15.0	29.9	10.2	2.0		
1945	24.5	21.1	26.5	6.1	2.0		
1949	21.1	22.4	23.1	8.2	2.0	9.5	
1953	10.9	15.6	12.9	16.3	2.0	17.7	
1957	15.6[d]	20.4	24.5	8.2	11.6	6.8	
1961	11.6	19.0	26.5	8.2	15.6		10.9
1965	2.0	4.1	13.6	10.2	55.8		12.2
1969	22.7[e]		16.0	10.0	36.7		14.7
1973	24.0		3.3	18.7	33.3		16.7

SOURCES: 1932–61, calculated from Urzúa Valenzuela (1968, 73–98); 1965–73, from McDonald and Ruhl (1989, 201).

　　PC: Partido Conservador (Conservative party)
　　PL: Partido Liberal (Liberal party)
　　PR: Partido Radical (Radical party)
　　PS: Partido Socialista (Socialist party)
　　PDC: Partido Demócrata Cristiano (Christian Democratic party)
　　PAL: Partido Agrario Laborista (Agrarian Labor party)
　　PCCh: Partido Comunista de Chile (Communist party of Chile)
　　[a]The 1973 legislative election was the last before the military seized power. No further elections were held until 1989.
　　[b]In 1945 the percentage in the table combines seats won by the Partido Socialista de Chile and the Partido Socialista Auténtico. The 1949–57 figures combine these parties with the Partido Socialista Popular.
　　[c]Prior to 1958, the core of what became the PDC was called the Falange Nacional. See Urzúa Valenzuela (1968, 84–100) for details of the evolution of the PDC.
　　[d]Combines seats held by PC and Partido Conservador Unido.
　　[e]The PC and PL merged to form the Partido Nacional. Figures in the table for 1969 and 1973 are for the PN.

zález Videla governed for the rest of the 1945 term and most of the 1949 legislative term. The coalitions supporting González Videla changed frequently. There were eight cabinet shuffles in six years, six of them involving changes in the identity of the parties supporting the president. All cabinets included the Radicals in various combinations with other parties; most excluded the Conservatives. Thus, during the González Videla administration (1946–52), extreme instability was added to other impediments to reform.

Furthermore, these coalitions were held together by agreements on the distribution of spoils among coalition partners (Valenzuela 1978; López 1972, 89). Even if the president's party had been willing to make an agreement with the opposition to eschew patronage, it could not have done so because of the almost certain disintegration of its governing coalition that would have followed. Such an agreement would, in effect, constitute defection in the ongoing reciprocal agreement between the president and his coalition partners, and he could expect to be punished for such defection. The relationship between the president and his co-alition supporters, in other words, affects calculations about the costs of reform in the same way that established patron-client relationships affect the cost of reform to other politicians.

A second characteristic of the Chilean democratic system also de-creased the likelihood of passing a reform: the open-list system of pro-portional representation. In open-list systems, a candidate's place on the list is determined by the vote received. Thus, a candidate runs not only against candidates from other parties, but also against other candidates from his or her own party. As a consequence of the open-list system, patronage becomes an even more valuable resource to those candidates who have access to it. Candidates can distinguish themselves from the candidates of other parties on the basis of programmatic appeals, offers of public goods, and ideology, but attention to casework and the distri-bution of private goods are among the few ways of distinguishing them-selves from other candidates in the same party. Incumbents have a great advantage over other candidates in terms of their ability to distribute favors. Consequently, incumbents of all parties that have historically been able to draw on patronage resources in an open-list proportional representation system can be expected to be especially reluctant to give up patronage. And they are the only ones who get to vote.

The game theoretic matrices shown in chapter 4 display the structure of the competition between members of different parties, but they do not show the competition among members of the same party in an open-list system. As in other overlapping or nested games, moves in one arena (here, the game between parties) have consequences in all others (here, the game among rivals in the same party). A matrix showing only one arena will not accurately predict outcomes because it does not take into account all the contextual factors that affect payoffs (cf. Tsebelis 1990).

In Chile, the costs of reform to incumbents in the game with rivals in their own parties raised the overall costs of reform to a level that made a vote for reform unlikely.

Given the fragmented party system, open-list proportional representation, and the need for coalitions in order to govern, no civil service reform could be expected in Chile, and none occurred. With regard to the occurrence or nonoccurrence of an initial reform, then, game theoretic predictions seem to be consistent with events in the real world.

BRAZIL

The early years of the Brazilian case are covered extensively in chapters 3 and 4. To summarize briefly, Getúlio Vargas established a career civil service in Brazil during the period of dictatorship from 1937 to 1945. Reform had made a fair amount of headway in imposing merit as the criterion for hiring and promotion by the time Vargas was overthrown. But, after the return to democracy in 1946, earlier reforms were to a considerable extent undermined by legislation that blurred the distinction between the career civil service and other public employees who had not been recruited by exam (Siegel 1966, 148–75).

During the 1950s and 1960s, as economic development became the most important goal of the Brazilian government, concern about administrative reform reached new levels. Presidents Vargas (during his second administration, 1951–54), Kubitschek, and Quadros all proposed major reforms (Graham 1968, 143–53). Public demand for reform was widespread. Even in the face of such expressions of public opinion, however, legislators refused to vote for it.

In chapter 4, Brazil's complex party system was simplified by combining legislators into the two blocs that dominated the political arena from 1946 to 1964 and using the average vote for each bloc as an approximation of its strength. Table 5 gives a more exact indication of the distribution of strength of the individual parties. The distribution of seats was markedly unequal. Brazil's open-list proportional representation system for electing the Chamber of Deputies gave incumbents in the PSD and PTB—the parties with greatest historical access to patronage—even stronger reasons to oppose reform. It thus seems unsurprising that reforms failed to pass between 1946 and 1964.

Reform laws were proposed at various times, but only two kinds of civil service laws made it through Congress: those that granted benefits to civil servants and thus involved no electoral cost to legislators; and

TABLE 5
DISTRIBUTION OF SEATS AMONG THE LARGER PARTIES IN THE BRAZILIAN CHAMBER OF DEPUTIES, 1946–1962[a]

Election Date	Party			
	PSD	UDN	PTB	PSP
1945	52.8	26.9	7.7	0.7
1950	36.8	26.6	16.8	7.9
1954	35.0	22.7	17.2	9.8
1958	35.3	21.5	20.2	7.7
1962	28.8	22.2	28.4	5.1

SOURCE: Santos (1986, 68).
[a] The last legislative election before the 1964 military coup was in 1962.

one that extended meritocratic norms into agencies controlled by one particular party and thus involved gains rather than costs for the majority of legislators. Congress increased the wages of civil servants and passed several laws granting job security and higher status to unclassified (that is, non-civil service) employees.

The one exception to the overall decline in the merit-based civil service during the 1946–64 democratic period occurred when Congress extended the merit system to cover the social security institutes. By voting to include these institutes in the merit system, legislators from other parties could decrease the resources available to one party, the PTB without incurring any cost themselves. Given the unusual circumstance of the existence of a group of agencies dominated by one particular party, parity in the legislature was not necessary as an inducement to vote to extend the merit system.

Since redemocratization in 1985, the party system has become even more fragmented and the distribution of seats has remained markedly unequal (see table 6). No reforms have occurred, and in fact, for reasons to be dealt with in more detail in chapter 6, politicization and corruption in the bureaucracy have increased (Geddes and Ribeiro 1992).

THE RETURN TO AN UNEQUAL DISTRIBUTION OF PATRONAGE

Up to now, this chapter has dealt with the situations in which the first step toward a merit-based civil service was taken. I turn now to consid-

TABLE 6
DISTRIBUTION OF SEATS AMONG THE LARGER PARTIES IN THE BRAZILIAN CHAMBER OF DEPUTIES, 1987–1991

Date Installed	Party					
	PMDB	PDS	PFL	PDT	PSDB	PRN
1987	53	7	24	5		
1989	26	6	18	8	12	6
1991	21	9	17	9	7	8

SOURCE: *Folha de São Paulo*, October 29, 1990, special edition, pp. 1–4.
   PMDB: Partido do Movimento Democrático Brasileiro (Party of the Brazilian Democratic Movement)
   PDS: Partido Democrático Social (Democratic Social party)
   PFL: Party da Frente Liberal (Liberal Front party)
   PDT: Partido Democrático Trabalhista (Democratic Labor party)
   PSDB: Partido da Social Democracia Brasileira (Brazilian Social Democratic party)
   PRN: Partido de Reconstrução Nacional (National Reconstruction party)

eration of whether these initial steps have been, or will be, followed by others. Given the notorious inefficiency of post-reform bureaucracies in Venezuela, Colombia, and Uruguay, one must conclude either that civil service reform does not work in Latin America or that initial reforms were subsequently undermined.

Evidence suggests that professionalization does occur and does increase competence and public service orientations in the parts of the bureaucracy in which it takes hold (Wahrlich 1964; Láfer 1970; Vieira 1967; Schmidt 1974; Mares 1990) but that initial reforms affect only a small part of the bureaucracy. Where conjunctures favoring the passage of reforms have lasted only a short time, initial reforms have not been followed by additional increments of reform. Further, reforms have sometimes been vitiated by subsequent legislation and executive decrees.

In the United States, where both parties enjoyed similar access to patronage from 1882 until 1896, merit-based civil service was gradually extended "by executive order, taking advantage of feeble statutory authorization" (Schattschneider 1942, 138). By 1896, the merit system had been extended to cover about half of all appointments, which included "the bulk of the offices which it was then either legal or politically and administratively practical to place under the merit system." (Van Riper 1958, 130). Most of these extensions occurred when the party in control of government had lost an election and expected the incoming party to dismiss its supporters (Skowronek 1982). This pattern of incremental extension was possible because, in a system of two approximately equal parties, occasions recur when it is temporarily in the interest of one party or the other to extend the merit system. In the long run, this series of instrumental decisions created a professional civil service.

The same thing is likely to happen in South America, but the long run will probably take longer because of differences in party systems. The initial establishment of a merit-based civil service, an agency to administer it, and, usually, a school to train civil servants creates islands of competence within the bureaucracy and concentrates advocates of further reform strategically within government. Though they lose many battles, they rarely disappear from the scene completely.

Reform continues to be strenuously advocated from these islands within the executive branch of government and, also, in the press. Elected officials, however, have often shown reluctance to extend reform. Multiparty systems in Latin America have so far not produced lasting periods of relative equality among the most popular parties or coalitions. And, in the two countries with two-party systems, the institutionalization of factions in the form of lists or *sublemas*[11] has transferred the struggle for patronage from a struggle between parties into a struggle among factions within each party. This makes it extremely unlikely that a parity situation can be maintained for any length of time, since it must be maintained among multiple factions, not just between two parties.

What has been the fate of these initial reforms as the distribution of patronage which made them possible changed? In the multiparty systems, one party or another has tended to dominate, and it has not served that party's interest to extend the merit system. If two approximately equal parties were to emerge as the only serious competitors for power in a multiparty system, however, as seemed to have happened in Venezuela prior to the Pérez impeachment in 1993,[12] the game theoretic model would predict further extensions of reform. And, as will be seen below, some extensions have occurred in Venezuela. In the countries

11. *Sublema* is the name given to party factions in Uruguay, where parties are called *lemas*, literally, slogans.

12. Recent constitutional changes in Venezuela and the scandals surrounding the Pérez impeachment may have undermined the party duopoly enjoyed for the last several decades by AD and COPEI. With barriers to entry at least temporarily lowered, it is possible that other parties will now be able to establish themselves as important political actors in the Venezuelan system.

with institutionalized factions, competition among the factions over patronage and the need to use patronage to hold coalitions of factions together have made agreements to extend merit-based civil service very unlikely.

VENEZUELA

In Venezuela, when Acción Democrática (AD) returned to its customary dominant role with the election of Carlos Andrés Pérez in 1973, non-partisan administration suffered a setback. Pérez won the presidency with a strong plurality (48.4 percent, compared with 36.7 percent for COPEI). He was the first post-1958 Venezuelan president to have an absolute majority of seats, as opposed to a coalition majority, in both houses of Congress (Karl 1982, 182–84). He asked for, and eventually got, special powers to enact by executive decree a package of proposals aimed at controlling and using effectively the windfall of oil money threatening to engulf the nation. Included among these projects were several administrative reforms. Pérez expressed strong support for administrative reform, including professionalization of personnel. His actions, however, tended to belie his words.

Decree 211, issued by Pérez, allowed the administration to increase the number of nonclassified public employees (that is, temporary and low-status employees who need not pass exams to enter the service) as well as the number of positions *de confianza*. Positions *de confianza* are high-status appointments in which loyalty is considered an appropriate criterion for recruitment. In practice, they are positions filled entirely at the discretion of supervisors. By the end of Pérez's term in office, employees *de confianza* included all division chiefs, those employed in budget departments, buying, supplies, document reproduction, and all secretaries in these areas. COPEI claimed that eighty thousand people had lost their jobs for political reasons during the administration turn-over when Pérez came to power (Karl 1982, 267).

Some administrative reforms have occurred since the Pérez adminis-tration. An anti-corruption law,[13] for example, was passed in 1982 when the Chamber of Deputies was again evenly split between AD and COPEI, as shown in table 3. The problem of professionalizing personnel, how-ever, remains unresolved (Petkoff 1978; Brewer-Carías 1985, 1988,

13. Ley Orgánica de Salvaguarda del Patrimonio Público, published in the *Gaceta Oficial* No. 3077, extraordinario (December 23, 1982). My thanks to Michael Coppedge for bringing this law to my attention.

167–99).[14] Partisan considerations still affect most hiring decisions, and turnover in the bureaucracy when a new administration comes into power is so high that administrative output falls noticeably during the first few months of each administration (Cova and Hannot 1986). Corruption continues to be a serious problem (Brewer-Carías 1988, 194–99; Capriles et al. 1989, 1990).[15]

URUGUAY

The situation in Uruguay resembled that in Venezuela, but in a more extreme form. The brief period of relative equality between two factions was unique in Uruguayan history. The two parties achieved near equality in 1962 and 1971 (see table 7), but, because the factions within each party were unequal, as shown in table 8, no reform occurred. Members of each faction compete not only with the other party, but with members of other factions within their own party. Consequently, reform would only appeal to members of the larger factions if the largest factions within each party enjoyed approximately equal amounts of patronage relative to each other as well as to factions in the other party.

Article 57 of the 1934 constitution mandated hiring and promotion based on merit, but did not establish an agency to conduct exams. Instead, each bureaucratic entity set its own standards (Taylor 1960, 215). Some evidence about the strictness of these standards can be inferred from education statistics. Forty-six percent of public employees in the mid-1950s had not finished primary school, and 70 percent had completed ten or fewer years of schooling (Taylor 1960, 218–19). Entrance exams in many agencies guaranteed little more than literacy. There was one important barrier to entry, however; applicants were not permitted to take the test without the consent of the neighborhood *sublema* boss.[16]

The 1952 constitution helped undermine earlier efforts to professionalize the bureaucracy by granting the right to name directors of state enterprises directly to the parties, three to the majority party and two to the minority. As a result,

The autonomous entities and decentralized services, in general, are refuges

14. "Burocracia: Ciudadano," *El Diario*, Caracas (August 2, 1987), pp. 22–23.
15. See virtually any 1992 or 1993 Venezuelan newspaper.
16. For a more extended discussion of neighborhood *sublema* organizations and their function in distributing patronage, see Biles (1972).

TABLE 7

DISTRIBUTION OF SEATS IN THE URUGUAYAN
CHAMBER OF DEPUTIES, 1942–1989[a]

Election Date	Party		
	Colorado (%)	Blanco (%)	Frente Amplio (%)
1942	58.6	23.2	—
1946	47.5	31.3	—
1950	53.5	31.3	—
1954	51.5	35.4	—
1958	38.4	51.5	—
1962	44.4	47.5	—
1966	49.3[b]	40.4[b]	—
1971	41.4	40.4	—
1984	41.4	35.4	21.2
1989	30.3	39.4	21.1

SOURCES: 1942–62, calculated from Fabregat (1950–63); 1966, Venturini (1984, 9); 1971 and 1984, calculated from Rial (1985, 11); 1989, *Latin American Research Review: Southern Cone* (December 21, 1989), p. 7.

[a] The 1942 legislative election was the first after the end of the Terra-Herrera pact. The 1971 legislative election was the last before the military seized power in 1973. The first postmilitary legislative election was held in 1984.

[b] The figures for 1966 are percentage of votes rather than percentage of seats.

for failed politicians, that is, candidates for deputy who have lost elections; this is a consolation prize; it assures them a salary and electoral possibilities through the illicit use of power. They have a duty to satisfy the demands of the party with regard to appointing employees, granting credits, pensions, giving prompt service. (Real 1965, 67)

Most legislation regarding the civil service and additional provisions added to the 1952 constitution dealt with job security and grievance procedures. These issues involved no cost to legislators as long as the number of jobs kept expanding, and, in fact, brought them electoral benefits in the form of support from government employees (estimated at 27.6 percent of the working population of Uruguay in 1956 [Taylor 1960, 100] and 31.6 percent in 1991).[17] In other words, later additions

17. The central government employs 262,000, and 117,079 work for state enterprises

TABLE 8

DISTRIBUTION OF SEATS BY LARGEST
FACTIONS WITHIN THE MAJOR URUGUAYAN
PARTIES, 1962 AND 1971

Date	Party	Faction (Sublema)	% Seats in Chamber	% Seats in Party
1962	Colorado	Por la Unión del Partido	28.2	63.6
		Unión Colorada y Batllista	7.1	15.9
	Blanco	Unión Blanca Democrática	20.2	42.6
		Dr. Luis A. de Herrera-Por la Reforma, etc.	20.2	42.6
		Dr. Luis Alberto de Herrera	5.0	10.6
1971	Colorado	Bordaberry (Jorge Pacheco)	28.3	68.3
		List 15 (Jorge Batlle)	12.1	29.3
	Blanco	Por la Patria (Ferreira)	15.2	37.5
		Aguerrondo	12.1	30.0
		Movimiento de Rocha (Pereyra)	8.1	20.0

SOURCES: 1962, calculated from Fabregat (1963, 31); 1971, calculated from Rial (1985, 12–13).

to the civil service laws were designed to appeal to civil servants' interests and thus to contribute to electoral gains for legislators rather than requiring further sacrifice of electoral interests.

As a result of this series of laws and constitutional provisions, by the 1960s it had become virtually impossible to dismiss government employees. Article 168, paragraph 10, of the 1952 constitution provides that the Senate must approve the dismissal of a classified employee. Even the dismissal of temporary employees could lead to serious political repercussions (Taylor 1960, 215).

The consequences of these legislative actions began to be felt during the 1950s. By then, such a large fraction of the budgets of many government agencies went for wages to pay patronage appointees that there were no funds left for operating expenses. For example, the Ministry of Public Health decided at one point to create 1,449 new jobs in public

out of a total working population of 1.2 million. *Latin American Research Review: Southern Cone*, RS-91–08 (October 17, 1991), p. 4.

hospitals. As a result, "the budget could no longer be made to purchase medicines and essential hospital equipment."[18]

In the Ministry of Public Works during one seven-month period, "313 new employees [were] hired in equipment repair and maintenance shops, although during this period no spare parts were bought, and at the end of the period there were no self-propelled road scrapers in operable condition although the Department owned a great many."[19] By the end of the period, all work on the roads had ceased. The "entire budget was being used to pay personnel and none was left for fuel, equipment, and materials" (Taylor 1960, 103).

To summarize, in Uruguay's factionalized political system, legislators supported those elements of career civil service that could be converted into electoral advantage, especially job creation and job security. They did not provide for the imposition of merit as the criterion for hiring and promotion. Such reforms would have reduced the ability of factions to service their clients.

COLOMBIA

The pattern of implementation of the 1958 reform in Colombia bears some similarity to that in Uruguay. Party parity continued during the other National Front governments of Colombia (Guillermo León Valencia, 1962–66; Carlos Lleras Restrepo, 1966–70; and Misael Pastrana Borrero, 1970–74). The National Front gave 50 percent of the seats in the legislature and 50 percent of all patronage appointments to each party. Within each party, seats and access to patronage were distributed on the basis of proportional representation to candidates on the various party lists. So, although legislatures after the Alberto Lleras Camargo administration (1958–62) were evenly divided between two parties, they were not, as table 9 shows, evenly divided among factions. After 1960, the cost of reform to legislators depended on the amount of patronage controlled by their faction relative to other factions within their own party, not on the even division of patronage between the parties.

A reform to further decrease patronage in these circumstances would only be rational for deputies (or faction leaders) if the largest factions *within* their party were approximately equal. Some support from the

18. *El Debate*, Montevideo (June 29, 1960), cited in Taylor (1960, 222).
19. Testimony by Minister of Pubic Works Luis Giannastasio before the National Council, reported in Taylor (1960, 178–79).

TABLE 9

VOTE FOR LARGEST FACTIONS IN THE
COLOMBIAN CHAMBER OF DEPUTIES
DURING THE NATIONAL FRONT

Election Date	Liberal Factions	% Vote	Conservative Factions	% Vote
1960	L. Oficialista	57.7	C. Unionista	22.3
	MRL[a]	13.9	C. Doctrinario	17.6
1962	L. Oficialista	35.0	C. Unionista	25.7
	MRL	19.5	C. Doctrinario	15.8
1964	Frente Nacionalista	32.7	Frente Nacionalista	35.1
	MRL Linea Blanda	12.6	C. ANAPO[b]	13.0
1966	L. Oficialista	38.1	C. Unionista	16.1
	MRL	13.6	C. ANAPO	14.4
			Lauro-Alzatista	11.8
1968	L. Oficialista	39.6	C. Unionista	23.2
	Oficialista-Disidente	7.9	C. ANAPO	12.8
1970	L. Oficialista	26.4	C. ANAPO	21.4
	L. ANAPO	14.2	C. Unionista	14.8

SOURCE: Ruddle and Gillette (1972, 77–79).
[a] MRL—Movimiento Revolucionario Liberal (Revolutionary Liberal Movement).
[b] ANAPO—Alianza Nacional Popular (National Popular Alliance).

other party would also be necessary to pass legislation. This would ordinarily pose no problem for reformers since the smaller factions in both parties should always favor reform. But in Colombia during the National Front the situation was complicated by the requirement until 1968 of a two-thirds vote to pass legislation. As can be seen in table 9, the only time when the factions in either party approached equality was 1966. That year, the largest faction of the Liberal party (the party in which factions were highly unequal) controlled more than a third of the seats and could thus block passage of the reform.

The Lleras Camargo administration, which preceded the consolidation of multiple factions, was thus the only one in which access to patronage was actually divided evenly between the largest competing groups. Consequently, no additional civil service reforms were passed, even though at least one later president, Carlos Lleras Restrepo, campaigned very vigorously for them.

Once parity between the two major parties was established, competition among the factions within each party for shares of the party's half of the spoils intensified. Struggles for patronage among factions of the same party became increasingly vitriolic over time. As in Uruguay, the party pact led to a sharp increase in the overall number of government jobs.

Most Colombian presidents during the pact made some effort at administrative reform, and quite a few reforms gained legislative approval. Merit-based hiring has been an exception, however. By 1966 when Lleras Restrepo came to power, 5 percent of public employees were included in the merit-based career civil service. He mounted an aggressive campaign against corruption and patronage and for administrative reform. Congress, however, successfully blocked his proposed personnel reform. Unable to extend the merit system to cover more jobs, near the end of his term, Lleras Restrepo issued a decree that would allow public employees to enroll themselves in the career service without taking the exam. This increased coverage to 20 percent, but undermined the meritocratic foundation of civil service.

As the party pact neared its end, struggle within and between the parties increased, and interest in administrative reform waned, even in the executive branch. Pastrana, the last president during the pact, showed little interest in reform, being more interested in consolidating his party's position before the first election unfettered by parity agreements.

Since the pact ended, factionalism has declined, but the Liberal party has dominated the legislature, as shown in table 10, and no further reforms have passed. As in Uruguay, civil service has come to mean inordinate job security and inflexibility in the administrative apparatus, rather than meritocratic hiring and promotion (Hartlyn 1988, 179–80).

The general assessment by observers of the current Colombian scene is that professionalization of some key sectors of the Colombian bureaucracy has occurred, but personnel reform in general has failed (Hartwig 1983; Perdomo 1982; Mares 1990). In spite of considerable presidential support, campaigns against corruption in the press, and supportive public opinion, legislators in the factionalized party system have not found it in their own interest to extend the merit system.

In brief, then, in all the countries examined, reforms initiated during periods of party equality or during a dictatorship suffered reverses when the distribution of power among the parties became unequal. Even in the United States, when the election of 1896 resulted in a reemergence of Republican dominance, the merit system was seriously threatened.

TABLE 10

DISTRIBUTION OF PARTISAN STRENGTH
IN THE COLOMBIAN CHAMBER OF DEPUTIES
AFTER THE NATIONAL FRONT, 1974–1990

Election Date	Liberal (% seats)	Conservative (% seats)
1974	55.6[a]	32.0[a]
1978	55.8	41.7
1982	57.3	42.2
1986	48.2	40.2
1990	59.0	31.2[b]
1991	54.0	16.0[b]

SOURCES: 1974, Hartlyn (1988, 150–51); 1978–1982, Wilkie and Perkal (1984, 730); 1986, Wilkie and Ochoa (1989); 1990, Murillo and Torres (1991, 58); 1991, "Definidos Congreso y governaciones," *El Tiempo*, November 26, 1991, p. 7A.
[a] Percent of vote.
[b] Partido Social Conservador.

President McKinley removed the exam requirement for ten thousand jobs. Further, during the McKinley administration, Congress passed legislation excluding thousands of new appointments from the system (Van Riper 1958, 171–75). If McKinley's assassination had not brought Theodore Roosevelt unexpectedly to the presidency, the United States might not look as different from Latin America as it does today.[20]

Civil service reforms generally include two kinds of provisions: requirements for merit-based hiring and promotion; and guarantees to employees of job security, fair treatment, union representation, and so on. In unequal or fragmented party systems, elected officials have been reluctant to increase the number of jobs included in the merit system since each new inclusion reduces the resources available to politicians

20. Theodore Roosevelt's extensions of the merit system can be credited to two causes. The first, an idiosyncratic factor, was Roosevelt's strong personal commitment to reform. The second was that Roosevelt, unlike presidents who had actually been nominated for the office, did not depend on the political machines for support. In fact, they opposed him. In order to consolidate his own control over the Republican party, Roosevelt needed to undercut the power of the Republican machines. He used the extension of civil service as one of his weapons against the machines. Roosevelt's commitment to reform is explicable as a consequence of the incentives he faced as an outsider in competition with the Republican party machines rather than dependent on them for support. See chapter 6 for a similar argument about the effect of being an outsider on Latin American presidents' attitudes toward administrative reform.

TABLE II

PARTY BALANCE IN LEGISLATURES
WHEN REFORMS PASSED

	President's Party		Other Largest Party	
	(% Seats)	*(% Votes)*	*(% Seats)*	*(% Votes)*
Lleras Camargo	50.0[a]	58.1	50.0	41.8
Caldera	27.6	24.2	30.8	25.8
Herrera	43.2	39.7	43.2	39.7

SOURCES: For Lleras and Caldera, Ruddle and Gillette (1972, 77, 101); for Herrera, Penniman (1980, 272).

[a] By the National Front pact, seats in each house of the legislature were divided equally regardless of the popular vote. In consequence, parity in the legislature and patronage existed even though the vote was unequal.

in their struggle with other politicians. Laws extending perquisites and job guarantees to larger numbers of employees have posed no problem for legislators, however, since they bring electoral benefits from grateful employees.

CONCLUSION

This chapter has reached two substantive conclusions: (1) Reforms are more likely to pass the legislative hurdle when patronage is evenly distributed among the strongest parties (and factions). (2) Initial reforms are more likely to be followed by further extension of reform where the electoral weight of the parties remains relatively even and stable.

Reforms that, like civil service, reduced the political resources of all parties were passed during only three administrations in the larger democracies of postwar Latin America, those of: Alberto Lleras Camargo of Colombia (1958–62); Rafael Caldera of Venezuela (1968–73); and Luis Herrera Campíns of Venezuela (1978–83). Table 11 above shows the distribution of votes and legislative seats during each of these administrations. In each one, the parties controlled almost equal numbers of seats in the legislature.

The rational actor assumptions on which the model used here is based also imply several expectations about the effects of certain institutions on the probability of reform. Electoral rules that encourage party fragmentation should reduce the likelihood of reform because equality among several parties occurs less often than equality between two parties. Open-list proportional representation, because it makes patronage a valuable resource to incumbents from parties that have traditionally had access to patronage in their struggle against challengers within their own parties, should reduce the probability of reform. Electoral rules that result in the proliferation of candidate lists within parties should also reduce the chances of reform, since reform will only be rational for members of the largest factions if the factions *within* the main parties are approximately equal, as well as the parties themselves.

Institutional features of the party system that give party leaders more influence over legislators, such as control over placement on the list, can work in either direction. Where party leaders have an interest in reform, their ability to impose party discipline increases the probability of reform, but, where party leaders have no interest in reform, their influence makes reform less likely.

The evidence examined in this chapter has proved consistent with these expectations. All the instances of initial civil service reform in democracies occurred during periods of rough party equality in countries with only two or three important parties. Reforms did not occur in democracies with open-list proportional representation. And the prevalence of multiple candidate lists seemed to undercut the ability of two-party systems to produce recurrent parity situations.

Evidence from these cases, furthermore, has proved inconsistent with other explanations of reform. It is, for example, sometimes suggested that administrative reform occurs when countries attain a level of economic development that makes the continuation of government incompetence economically costly. The dates of initial reforms in these cases, however, (Uruguay 1934, Brazil 1937, Colombia 1930–34 and 1958, Venezuela 1970, and Chile none prior to 1973) offer little support for a direct link between development and reform.

A related but more political argument hypothesizes that reforms occur when development causes changes in the distribution of social forces that make it possible for reformist parties supported by middle-class and manufacturing interests to defeat traditional political machines. Latin America offers few examples of victories by unambiguously reformist antimachine parties. The Christian Democratic Frei administration (1964–70) in Chile comes closest to what North Americans think of as a reform government. It did not introduce civil service reform; rather, the many administrative changes initiated by the Christian Democrats sought to monopolize offices for their own party. In contrast, the reforms that actually introduced meritocratic hiring—as demonstrated in the case histories above—occurred when traditional machine parties found themselves forced to share power with other traditional machines.

Latin American specialists have sometimes suggested that the Iberian colonial heritage shared by Latin American countries predisposes them toward clientelism and against impersonal procedures such as meritocratic recruitment to civil service. There may be some truth in this argument, but it obviously cannot explain the very considerable differences among Latin American cases.

The game theoretic model thus provides an explanation for the timing of reforms, whereas other arguments cannot. Claims about it have to be somewhat cautious because of the small number of cases examined here and the cultural and historical similarity of the cases. It may be that the domain of this model is limited to the Western hemisphere. Nevertheless, its implications are quite far-reaching. It suggests that administrative reforms will be difficult to achieve and maintain in multiparty democracies. Certain characteristics that are often thought of as increasing representativeness, such as open-list proportional representation and electoral rules that reduce barriers to the entry of small parties and thus result in a party system that reflects a wide spectrum of interests, may paradoxically cause elected officials to be less responsive to this particular public interest.

One of the promises of democracy is that it makes government services available to all citizens regardless of wealth, race, religion, gender or creed. The failure to professionalize public administration, however, makes that promise hard to keep. Stories abound in Latin America about the need for bribes or pull in order to get everyday services, such as the renewal of a driver's license. More seriously, inefficiency and incompetence in government agencies can be so extreme that clients' needs cannot be served at all. Thus, for example, Montevideo's *El Pais* reported in 1960 that the Fund for Pensions for Rural, Domestic, and Aged Workers was up to two years behind in the commencement of payments to nearly four thousand people.[21] During the democratic period, Chileans eligible for pensions routinely had to seek the help of elected officials to avoid the months or even years of red tape involved for the politically unconnected to initiate payments (Valenzuela 1977, 120–37; Tapia-Videla 1969, 300–313). By 1964, all but one of Brazil's

21. February 9, 1960, cited in Taylor (1960, 222).

many social security institutes had gone bankrupt, in part because of excessive employment of untrained PTB supporters (Malloy 1979, 119–22). In these instances—and many others could be cited—the failure of public service directly affects the quality of life of the ordinary people whom democracy is supposed to benefit.

It seems especially ironic that the reforms that would improve efficiency and fairness in the provision of government services should be impeded by the same representative institutions whose manifest purpose is to reflect constituents' interests.

SIX

The Political Uses
of Bureaucracy

Presidential Survival versus
Administrative Competence

I had a hungry party behind me. . . .
Grover Cleveland

Chapter 5 showed that legislators' decisions about voting for administrative reform depend on how they expect their votes to affect the likelihood of reelection. In this chapter, we turn to the role of the most important potential political entrepreneur, the president, in the struggle to build a more competent administration. The chapter focuses on the appointment strategies used by presidents to staff their administrations, a much neglected aspect of presidential politics. Some presidents appoint party loyalists and interest group "ambassadors"[1] almost without regard for competence; others rely heavily on technical criteria for staffing at least the most important sectors of their administrations; others relinquish effective control of the appointment process to allies, who are also potential rivals, within their party or governing coalition; and still others pursue mixed strategies. Which strategy presidents follow depends, as is shown below, on well-defined features of the political environment in which they find themselves.

Although presidential appointment strategies have attracted little scholarly notice, they have serious consequences. A president who, for example, appoints loyalists regardless of competence in order to maintain short-term viability may fatally cripple the government's ability to carry out policy of any kind. A president who, at the other extreme, appoints only technocrats may find that the legislature feels itself excluded from policy-making and therefore obstructs all the president's

---

1. This term comes from Polsby (1983).

policy initiatives. To govern effectively, a president must find an appointment strategy that secures both sufficient competence in the bureaucracy and also adequate political support. This chapter focuses on presidents' efforts to find an effective strategy.

To understand how presidents make choices among potential appointment strategies, we need first to consider their long-term goals. Legislators can be assumed to care about reelection, but sitting presidents face somewhat different incentives. Constitutions in virtually all Latin American countries preclude presidents from succeeding themselves and thus eliminate concern over immediate reelection from their calculations.[2] Nevertheless, many presidents hope to serve again after their immediate successors leave office, and this ambition is not unrealistic. Former presidents often compete in, and sometimes win, later elections. Even when they do not become viable candidates again, they usually continue an active political life as influential leaders of their parties or more informal followings. Speaking about Colombian presidents, John Martz (1992, 96) notes: "Former presidents neither die nor fade away, but instead remain powerful through their own news magazines, factional and family heirs, and the networks of linkages which generally extend throughout much of the nation's socio-economic elite. . . . Four of the six [presidents since 1958] actively sought a second term after the constitutionally mandated term out of office." Details differ from country to country, but many former presidents continue to head their parties, and many have permanent seats in the Senate from which to exercise influence.

Presidents thus are concerned about maximizing their long-term political power and influence, even if they cannot immediately run for reelection. To maximize their subsequent influence and chances for later reelection, presidents must do three things. First, they must survive in office, often overcoming serious threats from the military to oust them (Ames 1987). Second, they must govern effectively, creating a legacy of economic development and other achievements that will lead voters to want to return them to power when they next run for office. Third, they must build a political organization with strong loyalties to them person-

2. The only exception among the cases covered here is Argentina between 1949 and 1957. The 1949 constitution, written by a constituent assembly dominated by Peronists allowed immediate reelection for the first time. After Perón's ouster, military-sponsored efforts to write a new constitution floundered, and Argentina returned to the 1853 document that prohibits immediate reelection.

ally, so that they will have an organizational base that can be maintained even when the resources of the presidency are no longer available.

These goals partially conflict with one another. To govern effectively, presidents must get their programs passed by the legislature and implemented by the bureaucracy. Bureaucratic competence thus becomes essential to long-term presidential success. Winning support from the legislature for innovative policies, however, may require heavy political side payments in the form of patronage, particularistic benefits, or local projects, which can in turn undermine bureaucratic competence and dissipate resources needed to carry out key policies. Building a personal political organization may likewise require the diversion of limited resources from other tasks. And finally, maintaining oneself in office when threatened can require the wholesale abandonment of all longer-term goals.

How presidents choose among these competing imperatives is the subject of this chapter. Reasoning from the three goals that I have suggested all presidents share—current survival, effective government, and creation of a loyal machine—I hypothesize a set of strategic preferences with regard to appointment strategies for presidents operating in different political environments. These hypotheses generate a set of predictions about the kinds of appointment strategies presidents will choose in different situations. The chapter then compares these predictions with evidence from all the larger countries of Latin America that have had competitively elected governments since 1945.[3] Comparisons among these presidential administrations allow a test of whether focusing on the incentives of individual leaders has value for explaining presidential contributions to building administrative competence.

To preview the conclusions, the examination of the actual appointment strategies of forty-four Latin American presidential administrations shows that presidents building their parties or national support networks while in office tend to concentrate appointments among loyalists. The administrative reforms they initiate contribute to their overall goal of placing as many partisans in office as possible, often without regard for competence. Presidents who run as independents, supported by parties but not beholden to them, or who are nominated by their own parties in spite of opposition from most of the established party

3. Uruguay was excluded because its experiments with different forms of collegial executive modify the incentives facing presidents and thus make it unique.

leadership tend to hire more technocrats, and also more personal friends, than do presidents nominated more conventionally. They often try to build bureaucratic competence, but the fragility of their governments reduces their ability to survive and hence their long-term impact on state capacity.

Most presidents, who neither try to build a party while in office nor achieve the presidency without established party support, choose, like Juscelino Kubitschek whose administration is discussed in chapter 3, a middle strategy that I call "compartmentalization," the establishment of islands of competence in especially important agencies. The ability to establish islands of competence within the bureaucracy depends on the president's power relative to that of his or her political allies. Presidents who face only weak competition from rivals within their own parties and who can rely on party discipline to ensure legislative support tend, on average, to build compartmentalized bureaucracies in which the functions most crucial to economic performance are carried out by technocrats insulated from partisan pressures. Presidents who are weaker relative to party and coalition allies tend to make more partisan appointments and to have less success in building competent agencies.

Finally, presidents who face the threat of military overthrow usually have to expend all of their appointment resources to buy political support. They not only fail to increase bureaucratic competence but often, in their effort to survive, distribute the resources needed to maintain the islands of competence built by previous presidents.

THE POLITICAL USES OF BUREAUCRACY

Presidents, like other politicians, engage continuously in the exchange of benefits for political support. A president who, for example, presides over a rapid economic expansion can expect to be rewarded with the support of the populace. A president who gives a key government post to the brother of a legislative leader, or who arranges special consideration for the pension claim of the widowed mother of an impoverished voter, can likewise expect to enjoy, at least for a time, the political support of those helped. A president thus can exchange benefits for support at the level of the nation as a whole, the level of individual politicians and citizens, or any collectivity in between.

The executive bureaucracy is used in the ceaseless exchange of benefits for support in at least four ways.

1. As a source of particularized benefits for constituents.

2. As a source of patronage and other benefits to politicians whose support the president needs to remain in office and initiate new laws and programs.

3. As a source of benefits to members of a political organization loyal to the president.

4. As an instrument for effective implementation of policies and programs that benefit groups of citizens in both the short and long run.

The alternative uses to which the bureaucracy may be put are not fully compatible with one another. A president who, for example, turns an agency over to the brother of a legislative leader in exchange for the leader's support may not thereafter be able to use that agency's resources either to pursue his own policy initiatives or to build his own political organization; in all likelihood, the agency's resources will be turned to the service of the legislator's interests. Similarly, a president who distributes the resources of an agency in the form of particularistic goods to voters may find that the agency has few resources left to implement programs of general social value. A credit program for small farmers aimed at increasing food production and decreasing rural poverty, for example, may fail to serve its stated purposes If loans go to party loyalists regardless of the size of their farms or choice of crops.

The next few pages discuss in more detail these alternative uses of bureaucracy.

The Bureaucracy as a Source of Particularized Benefits. During a precampaign trip through the Venezuelan countryside by presidential candidate Carlos Andrés Pérez in 1985, Michael Coppedge observed hundreds of people making requests in writing for personal favors and was told by Pérez's national campaign organizer that the candidate had received more than 1,100 such requests during the four-day trip. As a sample of the kind of requests made, one illiterate petitioner, who relayed her request through Coppedge, asked for a job, a scholarship, and a new house. With three years to go before the election, "Pérez was making campaign swings in one state after another with just a few days rest in between, so the number of requests for favors he received must have been astronomical" (Coppedge 1988, 21–22). All requests were forwarded by staff members to appropriate government agencies with letters from Pérez asking officials to do everything possible to help; copies of these letters were, of course, also sent to the petitioners.[4]

Many programs initially passed as entitlements or elements of development plans end up transformed into particularistic benefits as they are implemented by a partisan bureaucracy. Supporters of the president or of the governing party are more likely to receive land during land reforms, small loans from state banks, vouchers for free lunches or milk, scholarships, construction materials for building a house, titles to small plots of land for housing, and so on, than equally deserving supporters of the opposition.

An official of the Brazilian Planning Ministry, for example, testified before a parliamentary commission of inquiry in 1987 that construction materials earmarked for slum dwellers in the poorest parts of the country had been distributed on the basis of two criteria: to guarantee a five-year term for President José Sarney and to launch the planning minister's electoral career in the state of Minas Gerais. Of resources distributed by the Planning Ministry in 1987, 16.5 percent went to Maranhão, the president's home state, and 10.4 percent to Minas Gerais, with 4.8 percent concentrated in the capital, Belo Horizonte, where the minister contemplated beginning his electoral career in the mayoral race. In contrast, the poor northeastern state of Pernambuco, governed by an enemy of the president, received only 0.1 percent (Dimenstein 1988, 53–54).

The distribution of benefits in this way requires an enormous expenditure of time and the maintenance of a massive political organization that extends from many agencies in the federal bureaucracy to the grassroots level. If presidents distribute benefits such as subsidized loans and jobs in state-run enterprises by the thousands, as they sometimes do, it can also be expensive. Yet, depending on a president's other opportunities and constraints, the distribution of particularistic benefits to masses of voters can also be an effective way to cultivate popular support. Individual benefits are highly visible and concrete, and thus easy for beneficiaries to understand and for politicians to take credit for.[5]

The Bureaucracy as a Source of Favors to Other Politicians. In Latin America as in other presidential systems, presidents who need the sup-

4. By way of comparison, U.S. members of Congress, whose reelection strategies also depend heavily on casework, receive an average of seventy-one requests for help per week; British members of Parliament average thirty-six (Cain, Ferejohn, and Fiorina 1987, 71).

5. See Fiorina (1978) for an argument that incumbent U.S. members of Congress also help maintain themselves in office by supplying particularized benefits.

port of other politicians to pass legislation or even remain in power rarely hesitate to "buy" the support they need with policy concessions, appointments, and projects that benefit the constituents or political dependents of particular legislators. In the example of the distribution of housing materials above, the beneficiaries included the deputies, mayors, and governors of the localities that received services, who got credit from grateful constituents for bringing the programs to their areas, as well as the recipients of the materials themselves.

Presidents differ in the extent to which they must buy support from other politicians. Presidents who lead disciplined majority parties naturally provide a policy package appealing to many of their copartisans, as well as substantial numbers of appointments. Normally, however, they need not negotiate with individual deputies for their votes on particular bills. Presidents such as Sarney and Fernando Collor de Mello, however, who lead small parties and have to hold together multiparty coalitions in a highly fluid and undisciplined party system, may be forced into a ceaseless search for support.

During the first seven months of 1992, the Brazilian press reported that 94 percent of the money distributed by the Secretariat of Regional Development had gone to the districts of deputies supporting President Collor (Bortot and Silva 1992). During the last two months before the legislative vote to impeach him, the effort to "buy" support became even more urgent and visible. The president of the Bank of Brazil, a close Collor ally, personally offered deputies the opportunity to choose, in return for their support, the municipalities that would receive appropriations for health expenditures worth between 50 and 150 million cruzeiros each. Projects offered to senators were reportedly worth 200 million each (Mossri and Krieger 1992, 1).

The Bureaucracy as a Source of Favors to the President's Organization. Presidents also use the bureaucracy to build their own political machines. On the one hand, they use appointments as rewards to followers to reinforce their loyalty, and, on the other, they need to scatter loyalists throughout the bureaucracy in order to be able to distribute benefits to other politicians and supporters as described above. In some cases, the president's political machine is more or less coterminous with a political party founded by the president, as was, for example, the Peronist party until 1955. In well-institutionalized parties, however, the president's organization usually forms a faction of the larger party. In fluid, uninstitutionalized party systems such as Brazil's, presidents often try to build loyal organizations that transcend parties.

Appointments are thus critical resources used in the political game. A secure if sometimes low-paid job with substantial health benefits and a good pension can make a major contribution to the welfare of a middle- or working-class political activist. A position as department head in a federal agency, manager in a state enterprise, or minister carries with it not only high income and prestige but the potential for building one's own network of political clients and dependents. High-level positions are the currency with which powerful political supporters are paid.

The Bureaucracy as a Tool for Implementing Policy. Effective governance depends, among other things, on (1) competent economic policy making; (2) progress in the provision of public goods such as roads, public transportation, education, potable water, sewerage disposal, and hospitals; (3) fair and effective collection of taxes; and (4) economically rational allocation of credit and various subsidies to the private sector. To achieve any of these goals, a president needs to command an honest, competent, public-service oriented bureaucracy. Even strictly distributive policies cannot be carried out efficiently by presidents lacking competent administrators and technicians.

Since the end of World War II, the voters of major South American countries have repeatedly elected presidents who advocated state-sponsored social and economic change. Until the middle 1980s, Latin American presidents led efforts to foster industrialization through increasing state intervention in their economies. With the aim of speeding growth, they manipulated the exchange rate, raised tariffs, proposed industrial policies aimed at overcoming bottlenecks in the supply of manufactured goods, provided investment capital to make possible the more rapid development of infrastructure and manufacturing, and increased state participation in the production of energy and basic goods essential to the industrialization process. These substantive programs included as inherent elements proposals for the creation of new administrative agencies, often with provisions for competent staffing and secure funding, to carry them out. Most notably, development-oriented presidents created monetary authorities, agencies charged with fostering industrial development, development banks, and scores of public enterprises in most of the large Latin American countries.

To gain the gratitude and loyalty of particular groups of citizens, presidents have also established programs to provide housing for middle-

and working-class urban residents; build roads that would allow farmers in inaccessible areas to market their crops; encourage the unionization and political mobilization of previously nonunionized workers; distribute land to the landless; and extend social security, medical care, education, sewers, and potable water to those who lack them. Given the level of competence of the public bureaucracies that presidents typically inherit, these programs also often require the creation of new, or reorganization of old, agencies and the securing of funds and competent, committed personnel to carry them out.

Since the mid-1980s, changes in international economic conditions have reduced the resources available to Latin American presidents for state intervention in the economy and forced most of them to concentrate on reversing traditional development strategies. This reversal generally involves trade liberalization, exchange rate reform, reduced state investment and employment, privatization of state-owned enterprises, and decreased provision of state services. These reforms hurt many who benefited from previous state intervention. Prominent among those most hurt are the party activists crucial to the success of incumbents' political machines, who had been disproportionate beneficiaries of state employment and services.[6] In order to survive in the new economic environment, politicians have had to be able to build quickly a new constituency of reform beneficiaries. Competent administrators have become even more important in the current situation than before. Politicians have much less to distribute and thus their support depends more heavily on successful macroeconomic performance. In the present stringent international economic environment, policy makers need high levels of both skill and luck to succeed.

Whether in the buoyant sixties or the distressed eighties, presidential aspirations for future power have depended on successfully carrying out innovations and programs such as those described above, which has in turn depended on building competent administrative agencies to handle day-to-day implementation. In other words, presidents have a powerful incentive to increase bureaucratic competence. Such efforts typically include the creation of new agencies, innovations in the supply of funding that protect resources needed for new agencies from legislative discretion, and an appointment strategy that concentrates competent, committed people in the new agencies.

6. For a more extended treatment of this issue, see Geddes (1991).

HOW APPOINTMENT STRATEGY AFFECTS
THE USES OF THE BUREAUCRACY

Appointments affect the ways the bureaucracy can be used. To deliver particularistic benefits to large numbers of voters, the president needs loyalists in all agencies that deal with the public for any purpose. Politicians must have bureaucratic colleagues on whom they can call to expedite pension payments, telephone hookups, and import licenses, approve loans, choose the teachers for local schools, and arrange, expedite, or find exceptions to anything else affected by government regulation.

To deliver benefits to more important political actors, such as other politicians and potential campaign contributors, the president needs to have loyalists in top policy-making positions. Presidents of state banks deliver loans to entrepreneurs who have made large campaign contributions and fund projects in the constituencies of loyal legislators. The minister and other high-level appointees in the Ministry of Health decide which legislators' constituencies get clinics, water purification projects, insect eradication programs, and free inoculations, as well as which builders and producers of hospital supplies and insecticides get contracts. The Ministry of Industry decides which manufacturers will be subsidized in various ways. The Ministry of Transportation and associated agencies determine which legislators' constituencies get paved roads and bridges and which contractors are hired to pave the roads and build the bridges. No claim is made here that these decisions are always based on political considerations, but under some circumstances—to be elaborated below—such considerations can weigh heavily, and they can never be entirely ignored.

To use the bureaucracy to govern effectively, presidents need to hire competent administrators, provide them with adequate funds, and allow them to establish fair, nonpartisan, and impersonal criteria for the distribution of their services, the application of regulations, the awarding of contracts, and so on. In the absence of these conditions, resources intended to further development goals or aid targeted groups of beneficiaries tend to end up in the pockets of the politically well connected, and experts whose skills are needed to successfully implement policy tend to become demoralized and to resign. These requirements for effective governance thus pose a potential challenge to other political uses of the bureaucracy.

Presidents have perceived the need for greater expertise, secure funding for new projects, and commitment to reformist goals on the part of officials. As noted in earlier chapters, these needs have been widely acknowledged by observers inside and outside of government. Foreign experts have reinforced presidents' beliefs about the need for greater administrative competence (e.g., Emmerich 1972; Currie 1966; IBRD 1950, 1961). The press has clamored for higher levels of efficiency and honesty in the bureaucracy in most Latin American countries for decades (López Pintor 1972, 103–4; Taylor 1960, 103, 178–79, 222; González 1980, 76–106; Brewer-Carías 1975a). Notwithstanding this broad support, however, presidents have found their ability to carry out administrative innovations limited. Administrative changes designed to facilitate carrying out new policies have sometimes proved more difficult to initiate than the policies themselves. The failure to establish adequate bureaucratic instruments has then, in its turn, caused slowness, mutation, and failure in the implementation of substantive programs.[7]

Proposed administrative reforms face opposition because, as detailed in chapters 4 and 5, politicians, bureaucrats, and party activists find them politically costly. Reforms deprive politicians and officials of discretionary control over important political resources. They limit the degree to which politicians can exchange jobs, contracts, and other favors for support.

WHAT DETERMINES A PRESIDENT'S PREFERENCES

The costs and benefits of reform to presidents differ in systematic ways from the costs and benefits to other political actors. Although the distribution of individual benefits plays an important role in presidential campaigns (as shown in the discussion of the Pérez campaign above), the use of innovative policies and new programs to attract support—as opposed to particularistic favors—is especially appealing to sitting presidents because they have a virtual monopoly on this weapon in the political game. Competitors can oppose and criticize, but they cannot initiate sweeping changes for which *they* can take credit. Moreover, the public goods distributed by new programs are "cheaper" to provide, from the president's point of view, than a comparable amount of private

7. No argument is being made here that this is the only cause of failure to implement new policies. Some policies are opposed by powerful interests, and some turn out to be unworkable. Many, however, are technically feasible and widely supported, but may nevertheless fall short of reaching their goals. When this happens, bureaucratic ineptitude or politically motivated diversion of resources is typically the culprit.

goods distributed as patronage (Cox 1986, 1987). Programs and policies, such as public housing projects or the extension of pension benefits to rural workers, provide benefits to very large numbers of people at the cost of relatively small per capita expenditures of the president's time and little of the president's large but nonetheless limited supply of patronage. Consequently, ambitious presidents try to establish themselves in the public's mind as leaders whose policies have led to a healthy growth rate and the extension of new benefits to citizens. While the distribution of individual benefits depends on an effective political machine, the design of effective policies and the routine delivery of services and entitlements both require a fairly high level of competence and honesty in the bureaucracy.

Though a record of prosperity and achievement will help a president's future chances, ambitious presidents cannot rely solely on the public's memory. They must attend as well to political organization. Here they cannot simply count on the party political machines, because someone else will have controlled the resources of the presidency for at least four years by the time they can run again. If they belong to stable, established parties, they cannot even count on controlling their own party machine, since they will face competition from others within the party. So they try to use some of the president's discretionary resources to build an informal political organization that includes both loyal party members and personal loyalists from outside the party.

PRESIDENTIAL APPOINTMENT STRATEGIES

The dilemma that presidents face in choosing an appointment strategy is that most potential appointees cannot contribute equally to attaining all three of their goals (current survival, effective governance, and building a loyal political organization). The appointees who can help gain the support of other political players and thus bolster chances of survival are not, in general, the same appointees who can help most to implement programs or build a loyal political organization. Hence, the greater the president's need to shore up current political standing by securing the cooperation of other political players, the fewer appointment resources available for personnel who can help attain longer-term goals. In the extreme case of a president on the verge of ouster from office, all appointment resources may need to be diverted to "buying" the short-term support of other players.

Reducing the complex motives of presidents to the desire for current and future political power is obviously simplistic and possibly unjust. But if one makes this simplifying assumption, one can deduce from it the preferences of presidents with regard to appointment strategies. And one can then predict outcomes based on the costs other players would be able to impose on the president for choosing particular appointment strategies. The test of the usefulness of this simplifying assumption lies in a comparison between predictions derived from it and real world events—a comparison made below.

Because of their interest in achieving program goals and maintaining a loyal political machine, presidents seek certain kinds of appointments. They would like to staff their administrations with people who are both technically competent and loyal to them personally, though in practice they must sometimes choose appointees on other grounds. The typology of presidential appointment strategies below attempts to capture the nature of tradeoffs between competence, on the one hand, and attributes that contribute to immediate political survival, on the other.

TYPOLOGY OF APPOINTMENT STRATEGIES

1. *Civil Service Reform*

   A. Political selection of top administrative personnel by the president on the basis of competence and loyalty.

   B. Meritocratic recruitment through centrally administered exams and promotion based on performance for all personnel who affect policy implementation (technicians and administrators, but also skilled workers, such as those who operate road maintenance machines, and clerks who provide services, such as driver's licenses and pensions).

   C. Partisan recruitment to jobs inessential to implementation (e.g., janitors, chauffeurs, routine office workers) largely controlled by president and his or her loyal lieutenants.

2. *Compartmentalization*

   A. Political selection of top administrative personnel by the president on the basis of competence and loyalty.

   B. Informal meritocratic recruitment and promotion based on performance in agencies president deems most crucial to program.

C. Recruitment of rest of bureaucracy through customary patronage channels, controlled by president, party, and coalition partners.

3. *Partisan*

A. Political selection of top administrative personnel from within president's party or coalition; loyalty and holding the coalition together take precedence over competence.

B. Informal meritocratic recruitment from within president's party or coalition in agencies president considers most crucial to program.

C. Recruitment to rest of bureaucracy also monopolized by the president's party and coalition partners on the basis of patronage criteria.

4. *Immediate Survival*

A. Political selection of top administrative personnel without regard to competence; appointments made to solidify relationships with key groups and to repay obligations. Appointment carries authority to recruit subordinates.

B. Recruitment to other decision-making posts based on political resources controlled by applicant. Appointment at this level also carries authority to recruit others.

C. Recruitment to other jobs through patronage controlled by president's supporters.

Section A within each strategy in the typology describes highest level appointments including the cabinet. All democratic political systems grant presidents the right to make a certain number of high-level discretionary, or *de confianza*, administrative appointments. Using this power, presidents can choose administrators who share their goals, who feel personally loyal, who have impressive technical qualifications and/or who can themselves command the loyalty of other important political players. Which of these qualities presidents emphasize depends on the political situation they face. With a few exceptions to be discussed below, presidents who feel reasonably secure will place a high value on expertise and commitment to the accomplishment of programmatic goals since these attributes will contribute most to fulfilling their long-term political aspirations. Presidents who owe debts to political allies or face threats to their current survival in office, however, will be forced to choose a less preferred strategy and to spend these resources on buying current support. If they deny their political allies these posts and the political resources they command, the probability of immobilism and overthrow increases.

Section B within each strategy describes second-tier appointments. Below the top administrative level, secure presidents prefer meritocratic recruitment for positions in agencies central to accomplishing their programs because they expect it to increase competence. Performance as the basis for promotion may be even more important, since it gives bureaucrats incentives to work hard and may even persuade those with opposing party loyalties (hired by previous administrations) to direct their efforts toward goals set by the current president.

Of course all presidents, even those famous for improving the competence of parts of the bureaucracy through meritocratic hiring, prefer to purchase political support with the jobs that do not contribute to carrying out electorally valuable programs. Section C in each strategy in the typology describes appointments to this level of bureaucracy. These appointments play an important role in linking the president's support network to the grassroots. Presidents cannot make all these appointments to the lower levels of the bureaucracy themselves. Although they would prefer to place all the hiring in the hands of loyalists, circumstance often prevents this. All presidents must delegate some hiring authority to potential rivals in order to gain their temporary support and cooperation. Moreover, since today's loyalists can become tomorrow's rivals as quickly as their power of appointment enables them to build a political base of their own, even delegation to current loyalists involves some risk.

PRESIDENTIAL CHOICES AMONG STRATEGIES

The initiation of civil service reforms involving meritocratic recruitment via competitive exams has some advantages for sitting presidents over more informal, merit-based recruitment. Presidents usually distribute a great many jobs to pay their political debts during their first few months in office. The distribution of presidential patronage then declines until shortly before the next election, when it rises again in an attempt to influence the vote.[8] The passage of a civil service reform after the first wave of distributions (earlier passage is unlikely since Congress must vote for such reforms) disadvantages the president's competitors. The

8. Ames (1987) finds the same pattern with regard to government spending in general.

president's own loyalists are safely in place and can be blanketed in later. The reform, however, will somewhat constrain competitors from within the president's party or coalition from using the next preelection distribution to build their own political machines to compete with the president's. It will also reduce the patronage resources available to the winner of the next election, who, in Latin America, will usually come from an opposing party. Although civil service reform forces presidents to give up some of their own patronage resources, they come out ahead relative to competitors.[9] Because of the reform's timing, others lose more than the president loses; moreover, presidents' advantage in the competition to supply public goods in exchange for votes reduces the relative importance of patronage in their electoral arsenals as compared to those of their rivals.

As noted in earlier chapters, however, civil service reforms require legislative approval. When, for the reasons discussed in chapters 4 and 5, legislators will not pass civil service reforms, presidents must settle for their second-best appointment strategies.

If the pursuit of civil service reform seems hopeless, the president's next best strategy for second-tier appointments is "compartmentalization." This strategy entails informal meritocratic appointments to positions considered essential to programmatic success, while permitting the president to use other appointments for short-term support and the development of a loyal following.

Presidents' preferences about how many jobs to give their own party depend, first, on the pool of technically competent people available in the party and, second, on the extent to which their own political success depends on party success. Some parties, such as the Chilean Christian Democratic party, have attracted large numbers of professionals and technocrats. This makes it easy to appoint people who are both competent and loyal. Other parties have fewer trained professionals on whom to call.

Presidents will prefer, all else being equal, to limit patronage to members of their own parties only if that is the best way of building their own personal followings. The most complete convergence between the president's and party members' interests occurs when the president's

9. U.S. experience, in which a series of presidents added increments to the proportion of the bureaucracy covered by civil service, after the Pendleton Act had supplied the "feeble" legal warrant needed to do so, seems to support the idea that civil service can play a role in presidents' electoral arsenals. See Van Riper (1958) and Skowronek (1982).

party has not existed prior to the campaign and must be built *during* the president's term in office. A president who has been elected as the leader of a newly formed party vehicle or movement (for example, Juan Perón in 1946) and who wants to build a party as a long-term political strategy, will tend to concentrate almost all appointments among party and personal loyalists.

As long as rivals do not challenge the leader's dominance in his party, appointments that benefit the party will benefit him or (hypothetically) her.[10] Generally, party founders need not worry about rivals within the party—at least not until after they have served a term as president. Usually competition becomes more severe in a party's second generation. Presidents who created their party vehicles also care about the achievement of programmatic goals, just as other presidents do. Top appointments usually go to individuals who are both qualified and loyal if such individuals can be found.

Presidents nominated by more established parties prefer to retain as much freedom as possible to choose the most competent people to implement their programs and to build a personal following. They want to attract respected and able independents and loyalists of other parties to their personal political network, whether or not they join the party. Kubitschek, for example, "who viewed his political base as broader than a party, showed little interest in using patronage politics just to strengthen the PSD" (Maram 1992, 130).

Presidents nominated by parties in which succession has become institutionalized cannot assume that any party member they appoint will be loyal to them rather than to some rival within the party. Their future electoral chances depend as much on competition from rivals inside the party as from outside,[11] so they are especially reluctant to

10. Although a very few women have served as presidents in Latin America, none have founded mass parties.

11. For an illuminating discussion of rivalry within Venezuela's Acción Democrática, see Coppedge (1988, ch. 4). Though it plays a large role, patronage is of course not the only weapon available to presidents in their struggle against party rivals. Coppedge reports that Jaime Lusinchi (President of Venezuela, 1983–88) "bought" the votes of state party secretaries for rule changes in the nominating process that would advantage his faction against its rivals by promulgating a rule that all state contracts must be signed by party secretaries as well as governors. This clever stroke opened new profit-making opportunities in the form of kickbacks to the secretaries, thereby gaining their cooperation without any direct expenditure of scarce presidential resources. On rivalry within APRA during the García administration in Peru, see Wise (1990) and Graham (1989). Within the Peronist party since redemocratization, see McGuire (1992). On Kubitschek's efforts to prevent the PSD from nominating a strong candidate to succeed him, "especially [one] that could

delegate control over appointments to party functionaries who may use it to build a base for themselves or some other potential rival.

Consequently, they will try to maintain personal control over appointments rather than delegate authority to the party apparatus. If they are politically strong enough, they will avoid granting power over appointments to potential future rivals in exchange for current support. And, since they can often attract independent supporters and supporters nominally committed to other parties, presidents generally prefer the freedom to appoint anyone they choose, regardless of party affiliation. That is, most presidents—unless they are building their parties while in office—prefer the leeway to appoint individuals from outside their parties. The extent to which presidents are able to pursue their own preferences is discussed below, but it should be mentioned here that presidents who lead very small parties and must hold multiparty coalitions together are often forced to use appointments to cement alliances with other parties, and thus to follow more partisan appointment strategies than they would prefer.

Finally, presidents who have achieved power in spite of opposition from most of the established leadership in their parties—such as Carlos Andrés Pérez in his second term or Carlos Menem—or as independents supported by but not beholden to parties—such as Jorge Alessandri or Carlos Ibáñez in Chile—see their own interests as most divergent from the party's. They are likely to prefer to fill large numbers of posts with personal loyalists and technocrats, since they owe the party little and, in fact, may have old scores to settle with party leaders who tried to block their nominations.

THE PREFERENCES OF OTHER PLAYERS

As noted above, a president's choice of strategies does not depend on his or her preferences alone. It also depends on the preferences of other players and their ability to impose costs on the president if he or she ignores their wishes. Other politicians, like presidents, want to remain in office, which, for legislators, depends on reelection. Even though all the countries discussed here use proportional representation to elect most of them, legislators' chances of achieving their goals depend heavily on delivering benefits to constituents and building personal electoral

---

be perceived as building up a power base independent of his own," see Maram (1992, 139).

machines. Legislators' chances also depend on their party's performance in office, the party's general ability to deliver benefits, and the effectiveness of the party's electoral machine.

Constituency service and hence personal machines play an especially large role in countries with open-list proportional representation, but they are also unexpectedly important in the other proportional representation systems because grassroots vote mobilization in all Latin American countries depends on the work of neighborhood bosses, *gamonales* (local party leaders), *cabos eleitorais*, and so on. These informal local political leaders form a crucial link between politicians and voters. They articulate demands for both private and local public goods, and whatever goods eventually arrive pass through their hands. Since they generally work within geographically defined areas, politicians have reason to supply goods to particular areas.

The concern with both party and personal performance determines the preferences of party politicians in the president's party or coalition with regard to appointment strategies. These preferences vary, depending on characteristics of the party and political system. Party politicians in well-institutionalized parties that already have well-developed electoral machines and networks for delivering benefits prefer to invest some appointment resources in developing technical expertise, in the hope that it will improve the party's performance in office. Members of parties that have not held national office for many years, if ever, and hence lack the resources needed to build effective distribution networks and electoral machines, will prefer to see all appointments go to party members. Such "hungry" parties will see the need to use party members with technical qualifications in certain jobs but will not favor hiring outside the party pool even if expertise within the pool is quite limited.

The preference ordering for members of established parties is:

1. Compartmentalization
2. Partisan
3. Civil Service Reform
4. Immediate Survival

The preference ordering for members of hungry new parties is:

1. Partisan
2. Compartmentalization

3. Immediate Survival

4. Civil Service Reform

Members of opposing parties, in contrast to supporting parties, would prefer either the maintenance of the status quo or civil service reform, depending on whether their party has gained a bureaucratic foothold in the past. They cannot expect any increase in the number of jobs under their control or any change in the pattern of distribution carried out by the opposition to help them. If opposing party members occupy a substantial number of bureaucratic posts because of past appointments, they will try to hold on to them by favoring the status quo. If, however, members of an opposing party have had little access to the bureaucracy in the past, they will favor civil service reform as a way of reducing the advantage of the other parties over them. Opponents of the president have no interest in increasing bureaucratic competence since presidential achievements will reduce their future electoral prospects. But, since reducing the other parties' control over patronage will increase their long-run chances of being able to compete on an equal footing, they campaign for civil service reform. Opposition parties, however, have little chance of getting what they want since, by definition, they control neither the executive nor the legislature.

Members of parties supporting the president, except in the special circumstances noted in earlier chapters, oppose civil service reform. Because of their alliance with the president, they benefit disproportionately from access to patronage, and reform would decrease current benefits and hence future chances of electoral success. Even when a president, such as Rómulo Betancourt of Venezuela's AD, strongly advocates reform, leads a disciplined party, and has a coalition majority in both houses of the legislature, he cannot persuade party members to favor civil service reform. Its political cost is simply too great.

Presidents in several countries have campaigned publicly for reform, but to no avail. Their lack of success has caused reform-oriented observers to question their sincerity. The argument laid out here, however, suggests that they bowed to political inevitability and abandoned this politically costly type of reform in order to pursue more effectively their substantive goals using second-best appointment strategies.

It might appear that presidents wanting civil service reform could, at least now and then, engineer a coalition of minority parties that shared their preference for reform in order to pass it. This has not occurred so far. The only countries with party systems sufficiently fragmented to provide the raw material for such coalitions are Chile before 1973 and Brazil since 1985. Chile and Brazil both employ the open-list system of proportional representation, which tends, as noted in chapter 5, to increase the costs to incumbents of reform; in addition, most of their parties have traditionally enjoyed access to a share of patronage. Thus, even in very small parties, incumbents would be reluctant to forgo the advantage patronage gives them over competitors within their own parties. These circumstances do not preclude the possibility of a reform coalition led by the president, but they substantially reduce its likelihood.[12]

Survival of the democratic regime is obviously a prerequisite for present and future success for most party politicians. When system survival is threatened, they will acquiesce in decisions to reduce partisan appointments, though to the outside observer they often seem slow to recognize threats. Such decisions can take various forms: the pact among AD, COPEI, and the Unión Republicana Democrática (URD, Democratic Republican Union) to share power and exclude the Venezuelan oil industry from partisan politics immediately after democratization in 1958; the similar pact between Conservatives and Liberals in Colombia to rely on technocratic criteria to fill high-level appointments in the economic policy bureaucracy and to divide the rest evenly during the years following redemocratization; the replacement of partisan appointments with military officers in the cabinets of Salvador Allende, Carlos Ibáñez, José Luis Bustamante y Rivero, and others severely threatened by military intervention; the offer of ministries to opposition parties in an effort to reduce dangerous levels of popular turmoil, as was done by Gabriel González Videla in the late forties, Getúlio Vargas in the early fifties, Allende in the early seventies, and Carlos Andrés Pérez in March 1992. (As the experience of Allende and Vargas shows, opposition parties sometimes refuse to cooperate in efforts to shore up the incumbent, even when the regime is threatened.)

DETERMINANTS OF PRESIDENTIAL POWER

If the interests of presidents conflict with those of other members of the governing party or coalition, what determines whose will prevails? Three factors affect the ability of presidents to follow their preferred appointment strategies: the legislative strength of a president's party; the degree

12. I am grateful to George Tsebelis for comments on an earlier version of this chapter that led me to think through this issue.

of discipline exercised by leaders over party members; and the amount of competition the president faces from rivals within his or her own party. Presidents who lead small parties and therefore need the support of larger parties, or several other small parties, may have to distribute more appointments in order to hold their coalitions together. Even when they can count on loyalty, shared ideology, or discipline to secure the legislative votes of members of their own party, the votes of coalition partners may have to be paid for with something more tangible.

Patronage is the glue that holds coalitions together in Latin America, and no president could hope to govern if he or she ignored the claims of coalition members. Even supporters who are not formal coalition partners expect rewards. Members of the Conservative and Liberal parties in Chile, for example, abandoned their own candidate and lined up behind the Christian Democrat Eduardo Frei at the last minute and without any formal coalition agreement in order to block a possible victory by Marxists in 1964. With their help, Frei won by a large margin, and the Christian Democrats won an impressive plurality in the legislature six months later, which enabled Frei to govern without consulting the other parties or offering them cabinet positions. Frei also appointed vast numbers of Christian Democrats to office while ignoring most of the claims of other supporters.

But the slighted parties took their revenge. From their entrenched positions in the bureaucracy, they hindered many efforts at reform and program implementation—not only programs such as land reform that many Liberals and Conservatives opposed, but also such innocuous activities as the housing program (Cleaves 1974). Furthermore, they refused to cooperate with the Christian Democrats in the next election, even though they again faced a serious threat from a Marxist candidate (Salvador Allende), in part because they felt that Frei had violated his implicit obligations to coalition partners (Valenzuela 1978). As this example shows, coalition partners who fail to get what they see as their fair share of patronage may have the power to inflict costs on the president and his party, even when they have insufficient legislative strength to block passage of bills.

Party discipline, whether in the president's party or in the parties that make up his or her coalition, also affects the power of the president relative to that of supporters. Where party discipline prevails, presidents are assured of support in the legislature by party members, and of coalition members once deals have been made with coalition party leaders. They need not trade additional appointments and other favors for legislative votes. In the absence of party discipline, especially if the president's party is small and the coalition fragile, he or she may be forced to trade everything available for support.

Party discipline varies across countries and across parties within countries. In highly disciplined parties, leaders can control placement on the party list and hence electoral chances, expel party members who fail to toe the party line, or impose other sanctions to enforce discipline. Alianza Popular Revolucionaria Americana (APRA, American Popular Revolutionary Alliance) deputies in Peru during the 1940s, for example, handed letters of resignation to party leaders before taking their seats so that the letters could be accepted in case of any breach of discipline (Bustamante i Rivero 1949, 30). In moderately disciplined parties, leaders' control is reduced by decentralization of candidate selection or open-list proportional representation, but deputies can still be expelled for violations of discipline, and party members cannot accept cabinet positions without party consent. At the undisciplined extreme, party leaders have few of these sanctions available and little ability to maintain discipline. At one end of the spectrum is AD of Venezuela, in which discipline is so effective that individual votes are not counted in the legislature; party leaders simply report the total. At the other end are most current Brazilian parties and the Partido Agrario Laborista (PAL, Agrarian Labor Party) of Chile, which repeatedly announced its withdrawal from the Ibáñez cabinet without being able to get all its members to resign.

Finally, the political strength of presidents relative to other members of their own parties affects whether they can pursue their preferred appointment strategies. Presidents who have built and led disciplined parties for many years before achieving office, such as Frei of the Christian Democrats in Chile, and Venezuela's Betancourt of AD and Caldera of COPEI, have great stature and power within their parties. They usually face little competition for the party's presidential nomination (at least until after they have held office once) and thus, though they often lead hungry parties, other party leaders have less leverage over their decisions. Consequently, they have more leeway for pursuing their preferred appointment strategies than do politicians who rise through the ranks of the party machine and owe their nomination to it. Candidates who rise within the party machine make commitments and develop reciprocal relationships along the way that they have to honor once they achieve power.

To summarize, presidents' preferences with regard to appointment strategies are to some extent inconsistent with the preferences of party members and coalition allies whose support presidents need in order to govern. The preferences of a president engaged in building a political machine while in office will resemble closely those of party members, because such presidents can best pursue their own long-run interests by hiring party supporters. In contrast, presidents who achieved office in spite of preexisting and well-established party machines will have little in common with party members. They will attempt to strengthen their own support base at the expense of established party professionals. Presidents supported by the machinery of established parties fall between these two extremes.

Presidents' ability to pursue their own preferred strategy depends on their vulnerability to demands from potential allies to exchange concessions for support. Presidents are more vulnerable to such demands if they face powerful rivals within their own party, if their party is small relative to others in the legislature, if they cannot wield the weapon of party discipline within their own party, and if the leaders of coalition parties cannot use party discipline to deliver predictable votes from deputies within the coalition. Without party discipline, the president may have to pay separately for nearly every vote. Except for party builders, stronger presidents choose strategies closer to the "compartmentalization" end of the continuum and weaker presidents near the "partisan" end.

These patterns can be radically altered, however, by the threat of military intervention. The threat of overthrow forces presidents to focus on immediate survival. Unless they can reach cooperative agreements with opposition parties to compromise on policy, insulate key elements of the policy-making apparatus from partisan pressures, and share the rest of the spoils, presidents threatened by overthrow tend to distribute everything at their disposal in a desperate search for support, regardless of long-term consequences.

AN EMPIRICAL TEST OF THE DETERMINANTS OF APPOINTMENT STRATEGIES

Given the preferences of relevant political actors and the factors that affect whether they can achieve their goals, one can predict the appointment strategies of presidents. This section subjects these predictions to some empirical tests. The "data," speaking loosely, are the appointment strategies of the forty-four constitutional presidents who served six months or more in Argentina, Chile, Brazil, Colombia, Venezuela, or Peru since 1945.[13]

In order to conduct tests, I developed a quantitative measure of the extent to which presidents used competence rather than partisanship or personal loyalty as the basis for selecting cabinet members and other administrative personnel. The measure does not capture all of the nuance in the typology of appointment strategies, but it does capture its central idea, namely, the tradeoff between technical competence and partisan loyalty. Having built the measure, I use it to test whether the factors identified in the preceding pages can explain variations in the importance of competence in the staffing of government agencies.

To measure the relative emphasis on partisanship and competence at the highest level of government, I used information on the professional backgrounds and party identification of cabinet members. At lower levels of government, I relied on descriptions of appointments in the secondary literature. This information was combined into an Appointment Strategy Index, which is described below.

The data on which the index is based have obvious weaknesses. Presidents usually reward the large parties in their legislative coalitions with cabinet posts and the appointments that go along with them. Cabinet selection, in other words, embodies a political strategy as well as an appointment strategy. Neither the president nor the analyst can disentangle the two. I should note here that cabinet members in Latin America are expected to be working administrators as well as formulators of basic policy. They are usually members of parties, but they are not usually sitting legislators or full-time party activists with a long history in electoral office. Information on cabinet composition is the only form of data comparable across countries on high-level appointments available to the researcher trying to compare several cases over time, so, despite its drawbacks, I have used it.

The use of secondary sources for descriptions of appointments at lower levels also has obvious shortcomings. Few scholars have been interested in this topic and thus little work specifically devoted to it is

13. The sample includes elected presidents and vice presidents who succeeded to the presidency after the president's death or resignation. "Elected" is defined as meaning elected in reasonably honest voting against competitors, even if the competition was somewhat limited. Juan Perón, for example, was included, but Manuel Odría and Marcos Pérez Jiménez were not, even though they were "elected." The idea was to include administrations that were minimally democratic while excluding those in which elections merely ratified a previous seizure of power. The inclusion or exclusion of a few cases would not change the results.

available. The discussions that exist are often sketchy and sometimes contradict each other. The "data," in other words, are likely to contain large amounts of measurement error. Nevertheless, it seems better to attempt some tests with inadequate data than to leave the argument to stand or fall on the plausibility of a few anecdotes.

The information sources from which the answers to the eight questions in the Appointment Strategy Index were gleaned are given in appendix B. Not all questions are appropriate for all countries. The question about partisan appointments in previously insulated agencies, for example, is meaningless in Peru during the 1950s because no previous insulation had occurred.

The Appointment Strategy Index is based on answers to each of the following eight questions for each of the forty-four constitutional governments. Scores on this index depend on the number of negative answers to the following questions for each administration.

APPOINTMENT STRATEGY INDEX

1. Was the criterion for choosing the finance minister primarily partisanship rather than competence?[14]

2. Were at least 90 percent of ministers members of president's party or coalition?[15]

3. Were second-tier appointments concentrated among party or coalition members?

4. Did party members refrain from public complaints about the president's appointment strategy or economic team?

5. Were public sector jobs of party members protected?

6. Did hiring in previously unpoliticized government entities or recently nationalized industries depend on partisan criteria?

7. Was there a lack of progress in insulating previously uninsulated agencies?

8. Did scandals about partisan hiring appear in the press?

The count of negative answers to these eight questions constitute each administration's score on the Appointment Strategy Index. Low scores

14. Fractions used where partisans occupied post part of the time.
15. Excluding military and other ministers appointed in what are unambiguously last-ditch efforts to stave off military coups. The point here was to capture the president's regular strategy, not desperate short-term attempts to prevent overthrow.

indicate a very strong concern for partisan criteria in administrative appointments. High scores indicate a strong opposition to partisan criteria and, in most cases, strong support for the maintenance and extension of existing "islands of competence" within the government.

It needs to be stressed that the Appointment Strategy Index focuses on the background and training of appointees, not their performance in office. Some partisan appointees exhibit high levels of administrative competence. A somewhat larger number of appointees with apparently good training turn out, in practice, to be abysmal administrators—in most cases because either they, their president, or both lack any understanding of the political requisites of effective administration. But, in any case, the reader should bear in mind that the index is intended to measure the kinds of appointee backgrounds that presidents sought rather than government performance per se.

Different countries and administrations vary greatly in terms of the number of ministries included in the cabinet and the identities of the ministries crucial to economic performance. All have finance ministers, however, and the finance ministry is always of central importance. The background of the finance minister is therefore used to assess the commitment to competence at the cabinet level. If even the finance minister has been chosen primarily for partisan reasons, we would not expect to find high levels of expertise elsewhere either.

The question about party members' complaints has been included because complaints by traditional party leaders about a president's failure to appoint party loyalists to key positions are among the surest signs that the president is pursuing an extreme compartmentalization strategy. Further details of construction of the Appointment Strategy Index are described in appendix B.

Table 12 shows the scores of all the cases on the Appointment Strategy Index. High scores indicate strong commitment to technical competence, with the highest suggesting executive isolationism or a failure to consider the realities of governing in a democratic system.[16] A score of two or less indicates a highly partisan strategy; a score between three and six indicates a compartmentalization strategy, in which competence dominates selection of appointees in key agencies, but the political needs of

16. There are a couple of what might be thought of as false positives among the scores on this index, that is, administrations that are markedly low in partisanship but not as competent as their scores imply. The Ibáñez administration is the most extreme case. Personal loyalty seems to have been the dominant factor in the Ibáñez appointment strategy. The president appointed an unusually large number of nonpartisan friends, cronies, and military officers without apparently giving much consideration to competence.

TABLE 12
SCORES ON APPOINTMENT STRATEGY INDEX

Argentina

J. Perón 1946–52	2.0
J. Perón 1952–55	1.0
A. Frondizi 1958–62	6.0
A. Illia 1963–66	2.3
J. Perón 1973–74	3.0
I. Perón 1974–76	1.5
R. Alfonsín 1983–89	3.0
C. Menem 1989–	6.0

Brazil

E. G. Dutra 1946–51	2.9
G. Vargas 1951–54	5.0
J. Café Filho 1954–55	7.0
J. Kubitschek 1956–61	4.0
J. Quadros 1961	7.0
J. Goulart 1963–64	1.4
J. Sarney 1985–90	1.0
F. Collor 1990–92	3.5

Chile

G. González Videla 1946–52	2.5
C. Ibáñez 1952–58	6.5
J. Alessandri 1958–64	7.0
E. Frei 1964–70	4.0
S. Allende 1970–73	1.0
P. Aylwin 1990–	4.0

Colombia

A. Lleras Camargo 1958–62	4.9
G. L. Valencia 1962–66	4.6
C. Lleras Restrepo 1966–70	5.0
M. Pastrana 1970–1974	3.5
A. López Michelsen 1974–78	4.0
J. C. Turbay Ayala 1978–82	3.0
B. Betancur 1982–86	3.0
V. Barco 1986–90	3.0
C. Gaviria 1990–	4.0

Peru

J. L. Bustamante 1945–48	6.6
M. Prado 1956–62	3.5
F. Belaúnde 1963–68	2.2
F. Belaúnde 1980–85	3.5
A. García 1985–90	1.0
A. Fujimori 1990–92 [a]	8.0

Venezuela

R. Betancourt 1959–64	5.0
R. Leoni 1964–69	5.0
R. Caldera 1969–74	5.0
C. A. Pérez 1974–79	4.0
L. Herrera Campíns 1979–84	3.0
J. Lusinchi 1984–89	4.0
C. A. Pérez 1989-93	7.0

[a] Although Fujimori continued to serve as president after 1992, Peru could no longer be called a democracy.

supporters are also attended to; and a score above six indicates an antipartisan strategy in which the claims of party supporters are pointedly ignored. Few presidents with scores in this range held on to power very long. The mean of the variable is 3.96, with a standard deviation of 1.86.

As discussed earlier, presidents, except for those trying to create a new party or national support network while in office, will prefer compartmentalization strategies when civil service reform appears impossible. Presidents whose nominations were opposed by established party leaders or who maintained their independence of established parties will prefer to insulate a larger part of the bureaucracy than others. Presidents are more likely to prevail if they founded their parties and hence face little internal competition, if they lead disciplined parties, and if they do not need to hold together a multiparty coalition in order to govern.

Table 13 shows all forty-four cases in a way that makes it possible to see the effects of most of these factors. Horizontally across the top of the table are categories indicating the closeness of the convergence of the president's interests with the interests of other party members: Party-building presidents (on left) are closest; independents (on right) have the most divergent interests; and nominees of established parties fall in between. Let us focus first on the effect of this variable.

The argument above leads to the expectation that, all else being equal, the greater the convergence between the president's interests and party interests, the greater the role of partisanship in appointments. The table confirms this expectation. The average score for party builders (shown at the bottom of the table) is 1.94, which indicates a strong emphasis on partisan criteria in hiring; for presidents nominated by the established parties and supported by established party leadership, the mean score is 3.63, which indicates a modest degree of compartmentalization; for presidents nominated over the objections of the party leaders, the mean score is 5.67, indicating a strategy of extensive compartmentalization; and for independents, the mean score is 7.02, which indicates almost complete inattention to partisan criteria. Thus, concern for technical competence increases as closeness to party decreases.

We might note that, on average, the antipartisan strategy followed by independents and a couple of others was not an effective survival strategy. Quadros resigned after seven months. Café Filho and Busta-mante were overthrown, and Alberto Fujimori joined the military in a coup that overthrew the constitutional government. Pérez survived two coup attempts before being impeached. Of the presidents who relied on

TABLE 13
EFFECT OF PRESIDENT'S PREFERENCES AND POWER ON APPOINTMENT STRATEGIES

President's Preferences

Building Party in Office		Conventional Nomination		Nomination Opposed		Independent	

PRESIDENT'S POWER: HIGH DISCIPLINE

Building Party in Office		Conventional Nomination		Nomination Opposed		Independent	
J. Perón		Frondizi	6.0	Menem	6.0		
1946–52	2.0	Illia	2.3	Gaviria	4.0		
J. Perón		J. Perón		Pérez			
1952–55	1.0	1973–74	3.0	1989–93	7.0		
Ave. = 1.5		Alfonsín	3.0	Ave. = 5.67			
		Frei	4.0				
		Aylwin	4.0				
		Lleras C.	4.9				
		Valencia	4.6				
		Lleras R.	5.0				
		Pastrana	3.5				
		López	4.0				
		Turbay	3.0				
		Betancur	3.0				
		Barco	3.0				
		García	1.0				
		Betancourt	5.0				
		Leoni	5.0				
		Caldera	5.0				
		Pérez					
		1974–79	4.0				
		Herrera	3.0				
		Lusinchi	4.0				
		Ave. = 3.82					

PRESIDENT'S POWER: LOW DISCIPLINE

Building Party in Office		Conventional Nomination		Nomination Opposed		Independent	
Belaúnde		I. Perón	1.5			Quadros	7.0
1963–68	2.2	Dutra	2.9			Ibáñez	6.5
Sarney	1.0	Vargas	5.0			Alessandri	7.0
Collor	3.5	Café Filho	7.0			Bustamante	6.6
Ave. = 2.23		Kubitschek	4.0			Fujimori	8.0
		Goulart	1.4			Ave. = 7.02	
		González	2.5				
		Allende	1.0				
		Prado	3.5				
		Belaúnde					
		1980–85	3.5				
		Ave. = 3.23					

COLUMN AVERAGES

1.94	3.63	5.67	7.02

antipartisan strategies in this sample, only Alessandri and Ibáñez completed their constitutional terms, and they both made significant concessions to established parties while in office—though the concessions fail to show up on the crude measure used here.

Among the party builders, the most assiduous in the pursuit of partisan strategies were Perón (especially after the 1949 Constitution allowed for immediate reelection) and Sarney.[17] In contrast to Perón, Sarney's low score was caused not by assiduous party building but by the initial weakness of his own political base, the need to hold a coalition together in an extremely fluid political environment, and the use of patronage on a hitherto unprecedented scale to secure passage of articles directly affecting the president in the 1988 Constitution. Belaúnde's[18] lesser emphasis on partisanship in appointments seems to have stemmed from idealism. He did not give as much attention to the organizational aspects of party building as did most other successful party founders,

17. Of the several Brazilian presidents whose categorization was difficult, Sarney was probably the hardest. I have labeled him a party builder even though he does not fit entirely comfortably into the category (he has changed party loyalties during his career and is not inextricably identified with a single party). But neither does he fit easily into any of the other categories. The purpose of the independent category is to identify those presidents who had built a powerful national support machine not limited to any one established party. Sarney does not fit into this category since, prior to his nomination for vice president on the PMDB ticket, he had been a long-time member and leader of the PDS, the most powerful party in the country during most of the period of military rule. He gained the vice presidential slot as part of a deal between Tancredo Neves, PMDB presidential candidate, and a dissident faction of the PDS that provided enough votes in the electoral college to elect Neves. The nomination of Café Filho, who was also given the vice presidential slot in a preelection deal, was classified as conventional since it was the result of a preelection coalition between two established parties. Sarney, however, was not given the vice presidency as the representative of an established party, but rather as the leader of a faction that then became a new party, the Partido da Frente Liberal (PFL, Liberal Front party). The PFL was transformed from a minority faction of the PDS into the second largest party in Brazil during the Sarney administration. Sarney's appointments were certainly not limited to members of the PFL, but this was unavoidable since he had to govern in coalition. If Sarney had not unexpectedly become president, it is not certain that the PFL would have survived as a party at all. For this reason, I have classified him as a party builder, though his efforts to build a national support network for himself have never been limited to members of the PFL.

18. Belaúnde began building his national political machine during his unsuccessful campaign for the presidency in 1956. This organization almost ceased activities after the election, but was revived and reorganized into the AP in preparation for the 1962 presidential election. Thus, although the roots of the AP can be traced back to an earlier period and to Belaúnde's initial regional support base, it did not exist as a well-organized national party much before the campaign leading up to the 1962 election. (None of the candidates in the 1962 election received the required third of the vote needed to win the election, which threw the election into Congress. The military intervened to invalidate the election in order to avert a coalition between Manuel Odría and APRA. A second election was held a year later among the same candidates, which Belaúnde won.)

and his party, Acción Popular (AP, Popular Action), has ceased to be a major contender since his second administration.

Collor's score is the farthest from what the argument predicts for party builders. In spite of having created a party vehicle to support his presidential campaign, Collor did not follow a party-building strategy. Such a strategy was not a feasible option for him, both because his party was tiny (8 percent of seats in the Chamber of Deputies at its peak) and because of constraints imposed by international economic conditions. Prior to the late 1980s, a president in Collor's position could have used state resources and jobs on a massive scale to attract party adherents. But when he came to power in 1990, Collor found himself under intense pressure to reduce state spending and intervention in the economy, which limited his options. In such a stringent environment, there was little real possibility of increasing the size of his party enough to make it a major political player. Consequently, his distribution of jobs, programs, and projects was aimed primarily at holding together an extremely fragile and restive multiparty coalition, rather than building his own party.

Table 13 also displays the effects of party discipline, which is dichotomized here into high or low, as shown down the left side of the table. Party discipline is one of the variables that affects the president's strength relative to that of his supporters. To make the table readable, only party discipline is shown here; the other strength variables are included in the regression below. Cases were categorized as less disciplined if the president's own party failed to maintain discipline (for example, Belaúnde's AP), if some of the parties essential to the president's coalition lacked effective discipline even though others were highly disciplined (as was true for Allende, González Videla, and Alessandri), or if the party system as a whole lacked the institutional foundations of party discipline (as, for example, in Brazil),[19] even though particular leaders might maintain reasonably high levels of effective discipline while in power (for example, Kubitschek).[20]

One would expect that presidents who enjoy high party discipline would be better able to act on their preferences, and the conventional nomination column shows this relationship. For presidents from estab-

19. See Geddes and Ribeiro (1992) for an extended discussion of the institutional and noninstitutional foundations of party discipline in Brazil.

20. Santos (1986, 86–92) shows that during the fifties rates of party voting were fairly high in Brazil, in spite of the lack of institutional foundations for party discipline.

lished parties, greater party discipline is associated with *less* partisanship in appointment strategies. The average score for presidents supported by more disciplined parties is 3.8, while the average among the less disciplined is 3.2.

There is no clear relationship between strategy and party discipline in the other categories of presidential preference. In the party-building category, we would expect no relationship because of the convergence between presidents' and supporters' interests. If presidents themselves want to make many partisan appointments, the issue of party discipline becomes irrelevant. There are too few cases in each cell of the party-building category to draw any conclusions. It is also impossible to tell from this table whether party discipline affects outcomes in the nomination opposed or independent categories. All of the cases in which presidents were nominated in opposition to the leadership of their parties have relatively disciplined parties (or in Colombia, factions).[21] All the independents were elected in countries with more fragmented party systems and less party discipline. In neither category is there any variation in party discipline.

Among the administrations in the conventional nomination category, a few with extreme scores seem worth discussing in a little detail. Arturo Frondizi received the highest score among the presidents backed by more disciplined parties. His unusually high score resulted from a shift in strategy early in his administration that involved appointing more technocrats and placing greater emphasis on economic orthodoxy in an effort to placate the military. Had he continued to follow his initial, and presumably preferred, strategy, his score would look like the others in this category.

At the other extreme, Alan García and Arturo Illia had the most partisan scores within this category. They both led hungry parties that had come to power for the first time in at least a generation. We would expect parties that had previously been excluded from office and access to spoils to make especially urgent demands for appointments.

Among those in the conventional nomination category backed by less disciplined parties, one score differs markedly from expectations: that of Café Filho. As the conventional nominee of a small undisciplined party, Café Filho should, according to the argument, have been con-

21. Argentina, Colombia, and Venezuela have all democratized nominating procedures during the last few years, which has created the possibility of official party candidates opposed by most party leaders for the first time.

strained to favor a relatively partisan appointment strategy. In fact, however, Café Filho scores at the extreme antipartisan end of the Appointment Strategy Index.

Examination of Café Filho's background resolves this anomaly. Café Filho was chosen by Partido Social Progressista (PSP) party founder and charismatic leader Adhemar de Barros to fill the vice presidential slot on the Vargas ticket in order to cement an electoral alliance between Vargas and Barros, Brazil's two foremost populist politicians at the time. Barros agreed to support Vargas in the 1950 campaign in return for Vargas's pledge of support for him in the next presidential election. Café Filho was a relatively unknown PSP congressman from a small northeastern state far from the São Paulo center of the PSP organization. He posed no threat to the continued domination of the PSP by Barros. When he unexpectedly attained the presidency after the death of Vargas, Café Filho attempted to form a stable multiparty caretaker government and carry out some unpopular but needed economic reforms. He seems to have been unique in this sample in apparently having no desire to be president again or maximize his personal political power.

This is a good time to reiterate that the kind of rational actor model used in this book assumes that individuals have certain preferences and have sufficient information and calculating ability to choose means that give the highest probability of achieving their goals. This kind of model is useful if most of the individuals examined either actually do have these characteristics or at least behave as though they did. We should expect to find some individual variation in all three areas: preferences, information, and calculating ability. The model, like any other, aims to explain average behavior, not every individual case.

To summarize, the main points in table 13 are: (1) presidents attempting to build parties while actually in office tend to follow partisan appointment strategies; (2) among conventionally nominated presidents, those backed by more disciplined parties can more easily follow compartmentalization strategies than can presidents who must rely on the support of less disciplined parties; (3) presidents who achieved their party's nomination in spite of opposition from established party leaders on average follow highly compartmentalized strategies; and (4) presidents who achieved national stature independently of any particular party tend to follow antipartisan hiring strategies.

These patterns appear to support the theoretical argument developed above. But to test more rigorously the fit between data and theory, I turn now to statistical analysis. Statistics can accomplish two things:

they can provide a rough idea whether the patterns identified could represent mere chance variation, and they allow the inclusion of more variables than can be intelligibly included in a table. The variables used in the regression analysis are as follows:

Presidential preference: A 4-point variable indicating the closeness of the convergence between the president's interests and supporters' interests. A score of 1 indicates that the president is a party builder, while a score of 4 indicates an independent. The variable is the same as shown in table 13.

Party founder: Coded 1 if the president founded his party and 0 otherwise.

Party discipline: Coded 1 if the president's party or coalition parties were reasonably disciplined, coded .5 if either the parties were somewhat disciplined or the president's coalition was made up of a mix of disciplined and undisciplined parties, and coded 0 if party discipline was very low overall.

Party size: Measured as percent of seats in the Chamber of Deputies occupied by the party most closely identified with the president.

Pact: Coded 1 if a pact to share power existed between the president's party and at least one other major party, and 0 otherwise. The pact variable was included because pacts to share power usually contain agreements to refrain from partisan appointments in areas crucial to economic performance, such as the oil industry in Venezuela. They thus contribute to maintaining administrative competence.

First time in office: Coded 1 if the administration was the first time that the president's party had achieved national office in at least fifteen years, and 0 otherwise. First time in office was included because I expected that party members would exert especially strong pressures for patronage if they had previously been excluded from a share of spoils.

Conventional nomination: Coded 1 if the president was nominated by an established party and supported by most of the party establishment and 0 otherwise. This variable identifies the middle category of the presidential preference variable in which most of the cases occur (see table 13). It is included in order to create the interaction described below.

Three of these variables—party founder, party discipline, and party size—are intended to measure the same underlying concept, namely, the political strength of the president. To avoid problems of multicollinearity among parallel indicators, I combined them into an index, *presidential power*.

Since "presidential power" is expected to affect only the strategies of conventionally nominated presidents, I have built an interaction term— *conventional nomination × presidential power*—to capture the effect of presidential power for these cases. Additional details about the construction of variables can be found in appendix C.

The variables have been scored so that positive coefficients indicate that the variable contributes to compartmentalization. Regressions were run both with and without the Café Filho administration. Since he seemed conspicuously to violate the assumption that presidents seek to maximize their long-term political power, it seemed legitimate to exclude him. The discussion of regression results below refers to the version that excludes Café Filho, but results of both regressions are shown in table 14.

Regression results confirm and extend the earlier analysis of the raw data in table 13. The effect of presidential preference, as in table 13, is quite large. Each point on the 4-point preference scale is associated with a nearly 1.28-point movement in the direction of greater competence on the Appointment Strategy Index that ranges from 1 to 8.

The interaction of conventional nomination × presidential power also shows an important and statistically significant effect. As their political power increases, conventionally nominated presidents follow more compartmentalized appointment strategies. A 1-point difference in presidential power (which ranges from 1.1 to 6.56 within the category of conventionally nominated presidents) is associated with a 0.63 point increase in the appointment strategy score. The effect of the difference between the lowest and highest presidential power scores is 3.5 points on the Appointment Strategy Index, or about half the actual range of the scale.

The dummy variables for pact and first time in office also show substantial effects in expected directions. The existence of a pact is associated with a 1.28-point increase in compartmentalization, all else being equal. And the dummy variable for first time in office is associated with a 0.68-point decrease. Both achieve conventional levels of significance.[22]

22. The presidential power variable entered into the regression alone shows a relatively small negative effect on appointment strategy that is not statistically significant. This coefficient probably has no substantive meaning. The coefficient for conventional

TABLE 14
COEFFICIENTS FOR REGRESSION
OF APPOINTMENT STRATEGIES ON
PRESIDENTIAL POWER AND PREFERENCES

	Café Filho Excluded	All Cases
Presidential Preference	1.28	1.21
(range: 0 to 3)	(4.34)	(3.31)
Presidential Power × Conventional Nomination	0.63	0.47
(range: 0 to 6.56)	(2.74)	(1.68)
Pact	1.28	1.17
(0–1 dummy)	(3.12)	(2.30)
First Time in Office	−0.68	−0.86
(0–1 dummy)	(1.94)	(1.98)
Presidential Power	−0.19	−0.20
(range: 1.10 to 7.64)	(1.05)	(.88)
Conventional Nomination	−2.77	−2.14
(0–1 dummy)	(3.22)	(2.04)
Intercept	3.51	3.72
$N =$	43	44
R^2	.78	.68

NOTE: T-ratios for coefficients appear in parentheses beneath each coefficient. Dependent variable, which has a range of 1 to 8, measures the extent of nonpartisanship in appointment strategy of president. High score indicates high level of nonpartisanship. See appendix C for details of the construction of this and other variables and for all raw data.

The cumulative effect of these variables is impressively large. A conventionally nominated president, who did not found his party, backed by a small (25 percent of the seats in the Chamber of Deputies) hungry party with little discipline, and unsupported by a pact, has an expected score of 3.15 on the Appointment Strategy Index—a score that indicates little concern with finding appointees with high levels of administrative competence. By contrast, a conventionally nominated president supported by a pact leading a large (50 percent of the seats in the Chamber of Deputies) disciplined party that he or she founded and that has not

---

nomination alone simply indicates an intercept shift: that is, all else being equal, administrations in this category scored lower on the Appointment Strategy Index.

previously been excluded from power, has an expected score of 7.15 on the index, which indicates a very high level of concern for competence.[23]

It thus appears that conventionally nominated presidents who govern under auspicious political conditions show as much concern for administrative competence as independent presidents (see lower right cell of table 13). The difference is that, as noted earlier, independent presidents, who attempt to ignore partisanship without having a strong base of political support, rarely govern effectively, whereas insider presidents can achieve both improved levels of bureaucratic competence and political stability.

The overall R^2 for the regression is .78, which seems about as good as could be expected, considering the crude measurement of key variables, especially the dependent variable. When the Café Filho administration is added to the data set, the R^2 drops to .68, and the estimated coefficient for the conventional nomination × presidential power variable decreases by about 25 percent. It remains large enough to be substantively important, but just fails to reach conventional levels of statistical significance. All other coefficients remain approximately the same. In a small and crudely measured data set, the effect of a single case that dramatically violates assumptions is substantial, but the basic pattern of effects can still be discerned.

THE EFFECT OF MILITARY THREATS

Up to this point, discussion has focused on the effects of presidents' preferences and power to get what they want in normal political times. I have argued above, however, that the threat of military intervention leads to a desperate search for support. Presidents whose survival is threatened have difficulty keeping resources out of the current political struggle in order to use them to build administrative competence. Instead, they will often have to distribute everything at their disposal in the effort to maintain minimal levels of political support. Threats to survival come from two sources: directly from the military in the form of coup attempts and public manifestos; or from widespread public disturbances involving illegal acts and violence—at the extreme, guerrilla warfare. The second is not a threat in and of itself. Democratic presidents in Latin America do not resign in response to popular protest. But protests and violence that reach certain levels of magnitude can

23. Expected scores calculated using coefficients in table 14 and variable values noted.

trigger military intervention, and presidents never know exactly where the intervention threshold is.

I have identified the cases listed below as threatened, either by overt military action or by extensive public disorder. I have included cases of guerrilla warfare or urban violence when they were associated with public military grumbling or widespread speculation about a possible coup. I have excluded a few cases, namely, the last few Colombian administrations in which the level of violence would have been high enough to provoke a coup in some countries but in which little danger seemed apparent in Colombia.

THREATENED ADMINISTRATIONS

Chile:	Carlos Ibáñez, after April 1957
	Salvador Allende
Brazil:	Getúlio Vargas, after June 1953
	João Goulart
Peru:	José Luis Bustamante y Rivero
	Fernando Belaúnde, after August 1967
	Fernando Belaúnde, from 1983 on
	Alan García, especially after mid-1987
	Alberto Fujimori
Argentina:	Juan Perón, especially after June 1955
	Arturo Frondizi, especially after March 1962 defeat
	by Peronists
	Arturo Illia, especially after January 1966
	Isabel Perón
Colombia:	Alberto Lleras Camargo
	Guillermo León Valencia
Venezuela:	Rómulo Betancourt
	Raúl Leoni
	Carlos Andrés Pérez, after February 1992

Where the democratic regime faces a clear danger of overthrow, democratic politicians from all parties should share an interest in maintaining the system. If they expect military intervention to reduce their own chances of holding office in the future, they should be willing to agree to cooperate in order to stave off a coup. Militaries do not intervene without substantial civilian support (Stepan 1971), so the behavior of opposition parties becomes crucial when a coup threatens.

Politicians' assessments of the likely effects of coups depend on how long they expect the military to remain in power and which parties they expect the military to favor. They derive their expectations from past experience and from talks with members of the military. Sometimes politicians make poor predictions about both the likelihood of a coup and its results, and so they make the wrong choices about whether to cooperate with the opposition in order to prevent military intervention. The Christian Democrats' failure to cooperate with Allende is probably the best example of this kind of miscalculation (Valenzuela 1978). Arguably, all the bureaucratic-authoritarian governments were helped to power by opposition politicians who, basing their expectations on past military behavior after interventions,[24] failed to predict that the military would remain in power so long.

Where both the president's party and the principal opposition party perceive their own interest in preventing military intervention and manage to achieve cooperation, one would expect to see the inclusion of opposition party members in the cabinet, as well as continued attention to technical competence, since both parties understand the importance of economic performance and honest public service to the maintenance of support for democracy. Charges of widespread corruption and incompetence often help legitimate military coups.

The most notable and successful instances of cooperation to ensure the survival of democratic regimes have occurred in the aftermath of periods of long or violent military rule in situations in which the threat of renewed intervention continued for some years—as it did in Colombia and Venezuela after redemocratization. In these circumstances, no great foresight was required for politicians to realize that their interests depended on the maintenance of the democratic regime. In consequence, party leaders reached cooperative agreements to include a broad range of parties in the initial governing coalition, while insulating sectors of the bureaucracy crucial to economic performance from partisan depredations.

In the aftermath of more recent democratizations, pacts have not formed, in most cases because the military has posed less of a continuing threat. The Argentine military, though restive, has had virtually no

24. See Stepan (1971) for discussion of the military's traditional role as moderator rather than ruler in its own right.

civilian support. The Brazilian military, though not discredited by its performance in office as was the Argentine, has demonstrated its reluctance to intervene again. Chile faces little danger of a coup, despite Pinochet's continued control of the armed forces, as long as the economy does well. Peru is the only exception, and there the opposition was given no opportunity to form a pact, as President Fujimori joined the army in overthrowing the government.

Fujimori's choice was almost unique and quite risky, however. As Uruguayan President Juan María Bordaberry discovered nearly twenty years ago, the lady who rides the tiger sometimes returns inside it.[25] In general, where the threat of military intervention exists, pacts are considered. When either the party in power or the primary opposition party underestimates the threat of intervention or sees its interests as likely to be furthered by intervention, one or both will refuse to cooperate, and we can expect the threatened president to devote all his appointment resources to a desperate effort to shore up support among potential allies and often within the military itself.

This argument suggests that presidents who form pacts with opposition parties (indicated by their inclusion in cabinets) should be able to follow compartmentalization appointment strategies. Appointments to posts in agencies essential to economic policy should go to qualified experts who, though sometimes members of the governing party, are not first and foremost professional politicians. Those threatened presidents who fail to achieve cooperation, in contrast, could be expected to follow appointment strategies focused strictly on survival. They would be expected to replace ministers frequently, changing both individual occupants and parties (where the party system provides this option) as they seek to shore up dwindling support. This rapid turnover would in turn undermine the coherence of economic policies, make the economic environment unpredictable to private actors, and hence reduce investment. Threatened presidents would also be expected to lose control of appointments to other actors whose support they need, to politicize previously professionalized agencies, and to fill high-level positions with military officers and with old friends whose loyalty they can count on.

To see if these expectations were fulfilled, I developed a quantitative measure of survival behavior, which I call the Survival Strategy Index.

25. Amid charges of immobilism and corruption in a context of economic crisis, President Bordaberry in collaboration with the military closed the Uruguayan National Assembly in June 1973. He then governed in alliance with the military until 1976, when he was himself overthrown by his erstwhile military supporters.

The Survival Index score for each of the forty-four cases is based on assigning one point (or fraction where appropriate) to each of the statements below that is true for a particular administration and adding them. Details of index construction are described in appendix B.

SURVIVAL STRATEGY INDEX[26]

1. Average cabinet duration of twelve months or less[27]

2. Average time in office of finance minister less than eighteen months

3. Partisan finance minister

4. Invitation to opposition to join cabinet

5. Friends and cronies of president occupy cabinet posts

6. Current or retired military officers occupy nontraditional cabinet posts[28]

7. More than three officers occupy nontraditional cabinet posts

8. Presidential interference with military promotions or replacement of military ministers with supporters

9. Politicization of appointments to previously unpoliticized government entities or newly nationalized firms

10. Press coverage of scandals involving hiring supporters in government agencies

Table 15 shows the average duration of cabinets, average time in office of finance ministers, and number of nontraditional military appointments for each threatened president. Table 16 shows the sum of each president's survival strategy score, with higher numbers indicating a greater use of appointments for survival purposes. The average score for threatened presidents, 4.9, is more than twice the average for unthreatened presidents (data not shown), 2.2, an indication that threatened presidents do on average behave as predicted.

26. There is some overlap between this index and the Appointment Strategy Index because there is in fact some overlap between a partisan strategy in normal times and a survival strategy. The selection of an unqualified finance minister or the politicization of previously insulated agencies, for example, can be caused by either excessive partisanship or the effort to gain support at any cost.

27. A cabinet reshuffle is defined as a change in personnel that involves at least three posts and at least one new minister (as opposed to a simple exchange of portfolios).

28. In countries where the military routinely occupies certain posts such as defense or army, navy, and air force, these were not counted.

TABLE 15
THREATENED PRESIDENTS AND SELECTED
INDICATORS OF SURVIVAL STRATEGY

Administration	Average Duration of Cabinets (months)	Average Time in Office of Finance Ministers (months)	Nontraditional Military Appointments
J. Perón, 1952–55	20.0	50.0	0
Frondizi	10.0	10.0	0
Illia	34.0	17.0	0
I. Perón	4.7	3.8	1
Vargas	10.7	21.5	0
Goulart	4.7	4.7	0
Ibáñez	6.0	9.0	16
Allende	4.3	6.8	10
Lleras Camargo	8.0	16.0	0
Valencia	12.0	12.0	0
Bustamante	5.6	5.6	18
Belaúnde, 1963–68	8.9	8.9	4
Belaúnde, 1980–85	6.7	15.0	2
García	8.6	8.6	5
Fujimori	5.0	10.0	5
Betancourt	12.0	16.0	1
Leoni	15.0	30.0	0
Pérez,[a] 1989–93	5.2	13.7	1

[a] Figures for Pérez calculated as of September 1992.

Table 17 compares threatened presidents who were able to form stable alliances with opposition parties to presidents who failed to do so. The average score among those who failed to form pacts (5.4) is nearly double the average score of those who succeeded (2.9). In other words, presidents who did not form pacts had to use more of their appointment resources in the struggle to survive than did presidents who formed successful pacts. Of those who failed to form alliances, many tried and some succeeded for a time. The Unión Cívica Radical del Pueblo (UCRP, Popular Radical Civic Union) entered Frondizi's cabinet

TABLE 16
SCORES OF THREATENED PRESIDENTS
ON SURVIVAL STRATEGY INDEX

J. Perón (1952–55)	5.0	Valencia	3.4
Frondizi	3.0	Bustamante	5.4
Illia	2.7	Belaúnde (1963–68)	5.8
I. Perón	5.5	Belaúnde (1980–85)	4.5
Vargas	5.0	García	7.0
Goulart	7.6	Fujimori	6.0
Ibáñez	6.5	Betancourt	4.0
Allende	7.0	Leoni	1.0
Lleras Camargo	3.1	Pérez (1989–93)	5.0

Average   4.9

NOTE: Higher scores indicate a greater reliance on survival-oriented appointment strategies.

during the last month before his overthrow, but too late to prevent a
coup. APRA accepted posts in Bustamante's cabinet for eleven months,
but the agreement broke down. Liberals, Conservatives, Christian Democrats, and members of other parties all entered the Ibáñez cabinet at
one time or another but later withdrew in irritation. COPEI entered
Carlos Andrés Pérez's cabinet after the coup attempt in February 1992
but withdrew again in July. Vargas and Allende attempted to placate
opposition parties by offering cabinet posts but failed to get opposition
party cooperation (though UDN sympathizers joined the Vargas cabinet
as individuals).

When it can be accomplished, the alliance and compartmentalization
strategy seems more likely to result in actual survival than does the
survival strategy itself. In this sample, all presidents who formed lasting
alliances finished their terms, while only 25 percent of those following
survival strategies without pacts did so. Lest it appear that the survival
strategy is counterproductive, however, note that those among the presidents who finished their terms in spite of failing to form stable alliances
had higher average scores on the Survival Strategy Index (6.0) than
those who were overthrown (who averaged 4.7).[29]

29. Pérez and Fujimori were excluded from calculations of the percent who survived

TABLE 17

APPOINTMENT STRATEGIES OF
THREATENED PRESIDENTS BY COOPERATION
WITH OPPOSITION PARTIES

Lasting Cooperation with Opposition	Unsuccessful Cooperation with Opposition
Lleras C.	J. Perón (1952–55)
Valencia	Frondizi
Betancourt	Illia
Leoni	I. Perón
Ave. = 2.88	Vargas
Survival Rate = 100%	Goulart
	Ibáñez
	Allende
	Bustamante
	Belaúnde 1963–68
	Belaúnde 1980–85
	García
	Fujimori
	Pérez (1989–93)
	Ave. = 5.42
	Survival Rate = 25% [a]

[a] Fujimori and Pérez were excluded from calculation of the survival rate. Fujimori neither survived as a democratic president nor was overthrown, but instead joined the military in carrying out the coup. Pérez was impeached after surviving two coup attempts.

To sum up, most presidents threatened by immediate overthrow turn to appointment strategies that decrease the competence and integrity of the bureaucracy in their desperate effort to trade tangible benefits for support. Forming stable alliances with the main opposition party is an effective alternative survival strategy, since the military rarely intervenes without substantial civilian support. Presidents who succeed in forming such alliances have no need to use appointments to shore up support and, in this sample, they do not.

and of average scores—Pérez because he was impeached rather than overthrown, and Fujimori because he neither survived nor was overthrown.

LONG-TERM CONSEQUENCES OF
PRESIDENTIAL APPOINTMENT STRATEGIES

Up to this point, the chapter has shown that, though they usually prefer compartmentalization strategies that build expertise, honesty, and commitment in selected bureaucratic agencies, presidents who are weak relative to their supporters use partisan strategies, and presidents threatened by overthrow usually end up trading jobs for support regardless of its effect on competence. Those presidents who can afford to, however, do employ compartmentalization strategies. Presidents, thus, see the bureaucracy as a political resource to be used to solve whatever political problems are most pressing. The long-term effects of this use of the bureaucracy in a politically unstable environment include retarding the growth of technical competence and extravagant overstaffing.

Although the compartmentalization strategy builds competence during particular presidential administrations (as shown in the description of the Kubitschek administration in chapter 3), it tends not to institutionalize administrative competence because recruitment remains *informal*. The highly trained individuals committed to goal achievement, who are recruited into some government agencies by presidents following compartmentalization strategies, themselves try to routinize the professionalization of their agencies, as noted in chapter 3. They sometimes initiate meritocratic recruitment procedures within agencies, for example, that are notably more stringent than those that apply to the rest of the career bureaucracy. Without support from the legal system, however, their capacity to insulate and professionalize their own agencies—especially given high rates of rotation through agencies—is limited. Generally, the survival of professionalism and nonpartisanship in administrative agencies depends on ongoing presidential support and consequently declines when, for whatever reason, presidential support declines.

Political instability heightens the more general problem of inadequate institutionalization. Military threats lead to the politicization of previously insulated agencies and thus not only to temporary declines in competent government performance but to the longer-term need to rebuild effective agencies or the postponement of their establishment in the first place. In this sample, the countries that had made the least progress in building a few competent bureaucratic agencies in key areas of policy making prior to the 1980s were Peru and Argentina, the same countries that had experienced the most military involvement in politics. Peru's weak state capacity is usually attributed to the more general backwardness of the Peruvian economy, and there does seem to be a loose relationship between development and state capacity. It should be remembered, however, that in the 1960s when the Colombians were initiating some of the reforms usually given credit for enhancing technocratic competence in the Colombian bureaucracy (Mares 1990 and 1993), Colombia's per capita income was the same as Peru's (United Nations 1971, 595). The Argentine case is unambiguous. Levels of state capacity failed to keep pace with development because of repeated partisan interventions and manipulations by military rulers and civilian politicians, both more concerned about ideology and loyalty than competence (Ascher 1975).

The military itself often initiates reforms aimed at professionalizing the bureaucracy (including civil service reforms in both Argentina and Peru), but these reforms tend to create little long-term legacy. They are not seen by most citizens as neutral, but rather as part of a more general attack on the supporters of the recently overthrown civilian government, and therefore have little support or legitimacy themselves after redemocratization.

Furthermore, in most circumstances the reemergence of party politics that inevitably follows military rule increases politicians' need for patronage to dispense and thus makes the insulation of bureaucratic agencies temporarily more difficult. During the period immediately before and after the return to civilian rule, parties and leaders compete intensely to attract new voters who have come of age under authoritarianism, casual adherents of the past, and members of any new groups who have become participants for the first time as a result of changes in electoral laws accompanying the transition (such as illiterates in both Peru and Brazil in the eighties). Promises of tangible benefits, including jobs, play a large role in this competition. And in addition, loyal members of parties that have been excluded from power for long years, as noted above, feel an especially strong hunger for spoils they have previously been denied. In short, even in the unlikely event that the military government itself follows exemplary policies with regard to building bureaucratic competence, transitions to and from military rule tend to undermine whatever progress had previously occurred.

The central place of patronage in building effective political machines also leads to systematic overstaffing and thus to inefficient allocation of scarce resources and upward pressure on the budget. Though some of the increase in personnel occurs as a result of hiring binges during periods of party building or survival efforts, most is the unintended consequence of routine partisan hiring along with partial civil service coverage that prevents dismissals for partisan reasons.

Whatever administrative appointment strategy they choose, all presidents who want to accomplish far-reaching goals such as land reform, rapid improvement of the infrastructure, or "fifty years development in five," will create new agencies charged with these new tasks and staffed by competent people committed to the new goals. Presidents create new agencies because they cannot count on either the competence or commitment of the public employees who staff preexisting agencies. These people represent the accretion of appointments, often patronage-based, of other politicians and parties over the years. In some countries, one can predict the party affiliation of bureaucrats by the years they were hired. Thus, new presidents have reason to feel uncertain about current employees' competence and to expect many of them to have little enthusiasm for the success of new programs.

Furthermore, the president has virtually no leverage for altering the behavior of the bureaucrats he or she inherits. Although civil service provisions for meritocratic hiring and promotion apply to only a small fraction of bureaucratic positions in Latin America, most of the larger countries have had administrative statutes that protect employees from politically motivated dismissal for many years. Advancement within the bureaucracy, moreover, depends almost entirely on seniority. Even where statutes exist that mandate tests of performance as determinants of promotion, they have little effect in practice. Typically all bureaucrats receive the same high scores on "performance" tests and thus the tests offer no basis for distinguishing among them (Nascimento 1965). This leaves presidents few effective tools for dealing with work avoidance or obstructionist behavior.

The desire to maintain a personally loyal machine also contributes to the appeal of job creation for presidents. Since they often cannot fire previous appointees, and natural attrition alone gives them insufficient positions to dispense, presidents have a strong incentive to create new ones. The result of this politically driven need to create new positions can be seen in the bloated bureaucracies that exist all over Latin America and in the extreme reluctance of presidents from established parties that have found comfortable niches in the bureaucracy to reduce public employment in order to reduce budget deficits. Outsider presidents such as Collor, whose supporters have few jobs in the bureaucracy, have shown much greater willingness to lay off public employees, but their efforts are often blocked by partisans, in the legislature and elsewhere, of the parties more historically linked to the bureaucracy.[30]

Job creation becomes especially pronounced when presidents are trying to build parties to serve their future electoral needs while actually in office. Juan Perón's massive use of his party supporters to staff government offices is probably the best known example.

Thus three long-term consequences of presidential appointment strategies in Latin America seem clear. First, though compartmentalization can result in effective bureaucratic performance during a presidential administration, it does not usually lead to the successful institutionalization of a professionalized sector of the bureaucracy. Second, periodic threats of overthrow, which lead to the politicization of previously insulated agencies, can undermine even those agencies that have achieved high levels of professional competence. And third, the routine use of patronage to build support tends to increase the size of the bureaucracy beyond what is necessary or can be afforded.

CONCLUSION

Presidential appointment strategies, which determine the competence and political loyalties of government officials charged with implementing the president's program, play a crucial role in determining whether "state" attempts to foster economic and social change actually work. Presidents who appoint able administrators committed to achieving presidential goals, who locate these appointees in agencies insulated from the obstructionist efforts of public employees hired by previous administrations, and who provide their appointees with secure and sufficient funding, will have a greater probability of carrying out successful policies.

What, then, determines presidential appointment strategies? This chapter has argued that presidential appointment strategies can be predicted from the assumption that presidents want to continue to exercise political power in the future even though they usually cannot run for reelection immediately, and from certain information about the president's relationship to the immediate political environment. One needs to know six pieces of information to make predictions: whether the

---

30. See Geddes (1991) for an extended discussion of the factors that influence presidential willingness to lay off public employees or privatize state enterprises.

president founded his or her party; whether the president can rely on the discipline of party members and members of coalition parties when seeking support in the legislature; the size of the president's party; whether the president is trying to build a support machine while in office; whether the president was nominated by an established party to which he or she had belonged for some years and is supported by party elites; and whether the military threatens the president's survival in office.

If the president is secure in office and seats in the legislature are more or less evenly divided between the strongest parties, then civil service or other political resource-reducing reforms can be enacted, as shown in chapter 5, regardless of other factors. Civil service, however, never covers more than a small part of the bureaucracy. For the rest, and where the uneven distribution of party strength in the legislature prevents the passage of reforms, the following expectations about presidential appointment strategies apply.

1. If survival is seriously threatened, then presidents either form pacts with the opposition if that is possible or follow a survival strategy, regardless of other factors.

2. Presidents attempting to build support organizations while in office follow partisan strategies, concentrating appointments among loyalists.

3. Presidents who win nomination in spite of the opposition of established party leaders or who run as independents or the nominees of parties to which they have not previously belonged tend to pursue strategies at the most nonpartisan end of the compartmentalization continuum.

4. For most presidents, who are nominated by established parties and supported by established party elites, the ability to follow compartmentalization strategies depends on their political strength relative to that of the party and coalition allies on whom they depend in order to govern. Presidents who founded their parties usually face little competition from within the party and hence have more power. Presidents who lead disciplined parties or coalitions made up of disciplined parties also have more power, as do presidents supported by larger parties.

An intensive examination of the appointment strategies of forty-four Latin American administrations carried out in this chapter has shown that these arguments do a good job of explaining patterns in presidential appointments in the larger democratic countries of Latin America. On average, threatened presidents who fail to form pacts dissipate their appointment resources in the effort to "buy" survival; party builders concentrate appointments among party loyalists; and independents often ignore the claims of partisan supporters. The appointment strategies of presidents nominated and supported by established party elites vary depending on the president's political strength relative to that of his or her allies. Founders and those who lead large, disciplined parties tend to follow compartmentalization strategies. Most who did not found their parties and who lead small and/or undisciplined parties must make more partisan appointments. Pressure for partisan appointments is especially strong when the party has not held national office for many years, if ever before. Pacts with opposition parties reduce threats to survival and increase the likelihood of successful compartmentalization.

SEVEN

The Effects of Institutions

This book began with a fanciful image of the state as an organism lumbering through halls. This image captures an essential element of many theories of the state, namely, that it is a unitary actor capable of pursuing its own interests and responding in a self-interested way to changes in its environment. This notion, though a useful simplification in international relations theory, impedes understanding of the role states play in domestic processes. States are not analogous to organisms made up of cooperating interdependent cells, but rather to agglomerations of single-celled animals who may or may not cooperate, depending on the costs and benefits they as individuals face. Consequently, in order to understand state behavior, one must understand the behavior of these individuals, as shaped by the political institutions that determine the costs and benefits of the different actions they can choose.

Such an approach, as demonstrated above, aids in understanding the development of administratively competent states. A focus on individuals assumed to behave rationally in the different political settings and roles they occupy leads to a series of predictions about when state-building reforms will occur. These predictions have turned out to be mostly consistent with evidence from Latin America.

The starting point for the explanation of reform is the observation that, from the point of view of most ordinary people, many of the actions that could be expected to contribute to bringing about reforms involve collective action problems. The struggle for civil service reform provides an extended example of such a collective action problem, but many other reforms aimed at improving the state's performance have the same characteristics. These reforms are costly to bring about, beyond the power of solitary citizens to achieve, and would benefit most citizens, whether they helped initiate them or not. So most citizens have insufficient reason to contribute their personal resources toward achieving them.

In contrast, many of the individuals most nearly affected by such changes—that is, the administrators, politicians, and bureaucrats who make up the system threatened by reform—have good reason to oppose changes. Changes in the criteria for recruitment to bureaucratic jobs involve a loss of resources for the politicians who previously had been able to use either the jobs themselves or the resources controlled by appointees for their own ends. And they threaten the job security, advancement, and general status opportunities of current holders of bureaucratic jobs. Consequently, these groups can be expected to oppose the change. Those who oppose such changes are already organized in the bureaucratic entities themselves, in parties, and in civil servants' unions, so that the costs of expressing their opposition are quite low relative to the costs of organizing new groups in order to represent the interests of those who would benefit from reform. The expected outcome for this class of possible reforms, then, is that, even if they are widely perceived as desirable, they tend not to occur.

In some instances, however, political entrepreneurs are capable of solving collective action problems such as these. Whether they do so depends on the incentives they themselves face. Where they can "sell" public goods for something of value to themselves (for example, votes) and where the political costs of such "sales" are not prohibitive, political entrepreneurs will do so.

Unfortunately, the most important category of potential political entrepreneurs in a democracy—elected officials—often face crosscutting incentives that undermine their impulses to supply collective goods. For legislators, the usefulness of patronage as a resource in the electoral competition with other candidates often outweighs the benefits of supplying reform as a public good to the country as a whole.

Patronage is especially valuable to legislators in systems of open-list proportional representation. In these systems, candidates compete against members of their own parties along with members of other parties. Under these circumstances, patronage conveys such an advantage to incumbents of parties that have historically had access to patronage vis-à-vis competitors from their own parties that it is never rational for them to agree to give up patronage, no matter what members of other parties might be willing to do. Among the cases examined here, no reforms occurred in open-list systems.

One of the most basic findings of this study is that the costs of reform to elected legislators decline when electoral strength, and, as a result, access to resources through clientele networks, are more or less equally divided among the larger parties in the political system. In these circumstances, legislators become willing to initiate reform.

The payoff matrices in chapter 4, which show the electoral game and the iterated patron-client prisoner's dilemmas superimposed on each other make this point more formally. When the distribution of costs to be incurred by the reform is equal, cooperation to bring about reform becomes the dominant strategy for members of all parties. When the distribution of costs is unequal, the dominant strategy of those for whom the costs will be higher, that is, those who benefit most from the old system, will be opposition to reform unless they expect to benefit very greatly from voting for it. This result is not sufficiently precise to predict outcomes deterministically. But it does lead to the prediction that the probability of the passage of reform will be higher where the distribution of costs is more equal. The case study evidence is consistent with this prediction.

To summarize, legislatures tend to pass reforms when electoral strength, and consequently access to patronage resources, is approximately evenly divided among the larger parties. They fail to pass them when one or two parties dominate, even if those parties have advocated reform during election campaigns.

Presidents, whose future careers depend more heavily than do legislators' on accomplishing promised programmatic goals, have stronger reasons for wanting to initiate reforms. Frequently, however, they also face more urgent pressures to jettison reform initiatives. They may need to preserve patronage resources not just for use in their own future campaigns but also to bolster their chances of surviving current threats of overthrow.

INSTITUTIONAL SOURCES OF REFORM

These conclusions have some important implications with regard to the effects of different political institutions on the probability of reform. A roughly equal division of access to spoils does not occur at random. It is caused by specific political institutions, notably the system of representation. Two-party systems are more conducive to achieving cooperation among legislators to initiate reform than are multiparty systems. Because the parties' time in office is likely to have been more equal in a two-party than in a multiparty system, the distribution of access to various forms of government largesse tends to be more equal, as do the costs of reform. In addition, as in all collective action situations, a smaller number of actors reduces transaction and enforcement costs.

Once the initial reform has occurred, two-party systems are also more likely to produce extensions of the reform. During periods of rough equality when two parties alternate in office, each party has an interest in blanketing in more positions before it turns power over to the other. This pattern, as exemplified by the history of civil service reform in the United States, results in an initial reform being extended incrementally over a decade or two until a major change in the bureaucracy has occurred.

At first glance, one might expect party parity to occur most frequently in systems with single-member district representation. Duverger's law predicts that single-member district systems of representation should result in two-party systems, and Anglo-American experience seems to confirm this expectation. In Latin America, however, the few single-member district systems of representation have resulted in one-party dominant political systems.

Most Latin American countries, including all those examined here, employ a mix of the two systems. Presidents, governors, and mayors (where they are elected rather than appointed) are chosen in winner-take-all elections from single districts. Deputies, in most cases senators, state legislators, and municipal councils are elected by proportional representation. Thus Latin American political systems include institutional features that impel them toward both more and less fragmented party systems at the same time.

Factors that increase the number of parties that can find viable niches in the party system include (1) large district magnitude, (2) easy party registration, (3) low representation thresholds, (4) nonconcurrent elections, and (5) runoffs. The first three have been fully discussed in the literature on parliamentary systems. As district magnitude (that is, the number of representatives selected from a single district) increases, smaller parties' chances of electing a few deputies increase (Taagepera and Shugart 1989, 112–25). The easier it is to register new parties, that is, the fewer signatures required and the simpler the other formalities, the more parties are likely to compete. The lower the minimum number of votes required for representation in the legislature, the easier it is for small parties to capture a few seats.

Runoffs and nonconcurrent elections have received less attention since they tend to occur in systems that combine features of presidentialism and proportional representation. Presidentialism, following the logic of Duverger's law, tends to reduce the number of parties. Only the larger parties usually have any hope of winning presidential elections. Smaller parties typically join coalitions with larger parties during presidential campaigns and, over time, might be expected to die out unless they can offer voters some advantage in other elections over belonging to larger parties.

Nonconcurrent elections, that is, the holding of legislative, gubernatorial, and municipal elections at times different from the presidential election, tend to increase the opportunities for small parties to attract voters (Shugart forthcoming). They increase the relevance of local and regional issues for vote choices. Small parties that have no chance of winning the presidency may be powerful contenders in local elections, and, in consequence, voters who might feel that they would be wasting their votes on them in a national winner-take-all election, readily vote for them in a local or proportional representation election. The most fragmented party systems among the cases examined here, Chile before 1973 and Brazil after 1985, have each held three separate sets of elections for different levels of government.

Runoff elections for president and governor also tend to increase party fragmentation (cf. Shugart and Carey 1992, 215–24). The existence of runoffs gives small parties an incentive to field candidates, and voters an incentive to vote for them, in the first round. The better they do in the first round, the more they can demand in return for their support of a larger party in the second round. Runoffs thus increase the bargaining power of small parties and the advantages they can deliver to voters, and therefore encourage the survival of small parties.

Runoffs, noncurrent elections, district magnitude, thresholds, and registration rules all affect whether party parity occurs spontaneously, but it has also sometimes been artificially maintained by a pact among party leaders. If party discipline is sufficient to enforce the pact, reforms then often occur. Pacts will be discussed in more detail below.

INSTITUTIONAL SOURCES OF
PRESIDENTIAL STRATEGIES

As in the analysis of legislators' incentives to initiate reforms, some political institutions increase the likelihood that presidents will follow appointment strategies that build bureaucratic capacity. Leaving aside for the moment presidents facing immediate threats of overthrow, those least likely to contribute to the growth of administrative competence are party builders trying to create a party machine while in office; independents, who try to follow an antipartisan strategy but usually fail to survive in office; and those who lead small parties in undisciplined coalitions. All of these conditions occur more frequently, though not exclusively, in more fluid, fragmented, uninstitutionalized party systems.

In such systems, more new parties are founded and hence party builders are more likely to achieve the presidency. The election of candidates who have neither founded nor risen through the ranks of major parties occurs only in relatively fragmented party systems. The election of presidents who lead small parties and thus must depend on multiparty coalitions also occurs only in fragmented party systems. In other words, presidents are more likely to help build administrative competence in stable, well-institutionalized, less fragmented, and more disciplined party systems.

During periods of threat, presidents are more likely to be able to improve or maintain levels of bureaucratic competence if they can form pacts to cooperate with opposition parties. Pacts can be understood as attempts to solve collective action problems; all participants must forgo some short-term benefits in order to achieve a longer-term arrangement more beneficial to all.

Though pacts can be formed by multiple parties, cooperation emerges more easily when it involves fewer, relatively stable, disciplined parties. As Mancur Olson (1965) noted long ago, collective action problems can be solved more easily when the number of actors is small. Stability in the party system and of leadership within parties makes bargaining easier, since it tends to reduce unpredictability and inconsistency in bargaining positions. Party discipline guarantees that deals made by party leaders can be enforced, that is, that individual party members will not be able to free-ride. Thus the probability that presidents will be able to weather threats of overthrow without dissipation of administrative capacity through the wholesale exchange of appointments for support increases in well-institutionalized party systems.

In short, whether threatened or not, presidents are more likely to contribute to the development of state capacity in stable, less fragmented, disciplined party systems. The institutional factors that limit the number of parties have been discussed above. The causes of party system stability deserve some attention here.

A stable party system can be defined as one that contains "a fairly constant set of parties, whose share of votes varies within roughly predictable limits" (Coppedge 1991, 2). Using this criterion, the cases examined in this study can be classified as follows: very stable—Colombia, Uruguay, Argentina, and Venezuela; moderately stable—Chile and Brazil (1946–64); unstable—Peru and Brazil (since 1985).[1]

The causes of party system stability in Latin America are not well understood. Latin American party systems do not fit the pattern posited by Lipset and Rokkan (1967). One might suspect that frequency of military intervention or levels of violence would affect party system stability, but no direct and obvious relationship exists (Geddes 1992). Historical explanations for party stability that link the survival of nineteenth century parties into the late twentieth century with early universal male suffrage and late civil wars have been suggested (e.g., Coppedge 1991). Proponents of this view argue that the extension of suffrage when partisan civil wars remain fresh in memory tends to create strong partisan loyalties at the mass level and raise barriers to the entry of new parties later. These are plausible explanations for Colombia and Uruguay, but they fail to explain the similar persistence of parties in Paraguay and Honduras, and make no effort to explain the relatively stable party systems in Venezuela and Argentina. In short, no general explanation of party stability in Latin America is widely accepted.

Nevertheless, one observation can be made. Although there is no inherent reason why a system composed of many parties could not be stable in the sense used here, that is, relatively unchanging, in fact a strong correlation exists between instability and the number of parties. It appears that the same institutional factors that limit the number of viable parties in a system also serve as barriers to the entry of new parties and thus contribute to party system stability over time. In other words, the same institutional features—low district magnitude, high representation thresholds, difficult party registration, concurrent elections, and plurality rule in winner-take-all elections—that limit the num-

1. Mainwaring and Scully (forthcoming) arrive at somewhat different categorizations since they look only at the last twenty or so years for most countries.

ber of parties in presidential proportional representation systems also increase party system stability.

Party discipline also contributes to presidents' ability to follow appointment strategies that enhance bureaucratic capacity. Institutional sources of party discipline are located in both electoral rules and internal party procedures. Electoral rules that increase the influence of party leaders over candidate selection and the likelihood of winning give party leaders powerful levers with which to enforce discipline. Rules that allow multiple faction lists to run under the same party label or that allow voters to determine candidates' position on the party list decrease this leverage and thus, all else being equal, decrease discipline.

Party discipline can also be generated within parties, even in political systems in which the electoral rules offer party leaders little leverage over members. APRA in Peru, the Partido dos Trabalhadores (PT, Workers' Party) in Brazil, and Conservatives, Communists, and Christian Democrats in Chile all developed high levels of party discipline in such systems. The kinds of internal party rules that result in disciplined behavior by legislators and other party activists are fairly straightforward: tight control over candidate selection, the ability of the leadership to expel members and force officials to resign from their posts, control over campaign financing, and so on.

Many of the highly disciplined, mass-based parties in Latin America were first organized a number of years before achieving power, and managed to survive and maintain support despite having few tangible benefits to offer voters. I would include in this category AD in Venezuela, APRA in Peru, and the Christian Democrats and Communists in Chile. I would suggest that the relationship between early exclusion and discipline exists because only parties that developed effective discipline—whether as a consequence of the personalities of early leaders or through trial and error—were able to survive many years out of office.

Party discipline also seems to have gotten a boost during Latin America's only lengthy experiment with parliamentarism.[2] Chilean parties, especially the Conservative party, developed grassroots organizations and much more effective party procedures, stimulated by the competition for seats in the legislature during the parliamentary interlude (Rem-

2. Chile experimented with what should more accurately be called a semiparliamentary system between 1891 and 1925. During this interlude, Chile had an elected president with limited powers and a legislature that in effect controlled cabinet appointments. Brazil's semiparliamentary interlude between 1961 and 1963 was both short and extremely unstable, and thus had little effect on parties.

mer 1984). These organizational changes occurred, however, prior to the initiation of the open-list system. There is no way of predicting whether or not parliamentarism in the absence of electoral rules conducive to party discipline would lead to the strengthening of party organizations.

AUTHORITARIANISM AND REFORM

In the quest for bureaucratic competence in democratic systems, the problematic element is the uncertainty over whether potential political entrepreneurs will face incentives that lead them to supply this particular collective good, even if all would agree that they favor reform in principle. Electoral competition and insecure tenure in office force politicians to compare the "profit" to be gained from supplying this kind of collective good with that available from the supply of other public goods or from the conversion of the public resources needed to create public goods into private goods. Different institutional arrangements, as detailed above, set different limits on politicians' choices. Some are more conducive to creating appropriate incentives for potential political entrepreneurs than others.

Nevertheless, the provision of public goods always remains problematic. In developing democracies, those who might provide leadership for solving collective action problems frequently have good reasons for failing to do so. This book has focused throughout on impediments to the development of state capacity in democratic political systems. Does authoritarianism offer ways around any of these obstacles?

Political competition is a double-edged sword. It can sometimes, as shown above, undermine the desire of politicians to initiate reforms. But it also provides them with the principal incentive for providing this and other public goods, since competition for votes leads politicians to supply voters with public as well as other goods. In the absence of competition, collective action problems would be solved *only* when privileged groups or adequate selective incentives existed within the latent interest group itself.

This book so far has dealt with politicians' uncoerced decisions to initiate reforms. Voluntary cooperation to bring about change, however, is not the only means of securing such reforms. Important bureaucratic reforms in France and Prussia as well as Brazil occurred under the auspices of dictatorial rulers (Rosenberg 1966; Suleiman 1974). For leaders impatient for major reform, the advantages of dictatorship are obvious: like Vargas in the late thirties, they need not wait for other political actors to agree to cooperate. Instead, the dictator can, in principle if not always in practice, impose costs that ensure changes in behavior. This accounts for some of the appeal of authoritarianism to Third World leaders committed above all else to bringing about rapid state-led change and for some of the speculations by scholars on the utility of authoritarianism during certain stages of development.

Two characteristics of Third World polities make authoritarian solutions to development problems especially tempting to some elites and sometimes also to ordinary citizens. The first is that representative institutions have been slow to initiate all kinds of reforms, sometimes for the reasons noted above. At the initiation of authoritarian interludes, developing countries generally have a large backlog of problems for which solutions have been identified (not always correctly) but not carried out because of their political infeasibility.

The second factor that increases the temptation toward authoritarianism is heavy state involvement in the economy. The more the government intervenes in the economy, the larger the potential effect of political and administrative reforms on national well-being. If patronage appointments lead to incompetence and malfeasance in city services, the post office, and the port authorities, as happened in the United States in the nineteenth century, support for reforms will develop. It seems doubtful, however, that anyone would think these sufficient causes for overthrowing a government. But when patronage appointments lead to incompetence and malfeasance in the state-owned steel and oil industries, in the banks that provide most of the loans to manufacturers, and in the agencies that supply foreign exchange and regulate international trade, the economic costs of maladministration rise and may add to other inducements people have to consider extreme measures.

Authoritarianism may seem to offer solutions to development problems because it can insulate government decision makers from many of the political clientele networks that pervade society, as well as from most organized interest groups. It thus, in theory, frees decision makers to devise rational policies in the national interest. Most obviously, authoritarian governments weaken or destroy party-based patronage networks. Elected politicians can no longer divert state resources to their own survival needs.

Where authoritarian governments impose tight control on political parties and other forms of autonomous political organization, they severely reduce traditional politicians' influence and, as a result, their ability to broker exchanges. Ordinary citizens still want jobs and other favors, and they remain willing to trade support for them. Many legislators, if the legislature still exists at all, are still willing to grant jobs and favors in exchange for support. But, if they are shorn of most of their traditional power by the authoritarian regime, they have little to offer administrators in exchange for agreeing to hire their protégés or grant other kinds of favors.[3] Neutralization of the electoral connection in these ways removes one of the major impediments to carrying out administrative reforms.

Additionally, in authoritarian regimes committed to development, administrators are themselves under greater pressure to perform. Some will be new appointees who share the new regime's concern for competence and efficiency. Others who do not share regime values will nevertheless feel greater pressure to perform, as their success in office depends on satisfying the new leaders. This pressure raises the cost to them of hiring incompetents while, at the same time, the benefits of doing so drop with every reduction in the decision-making power of Congress. In a democratic system, the cooperation of legislators may be very valuable, especially at appropriations time. In an authoritarian regime, congressional cooperation is worth much less—if a congress exists at all.

More generally, to the extent that electoral considerations have stood in the way of reform initiatives that would increase the competence of the bureaucracy, that impediment no longer exists in an authoritarian political system. And the same could be said for any other collective good which it did not pay elected leaders to provide. Certain alternatives simply lose their attractiveness.

This does not, however, imply that authoritarian governments will be better providers of collective goods—only that their efforts to do so, assuming they make any, will face different obstacles. Authoritarian governments create their own characteristic set of impediments to carrying out reforms. Starting at the top of the hierarchy, the dictator may plunder the national treasury or employ incompetent relatives or cronies. Only a countervailing force located in the military or ruling party will have any power to restrain a corrupt dictator. Even a dictator who values power or national development over personal wealth may not be

3. The degree to which authoritarian regimes actually impose limits on traditional political power varies across countries and over time. As Frances Hagopian (forthcoming) and Barry Ames (1987) have both shown, the Brazilian military government after 1974 permitted and even encouraged the resurgence of traditional political networks.

able to prevent government officials from plundering the nation. As in a democracy, the more the state intervenes in the economy, the greater the opportunities for plunder. In the absence of institutions that would make officials accountable to the populace, official depredations on the economy may reach astounding proportions.

Officials can always further their own interests by diverting funds earmarked for development projects to their own use. Many will do so unless the cost and risk of being caught outweigh the expected benefits (Shackleton 1978; Rose-Ackerman 1978). Corruption is an especially severe problem in authoritarian governments because of the absence of norms of public disclosure and accountability.

The national leaders of authoritarian regimes often seek to develop bureaucratic capacity. The only incentives to lower-level officials of authoritarian governments to supply the public goods that would contribute to building such capacity, however, come from the costs and benefits which the party, military corporate group, or government itself can impose on them. Thus, the central problem for authoritarian regimes is the creation of an appropriate set of incentives to shape the behavior of their own officials.

If these officials are embedded in organizations that effect a convergence between individual interests and regime goals, one can expect that goals will be reached more frequently than when individual interests diverge from regime interests. Such convergence occurs when organizations offer benefits to individuals—whether in the form of power, status, wealth, or promotions—for expending their energies to pursue regime goals (and, of course, impose costs for failing to do so) that outweigh the benefits associated with the various behaviors that undermine the pursuit of these goals.

Leninist parties and some highly professionalized militaries have demonstrated greater capacity to shape the incentives of member-officials than have other governing parties and less professional militaries. Each of these organizations, during some phases of its existence, has features that can shape the incentives of members: opportunities for upward mobility within the organization, along with strictly enforced criteria for advancement based on compliance with directives from above; boundaries between the organization and the rest of society that reduce opportunities for contact with groups that compete for the official's loyalty; intensive socialization to organization norms and values, which reduces the discrepancy between the informal subculture of members and the formal culture of the organization, and consequently reduces the incidence of members' taking advantage of their official positions to pursue personal gain (Jowitt 1971; Selznick 1960; Berman 1974). The creation of such organizations, however, has proved difficult in Third World authoritarian regimes.

Consequently, authoritarian governments have not, on average, performed better as sponsors of development or reform than have democratic governments (Remmer 1990 and 1993). As a result, although authoritarianism has posed a recurrent temptation, it has been as unstable as democracy, and Latin American countries have veered erratically between the two.

TRANSITIONS

Frequent transitions between democracy and authoritarianism have particularly deleterious effects for building competence in state bureaucracies. The threat of overthrow is the most powerful solvent of bureaucratic competence encountered in this study. Fragile presidents whose governments hover on the edge of ouster will often exchange everything at their disposal, including positions in key policy-making agencies that have functioned with competence for many years, for short-term support. Several decades of incremental progress can be lost in a few months during an episode of threat.

Once an authoritarian government takes power and begins trying to accomplish its own aims, it faces all the obstacles noted above. Should it succeed, against all odds, in building up the competence of sectors of the state apparatus, these levels of competence are unlikely to survive the transition to democracy. Except when the authoritarian regime has been extremely successful in the economic sphere, and in consequence garnered some support for its methods, procedures initiated by dictators tend to be seen as illegitimate, as motivated by the thirst for power and control, and thus to be abandoned during transitions to democracy.

Unless accompanied by pacts that curtail party competition, new democracies are infertile ground for the growth of bureaucratic competence. Party systems tend to be more fluid, with new parties emerging and all parties struggling to establish or reestablish themselves in stable electoral niches. Parties scramble to attract the large number of potential voters who have come of age since the last real election, those whose party loyalties have eroded through disuse or cynicism during the authoritarian interlude, and those—such as illiterates in some instances—

who have only become eligible to vote during the transition. Party and politician survival depend on success in the initial competition for votes, and party identification and loyalty play lesser roles in outcomes than during normal times. As a result, the distribution of all kinds of goods— including appointments—plays an unusually large role.

Party pacts, as shown in chapter 6, can curtail these excesses. Pacts, as the term is used here, are cooperative agreements among two or more parties, which together can attract most votes and account for more than half of the political spectrum, to limit competition and share the fruits of office. Parties agree to pacts in order to secure civilian rule against the return to power by uncowed military leaders. Since adequate economic performance plays an important role in limiting civilian support for coups, pacts have often included provisions for insulating from partisan pressures those state agencies key to economic performance.

Pacts, however, have high costs for the parties that would otherwise have dominated government. Where the military either seems to have reached a consensus in favor of returning to the barracks (as did the Brazilian military after mid-1984) or has discredited itself through abysmal performance in office and, as a result, has demonstrably lost virtually all civilian support (as in Argentina), parties and politicians can expect a return to civilian politics even without pacts, and therefore do not create them.

Preventive pacts, that is, pacts to prevent the initiation rather than the resumption of military rule, seem even more costly and hence less likely to emerge. The disincentives to the formation of preventive pacts include not only the cost to the ruling party of lost spoils, changed policies, and broken campaign promises, but also the cost to opposition parties that face a high risk of losing the next election if they are linked in the public mind to the failed programs of the threatened president. If opposition parties underestimate the threat of overthrow or expect the military intervention to be brief, the cost of joining the government of the threatened president will appear higher than the cost of letting things take their course. For these reasons, pacts occur infrequently, and state capacity often declines in the periods preceding and following military rule.

In short, authoritarianism, although seeming to offer a quick fix for stalled efforts to build state capacity, rarely works in practice. It overcomes certain obstacles characteristic of competitive electoral systems, but brings in its train others at least as intractable. The worst of both worlds is the oscillation between democracy and authoritarianism caused by the alternation between the temptation to try authoritarian rule and disillusionment with it. Frequent transitions between democracy and authoritarianism lead to the recurrent dissipation of competence in previously professionalized agencies during periods of political stress both before and after authoritarian interludes.

Assessment of Achievement for the Various Targets in the Target Plan

All the targets in the Target Plan are arrayed in tables 18–22, categorized in terms of the kinds of agencies and actors involved in achieving them, as in table 1. The figures shown in table 1 are averages of the percentage achieved of each target shown in tables 18–21. (Table 22 shows targets for which a quantitative assessment of achievement is not possible.) Where a single target listed several sub-goals, these were first averaged to get an overall figure for the target as a whole. Where possible, I used 1961 figures for the averages. In cases where production was increasing rapidly, it seemed fair to allow an extra year before assessing achievement. In cases where 1961 figures were lower than 1960 figures, it also seemed appropriate to use them since there seemed some possibility that 1960 figures might in some instances have been inflated to give the appearance of achievement. In a few cases, 1962 figures were used. Where targets included an endpoint other than 1960 (e.g., 4,852,000 kw installed capacity for electricity by 1965), I used the year after the specified endpoint where possible.

Targets used to calculate the figures in tables 18–22 come from *Programa de Metas do Presidente Juscelino Kubitschek* (1958, 23–96). Where there were differences between the detailed discussion of a target and the summary statement of it, I used the detailed version. Several of the targets were reassessed and revised as more information became available during the course of the Kubitschek administration. I used the 1958 version because the targets at this date were somewhat more realistic than the earliest statement of the plan, but not simply a reflection of what had already been accomplished, as one might suspect about the final iteration of the plan.

"Targeted Increases" were calculated by subtracting 1955 figures (drawn wherever possible from standard sources, not from the Target Plan itself, which often differed from standard sources and from one version to the next) from target figures. "Actual Increases" were calculated by subtracting 1955 figures from 1960 and 1961 figures, unless other dates were mentioned in the Target Plan, again drawn wherever possible from standard sources.

As is apparent from the source notes to the tables, Brazilian production statistics from the fifties and sixties are not entirely reliable. Wherever possible, I checked one source against others. When three or more sources disagreed, I chose the middle figure. When two disagreed, I chose the conservative one, that is, the one that, if incorrect, would bias calculations against my argument. Sources for particular figures and discussion of disagreements among sources can be found in the source notes to the tables. There is also quite a bit of ambiguity in the Target Plan itself. I have noted targets in which there were multiple possible interpretations of goals and my reasons for interpreting them as I did in the source notes to the tables.

TABLE 18

TARGETS DEPENDENT ONLY ON SPECIAL
FUNDING AND EXCHANGE PROVISIONS

	Pre-Target Level[a]	Increase Targeted	Increase Actual	Achieved (%)
TARGET VI IMPORT OF RAILROAD CARS AND TRACK				
Modern Engines	—	412	389[b]	94
Freight Cars	—	10,943	6,498	59
Passenger Cars	—	1,086	554	51
New Track (mil. tons)	—	791,600	613,259	77
Cargo (mil. ton-km/km)	—	131,155[c]	62,545	48
1962			133,765[d]	102

**TARGET XI   INCREASE IN TANKERS, COASTAL AND
LONG-RANGE SHIPPING FLEET** (1,000 deadweight tons)

	Pre-Target Level[a]	Increase Targeted	Increase Actual	Achieved (%)
Tankers	217	330	299[e]	91
Other	724	200	243	122

SOURCES:

[a] Pre-target level 1955 unless otherwise noted; date for target completion 1960 unless otherwise noted.

[b] For engines, cars, and track imported, see Láfer (1970, 172).

[c] Figures for 1955 and 1960 calculated from *United Nations Statistical Yearbook* (1963, 375). Figures somewhat higher than those used here can be found in Brazil, Conselho Nacional de Economia, *Exposição Geral da Situação Econômica do Brasil* (1962, 2/3), and figures somewhat lower in *Anuário Estatístico do Brasil* (1957, 139 and 1962, 108).

[d] Calculated from *Exposição Geral* (1964, 41).

[e] Láfer (1970, 179).

TABLE 18 (*continued*)

	Pre-Target Level[a]	Increase		Achieved (%)
		Targeted	*Actual*	

TARGET XII   RENOVATION OF THE COMMERCIAL AIR FLEET (mil. tons/km)

Domestic Capacity	90[f]	495[g]	300[h]	61
Total Capacity	—	—	499	100

TARGET XVII   INCREASE IN THE NUMBER OF TRACTORS IN USE

	28,928[i]	43,072	34,565	80

SOURCES:

[f] No capacity figures are available for 1955. The figure here refers to amount actually shipped. *Exposição Geral* (1962, 273).

[g] Since no capacity figures are available for 1955, the targeted increase was calculated by subtracting the actual amount of cargo carried in 1955 from the Target. This overstates the targeted increase since capacity is always greater than utilization. If capacity figures were available, the percentage achieved would be larger than it appears here.

[h] Domestic and total figures are both from *Exposição Geral* (1965, 54). It is not clear from the description in the *Programa de Metas* whether the target refers to total shipping by air or only cargo shipped by Brazilian airlines.

[i] Average of 1952 and 1956; these and 1960 figures from *United Nations Statistical Yearbook* (1968, 113).

TABLE 19
TARGETS INVOLVING PRODUCTION WITHIN INSULATED AGENCIES OR ENTERPRISES ALONG WITH SPECIAL FUNDING, EXCHANGE, AND TARIFF PROVISIONS

	Pre-Target Level	Increase Targeted	Increase Actual	Achieved (%)
TARGET I INCREASE IN INSTALLED CAPACITY FOR ELECTRICITY (1,000 kw)				
1960	3,148[a]	1,852	1,653[b]	89
1961			2,057	111
1965		4,852	4,264	88
1966			4,418	91
TARGET IV INCREASE IN THE PRODUCTION OF PETROLEUM (barrels per day)[c]				
1960	5,569	92,431	75,759	82
1961			90,028	97
TARGET V INCREASE IN OIL REFINING CAPACITY[d] (barrels per day)				
1960	108,300	197,700	109,700	55
1961		221,700	200,300	90
TARGET VIII PAVEMENT OF FEDERAL HIGHWAYS (km)				
	2,376[e]	5,000	6,643	133

SOURCES:

[a] *Exposição Geral* (1962, 69).

[b] Figures for 1960–66 from *United Nations Statistical Yearbook* (1968, 353).

[c] Target was expressed in barrels per day. Figures in this section of the table were calculated from tons per year data in the *UN Statistical Yearbook* (1963, 172), using the formula 1,000 barrels = (6.2898) (tons per year) (1/.82), where .82 is the average specific gravity of Brazilian crude oil.

[d] Figures for this part of table from Láfer (1970, 169), and Lessa (1964, 164). They cannot be confirmed from standard sources because other sources report production rather than capacity. Production reported in *Anuário Estatístico do Brasil* (1962, 86), and *Exposição Geral* (1964, 28), are consistent with the amounts of installed capacity reported here.

[e] *Exposição Geral* (1962, 79).

TABLE 19 (*continued*)

	Pre-Target Level	Increase		Achieved (%)
		Targeted	Actual	

TARGET IX CONSTRUCTION OF NEW FEDERAL HIGHWAYS (km)

	22,250[f]	12,000	11,801	98

TARGET XVIII INCREASED PRODUCTION OF CHEMICAL FERTILIZERS (tons)

1960	25,060[g]	274,940	260,823[h]	95
1961			264,651	96

TARGET XIX INCREASED PRODUCTION OF STEEL (1,000 tons)

1960	1,162[i]	1,138	681	60
1961			833	73
1965		2,338	1,271[i]	54
1966			1,939	83

SOURCES:
[f]*Exposição Geral* (1962, 79).
[g]Lessa (1964, 168).
[h]*Anuário Estatístico do Brasil* (1962, 89).
[i]1955, 1960, and 1961 from *UN Statistical Yearbook* (1963, 283). Confirmed by *Anuário Estatístico do Brasil* (1962, 74).
[j]1965 and 1966 calculated from *UN Statistical Yearbook* (1968, 305). For these years, the UN reports data for ingots and castings together, but in earlier years and in other sources, ingots are reported separately. To approximate the amount of ingots only in 1965 and 1966, I multiplied the total figure by .82, the percentage of ingots in the total in 1960, the only year for which I had data for both ingots and total from the same source. The official target refers to ingots, so I have reported production of ingots. If, however, one looks at total crude steel production, the 1960 target was more than achieved and the 1965 target had been surpassed by 1966.

TABLE 19 *(continued)*

	Pre-Target Level	Increase		Achieved (%)
		Targeted	*Actual*	
TARGET XXIII INCREASE IN INSTALLED CAPACITY FOR THE PRODUCTION OF ALKALIS (1,000 tons)				
Caustic Soda	35[k]	105	105[l]	100
Sodium Carbonate	0	72	100[m]	139
TARGET XXV PRODUCTION OF SYNTHETIC RUBBER (dry weight tons)				
By 1967	0	40,000	54,726[n]	137
TARGET XXVI INCREASE IN IRON EXPORTS (1,000 tons)				
1960	2,565[o]	5,435	2,595[p]	48
1961			3,672	68
1962			4,963	91

SOURCES:

[k] Lessa (1964, 167). Other sources report production rather than capacity, but *UN Statistical Yearbook* (1963, 264) and Brazil, Ministério do Planejamento e Coordinação Econômica, *Plano Decenal de Desenvolvimento Econômico e Social* (1967, Bk. 5, V. 5, p. 30), report production amounts consistent with the installed capacity used in the table.

[l] Production of caustic soda lagged far behind capacity because it can only be produced efficiently if a by-product of the production process, chlorine, can be sold. The market for chlorine was limited in Brazil.

[m] 1962 production figures, *Plano Decenal* (1967, Bk. 5, V. 5, p. 35).

[n] 1966 production figures, Brazil, Ministério da Indústria e do Comércio, Superintendência da Borracha, *Anuário Estatístico: Mercado Nacional* 3:5 (1969, 14).

[o] *Anuário Estatístico do Brasil* (1957, 237).

[p] *Anuário Estatístico do Brasil* (1962, p. 165).

TABLE 20
TARGETS INVOLVING SPECIAL FUNDING
AND SUBSIDIES, DISTRIBUTED BY
TRADITIONAL UNINSULATED AGENCIES

	Pre-Target Level	Increase Targeted	Increase Actual	Achieved (%)
TARGET VII CONSTRUCTION OF NEW RAILROADS (km)				
1960	37,092[a]	2,100	1,195[b]	57
1961			1,247[c]	59
TARGET XIII INCREASED PRODUCTION OF WHEAT (1,000 tons)				
1960	858[d]	342	−145	0
1961			−313	0
TARGET XIV CONSTRUCTION OF NEW WAREHOUSES AND SILOS (tons storage)				
	—	742,000	569,233[e]	77

[a] *Anuário Estatístico do Brasil* (1957, 138).
[b] *Anuário Estatístico do Brasil* (1962, 107).
[c] *Exposição Geral* (1963, 46).
[d] Average production 1952–56, *United Nations Statistical Yearbook* (1967, 145).
[e] Láfer (1970, 183–84).

TABLE 20 *(continued)*

	Pre-Target Level	Increase		Achieved (%)
		Targeted	Actual	

TARGET XXV   INCREASE IN THE PRODUCTION OF NATURAL RUBBER (dry weight tons)

	Pre-Target Level	Targeted	Actual	Achieved (%)
1960	21,191[f]	3,809	2,271	60
1961			1,545	41

TARGET XXX   INCREASED PRIMARY EDUCATION AND TECHNICAL TRAINING (children in primary school)

	Pre-Target Level	Targeted	Actual	Achieved (%)
1957–58	—	424,300[g]	398,000	94
1958–59		528,180	326,000	62
1959–60		647,740	347,000	54
1960–61		788,560	350,000	44

[f] Superintendência da Borracha, *Anuário Estatístico: Mercado Nacional* 3:5 (1969, 3).

[g] The meaning of targets listed in the Programa de Metas is somewhat ambiguous. The quantitative targets are so low that they indicate either (1) that planners had no idea how many additional children normally entered primary school every year; or (2) that targets refer to an increase above the rate of normal increase. The latter interpretation seems more consistent with internal evidence so I have used it. The average increase in primary school enrollments during the years immediately prior to Kubitschek's administration was 6% per year. The targeted increases shown in the table equal 6% of the previous year's enrollment plus the additional increase stated in the Plan. A more general assessment of Kubitschek's effect on primary education can be obtained by comparing the average increase between 1957 and 1961 with the general trend to see if it differs. The average increase from 1957 to 1961 was 5.25% per year. From 1952 to 1961, it was 6% per year. In other words, there was no increase in the rate of increase during the period of the Target Plan. In contrast, the number of children enrolled in primary school increased by 24% between 1963 and 1964. All data from Brazil, Ministério do Planejamento e Coordenação Econômica, *Plano Decenal de Desenvolvimento* (Versão Preliminar) (Bk 6, V 1, pp. 49, 193). The *United Nations Statistical Yearbook* and *Anuário Estatístico do Brasil* show somewhat lower figures for virtually every year, but the same general trends. I used the figures in the *Plano Decenal* because it provided the longest continuous complete series.

TABLE 21
TARGETS ADMINISTERED BY INSULATED AGENCIES INVOLVING PRODUCTION BY THE PRIVATE SECTOR, SPECIAL FUNDING, AND SUBSIDIES

		Increase		
	Pre-Target Level	Targeted	Actual	Achieved (%)
TARGET III INCREASE IN COAL PRODUCTION (1,000 tons)				
	2,349[a]	791	−189[b]	0
TARGET XV CONSTRUCTION OF NEW REFRIGERATED WAREHOUSES (tons storage)				
	36,600[c]	45,000	8,014	18
TARGET XVI CONSTRUCTION OF INDUSTRIAL SLAUGHTERHOUSES				
Cows/day	15,300[d]	2,750	2,200	80
Hogs/day	0	1,100	700	64
Cold Storage (tons)	—	13,030	817	6
TARGET XX INCREASE IN ALUMINUM PRODUCTION (1,000 tons)				
1960	1.7[e]	23.3	16.5	71
1962		40.8	18.4	45
1963			15.9	39
TARGET XXI INCREASE IN PRODUCTION AND REFINING OF NON-FERROUS METALS (tons)				
Lead	4,027[f]	13,973	5,949	43
1961			8,500	61
Copper	399	2,601	813	31
1961			1,260	48
Tin	1,203	8,797	1,127	13
Nickel	39	161	56	35
Zinc	0	10,800	0	0

TABLE 21 *(continued)*

	Pre-Target Level	Increase Targeted	Increase Actual	Achieved (%)

TARGET XXII   INCREASE IN CAPACITY FOR PRODUCING CEMENT (tons)

	Pre-Target Level	Targeted	Actual	Achieved (%)
	3,335,550[g]	1,334,450	1,348,640	101

TARGET XXIV   INCREASED PRODUCTION OF CELLULOSE AND PAPER (1,000 tons)

	Pre-Target Level	Targeted	Actual	Achieved (%)
Pulp	72[h]	189	88	47
1961			158	84
Newsprint	37	188	29	15
1961			25	13
Other Paper	232	84	74	88
1961			73	87

TARGET XXVII   IMPLANTATION OF THE AUTO INDUSTRY (Vehicles/year)

	Pre-Target Level	Targeted	Actual	Achieved (%)
1960	—	170,000[i]	133,078	78
1961			145,674	86

[a] *Exposição Geral* (1962, 74). The *UN Statistical Yearbook* (1957, 147), reports 2,268,000 tons produced in 1955. This difference does not affect the assessment of the outcome.

[b] *Exposição Geral* (1962, 74). The *UN Statistical Yearbook* (1962, 143), and the *Anuário Estatístico do Brasil* (1962, 43), both report production of about 2,330,000 tons in 1960. Whichever figures are used, production did not rise significantly between 1955 and 1960.

[c] 1955 and 1960, Láfer (1970, 184).

[d] All figures from Láfer (1970, 184–85).

[e] 1955 and 1960 from *UN Statistical Yearbook* (1963, 289). 1962 and 1963 from *UN Statistical Yearbook* (1968, 306).

[f] Data for all years from Lessa (1964, 168). The *United Nations Statistical Yearbook* (1963, 287), reports approximately the same amounts of lead and tin produced. Amounts produced of other minerals are so small that they are not included in standard sources.

[g] Data on installed capacity in 1955 and 1960 from *Plano Decenal* (1967, Bk 5, V. 7, p. 71).

[h] All figures in this part of the table from *UN Statistical Yearbook* (1963, 259–61). Figures for pulp and paper production are unusually unreliable. 1955 figures for other paper vary from 232,000 to 346,081 tons. 1960 figures for pulp vary from 160,000 to 210,300 tons; for other paper, from 306,000 to 505,089 tons. Figures on newsprint are approximately the same across sources. I used UN figures because they were complete for the whole series and thus involved less chance of inadvertently comparing figures based on different definitions of what to include or different kinds of measurement.

[i] All figures in this part of table from *Anuário Estatístico do Brasil* (1962, 75).

TABLE 22

TARGETS THAT CANNOT BE
QUANTITATIVELY ASSESSED

TARGET II DEVELOPMENT OF NUCLEAR ENERGY CAPACITY

Specific   National Production of Nuclear Materials
Goals   Technical Training of Personnel
             Planning and Installation of Nuclear Energy Plants
             Creation of Laws to Regulate the Nuclear Industry

Achieved   First Nuclear Reactor in Latin America Installed
             Creation of National Storage of Nuclear Materials
             Distribution of Scholarships[a]

TARGET X RENOVATION AND ENLARGEMENT OF PORTS;
          ACQUISITION OF DREDGING EQUIPMENT

Specific   Increase Number of Ports and Port Facilities
Goals   Acquisition of Equipment for Cargo Handling
             Dredge about 25 Million Cubic Meters in 23 Harbors
             Acquisition of Dredging Equipment

Achieved   Equipment for cargo handling and dredging was imported.
             Quantitative data on dredging and port facilities are not available,
               but Láfer suggests that goals in these areas, under the control of
               traditional administration, were not achieved.[b]

TARGET XXVIII IMPLANTATION OF SHIP BUILDING INDUSTRY

Specific   Reequipment of 14 Shipyards
Goals   Creation of Two Shipyards for the Production of Large Ships, with
               Capacity to Turn out 130,000 dead weight tons/year
             Build Three Dry Docks for Smaller Vessels

Achieved   By 1960, projects were nearing completion capable of producing
               158,000 dwt/yr.[c]
             Two large shipyards had been approved, and one ship launched.
             This project was managed by insulated agencies (Grupo
               Executivo da Indústria de Construção Naval and SUMOC).

---

[a] Láfer (1970, 167).
[b] Láfer (1970, 178–79).
[c] Láfer (1970, 204). Other sources report gross tons registered or deadweight tons
contracted in particular years, but not production capacity.

TABLE 22 *(continued)*

TARGET XXIX   IMPLANTATION AND EXPANSION OF ELECTRICAL AND
              HEAVY MECHANICAL INDUSTRY

Specific   Production of Generators with Capacity of 450,000 kva/yr
 Goals   Production of Transformers with Capacity of 960,000 kva/yr
            Production of 40,000 motors with up to 1,800,000 hp

Achieved   Láfer reports that production of heavy machinery increased by
            100% and electrical equipment by 200% during the period.[d]
            No quantitative data are available to make an independent
            assessment.

---

[d] Láfer (1970, 205).

Creation of Appointment and Survival Strategy Indices

Scores on the Appointment Strategy and Survival Strategy indices are based on information gathered about cabinets and executive bureaucracies during each of forty-four presidential administrations. Judgment criteria for the various items in the indices were as follows:

Partisan finance minister

Most finance ministers are both members of the president's party and technically competent. Finance ministers were considered mostly partisan if they had little or no relevant training, if their careers had been spent mostly in party and electoral politics, if they were members of the party central committee, or if contemporary press reports identified them as insufficiently qualified. In the few instances in which military officers held finance portfolios, they were counted as partisan, though they were not usually partisan in the literal sense, because their main appeal to presidents was not technical competence but rather their contribution to the maintenance of support.

Ministers as members of president's party or coalition

Ministers were counted as part of the party or coalition of the president unless they were affiliated with no party, affiliated with a very small party that brought the president no legislative support, or serving in cabinets as individuals even though their party had refused official participation. Military ministers in posts traditionally held by the military were excluded from calculations, as were military or opposition party ministers appointed in what were obviously last-ditch efforts to stave off a coup. The aim was to capture a facet of the appointment strategy in normal political times for a particular president, not at the peak of a crisis.

Second-tier appointments

Second-tier appointments include managerial posts below the ministerial level in the federal bureaucracy, state enterprises, and other government agencies outside the central bureaucracy.

Public complaints

Complaints in the press by members of the president's party or coalition partners about appointments were taken as an indication that the president was making fewer partisan appointments than was customary in a particular political system.

Public sector jobs protected

A president failed to protect the jobs of supporters if (1) substantial numbers of members of his own party or coalition occupied positions in the state bureaucracy, and (2) either wholesale layoffs of bureaucrats occurred, or public enterprises were sold or closed.

Politicized hiring in previously unpoliticized entities

Presidents were given credit for politicizing hiring in previously unpoliticized government agencies if they used partisan criteria as the basis of hiring either in previously professionalized agencies or in newly nationalized enterprises.

Progress in insulation

Presidents were given credit for insulating previously uninsulated agencies if there were reports in the literature or the press indicating that technocratic criteria were being used to staff agencies that had previously recruited through customary channels.

Hiring scandals

Press coverage of scandals involving the hiring of presidential supporters in government agencies was taken as an indication that partisanship in hiring exceeded customary bounds.

Cabinet duration

A new cabinet was defined as involving changes in at least three portfolios, at least one of which was staffed by a newly appointed individual. Average cabinet duration was measured as the number of months the president held office divided by the number of cabinets. Average cabinet duration of less than a year was taken as indicating instability.

Time in office of finance minister

The number of months the president spent in office was divided by the number of finance ministers. Where a particular individual was appointed more than once during the same administration, each appointment was counted separately.

Invitation to opposition to join cabinet

Invitations reported in the press or elsewhere were counted, whether they were accepted or not. An administration scored one if one or more invitations were reported and zero otherwise.

Friends and cronies

Individuals were counted as friends or cronies if the press or other literature described them in these terms and if their backgrounds did not offer other obvious explanations for their appointments.

Military in nontraditional posts

In different countries, different cabinet positions are traditionally reserved for members of the armed forces. Administrations received a one if one or more officers were appointed to a post not traditionally reserved for the military and zero otherwise. Retired officers were counted if they were appointed because of continuing influence in the armed forces, but not if they seemed to have been chosen primarily because of technical expertise. In several Latin American countries, officers have often received better technical and scientific educations than most civilians. *Anfíbios* ("amphibians"), former officers who had become full-time politicians, a not uncommon occurrence in Brazil, were not counted.

Three or more military officers

Counting the number of officers in a cabinet is not as straightforward as it would at first seem. For this index, I added one to the count each time an officer was appointed minister for the first time, moved to a new ministry during a cabinet reshuffle, or reappointed after a period of time out of office. If an officer held two ministerial posts at once, I added two to the count. As can be seen in table 15, a few presidents appointed a large number of officers to their cabinets. This was taken as indicating, on average, a more intense effort to respond to the threat of overthrow, and therefore administrations that included three or more officers were given an extra point on the Survival Index.

Interference with the military

In countries in which the military customarily has several representatives in the cabinet, threatened presidents do not usually appoint more. Instead, they try to reduce the military threat by promoting officers who support them and forcing into retirement officers they distrust. Administrations were given a one if the press reported presidential interference with promotions or forced retirements and zero otherwise.

Before making the judgments described above, the members of each president's initial cabinet were identified by name and then all changes over time were noted. As much information as possible was collected on cabinet members' party identification, professional background and qualifications, political background, personal and political relationship with the president, length of time in office, and cause of resignation. This information was then used to generate scores on the parts of the indices that refer to cabinets. For some administrations, information was readily available in secondary sources. For others, local newspapers had to be used.

The names of most cabinet officials are from *Keesing's Contemporary Archives* (1946–92). *Keesing's* was supplemented with information on both cabinets and the rest of the bureaucracy from the following sources:

Hispanic American Report, various issues (1949–64); Mallory (1956–62); Mallory (1963–69); Stebbins and Amoia (1970–74); Banks (1975–90); *Countries of the World and Their Leaders*, (1975); *Latin American Regional Reports*, various issues (1988–92); *Latin American Monitor*, various issues (1985–92); *Latin American and Caribbean Contemporary Record*, various volumes (1982–85); Corke (1984).

ARGENTINA

Acuña (1984); Ascher (1975); Imaz (1970); *Quién es quién en la Argentina* (1955, 1958–59, 1963); Snow (1965, 1971a, 1971b); Wynia (1978).

Frondizi: Pisarello and Edda (1988); Sikkink (1988); Smulovitz (1991); Uzal (1963).
Illia: Sánchez (1983); Smulovitz (1991).
I. Perón: *Quién es quién en la sociedad argentina* (1982).
J Perón: Crassweller (1987); Page (1983); Smith (1974).
Menem: McGuire (1992); Nash (1992).

BRAZIL

Amorim Neto (1991); Beloch and Abreu (1984); Benevides (1989); Graham (1968); Hippólito (1985); Leff (1968); *Quem É Quem no Brasil 1955–1967* (1967); Santos (1986); Siegel (1966); Skidmore (1976).

Dutra: Leite and Novelli (1983); Mourão (1955); Newspaper and journal articles: "Brazil Names 2 Ministers," *New York Times*, September 29, 1946, p. 22; "4 Brazilians Quit Cabinet," *New York Times*, October 15, 1946, p. 21; "New Brazilian Minister," *New York Times*, November 15, 1946, p. 6.
Vargas: D'Araújo (1982).

Kubitschek: Benevides (1976); Láfer (1970); Maram (1992).

Sarney: Newspaper and journal articles: "A dança das cadeiras," *Veja*, January 30, 1985, pp. 20–27; "Deu Leão na cabeça," *Veja*, February 20, 1985, pp. 16–22; "Estocada no PMDB," *Veja*, February 19, 1986, pp. 20–26; "Sarney oferece a Archer Ministério da Previdência," *Jornal do Brasil*, October 21, 1987, p. 3; "Reforma vira só troca de 4 ministros," *Jornal do Brasil*, October 22, 1987, p. 1; "Sarney troca 4 ministros e muda nome de ministério," *Jornal do Brasil*, October 22, 1987, p. 4; "Ulysses tira seus três ministros," *Jornal do Brasil*, July 29, 1988, p. 1; "Maílson acha difícil ficar no governo," *Jornal do Brasil*, August 8, 1988, pp. 1, 13; "Maílson não sai e manda pagar a URP," *Jornal do Brasil*, August 11, 1988, p. 1; "Uma Presidência de vice," *Veja*, March 14, 1990, pp. 32–37.

Collor: Newspaper and journal articles: "Time da retaguarda," *Veja*, March 21, 1990, pp. 104–7; "O amor fulminante," *Veja*, October 17, 1990, pp. 30–35; Bardawil (1990, 28–29); "Conchavar para reinar," *Visão*, November 7, 1990, pp. 6–9; Viotti (1990, 32); "Ciranda de alianças," *Veja*, May 29, 1991, p. 21; "Sucessão de fracassos derruba Chiarelli," *Folha de São Paulo*, August 22, 1992, pp. 8–9; "Rosane anuncia sua saída da LBA no dia da queda de Chiarelli," *Folha de São Paulo*, August 22, 1991, p. 3; "Denúncias de corrupção provocam a maior reforma ministerial de Collor," *Folha de São Paulo*, March 31, 1992, p. 1; "Collor definiu mudança há três semanas," *Folha de São Paulo*, March 31, 1992, p. 6; "Collor mantém Cabrera, atende PDS, PL e PTB e convida 3 ex-ministros," "Reforma de Collor recria três ministérios," and "Cabrera assina ficha no PRN para continuar," *Jornal do Brasil*, April 10, 1992, pp. 1, 3, 4; "Collor refaz o ministério com mais cargos e nomes do regime militar," and "Presidente está nos braços da fisiologia," *Folha de São Paulo*, April 10, 1992, p. 1; Rossi (1992, 6); Gabeira (1992, 6); Dimenstein (1992, 7).

CHILE

Ascher (1975); Caviedes (1979); *Diccionario Biográfico de Chile* (1948–49, 1953–55, 1972–74); López Pintor (1972); Stallings (1978).

Ibáñez: Bray (1961); Olavarría Bravo (1962); Newspaper and journal articles: "Asumieron sus funciones los ministros de cinco carteras," *El Mercurio*, March 3, 1953, p. 15; "Nueva etapa ministerial," *El Mercurio*, March 4, 1953, p. 3; "Crisis ministerial quedó solucionada con la organización de un Gabinete administrativo," *El Mercurio*, October 15, 1953, pp. 1, 19; "Min. de Relaciones Exteriores designado D. José Serrano P.," *El Mercurio*, January 3, 1956, p. 1; "Quedó planteada ayer la crisis total de Gabinete," *El Mercurio*, April 23, 1957, pp. 1, 20; "S.E. aceptó renuncia del Min. de Interior y designó para ese cargo al Vicealmirante O'Ryan," *El Mercurio*, July 4, 1957, pp. 1, 20; "Con designación de seis nuevos ministros S.E. resolvió ayer la crisis parcial de Gabinete," *El Mercurio*, October 29, 1957, pp. 1, 18.

Alessandri: Urzúa Valenzuela (1968); Gamonal (1987); Newspaper and journal articles: "Personalidad de los Secretarios de Estado," *El Mercurio*, September 16, 1960, pp. 1, 20; "Renuncia colectiva del Gabinete ante transgresión del principio de autoridad," *El Mercurio*, September 13, 1963, pp. 1, 28; "Nuevos miembros del Gabinete prestaron juramento ante S.E.," *El Mercurio*, September 27, 1963, pp. 1, 22.

Frei: Cleaves (1974); Sigmund (1977).

Allende: Valenzuela (1978).

COLOMBIA

Barrero Restrepo (1991); Blanco et al. (1991); Hartlyn (1988); Hartwig (1983); Juárez (1992); Kline (1988); Leal (1984); Leal and Dávila (1990); Leal and Zamosc (1990); Martz (1992); Morcillo (1975); Osterling (1989); Pécaut (1989).

Lleras Camargo: *Quién es quién en Colombia* (1962–63); Vidal (1982).

Barco: Lanzetta et al. (1987).

Gaviria: Newspaper and journal articles: "Justice Minister in Colombia Is Out in Dispute with Army," *New York Times*, August 7, 1991, p. A6.

PERU

Hopkins (1967); Rojas Samanez (1984); Wise (1990, 1992).

Bustamante: Bustamante i Rivero (1949).

Prado: Payne (1968).

Belaúnde (1963–68): Bourricaud (1970); Gómez (1969); Kuczynski (1977).

Belaúnde (1980–85): Pease García (1981); Woy-Hazelton and Hazelton (1987).

García: Guimarey and Garay (1986); Graham (1989); Pease García (1988); Wise (1990 and 1992). Newspaper and journal articles: "El Duque y los audaces," *Oiga*, June 29, 1987, pp. 12–17; "Este es el APRA: ¿Que les parece?" *Oiga*, June 20, 1988, pp. 15–16; "Salinas candidato," *Oiga*, December 5, 1988, p. 20; "De la mecedora al adormecimiento," *Oiga*, June 12, 1989, pp. 17–23.

Fujimori: Newspaper and journal articles: "¿Quienes son?" *Caretas*, July 23, 1990, p. 16; "Peru's Premier Quits Amid Report of Feud," *New York Times*, February 15, 1991, p. A3; "Presidente Fujimori enfrenta primera crisis de gabinete," *El Mercurio*, February 15, 1991, pp. A1, 16.

VENEZUELA

Blank (1984); Brewer-Carías (1975a, 1975b, and 1985); Groves (1967); Hellinger (1991); Martz (1992); Penniman (1980); Peña (1978); Stewart (1978).

Betancourt: Alexander (1964); Levy (1968).

Caldera: Herman (1980).

Pérez (1974–79): Karl (1982).

Lusinchi: Coppedge (1988).

Pérez (1989–93): Newspaper and journal articles: "President Goes It Alone," *Latin American Economy and Business*, February 1992, p. 7; "CAP juramenta hoy su nuevo gabinete," *El Nacional*, August 27, 1989, p. D1; Vinogradoff (1989); García (1989 and 1992); Ramírez (1989); Garay (1989a and 1989b); "Renunció Gabinete en pleno y CAP juramentará hoy nuevos ministros," *El*

Nacional, July 27, 1990, p. D1; "El Presidente juramentó gabinete tecnocrático," *El Nacional,* July 28, 1990, p. A1; Sánchez (1990); "Las tribus judiciales no son un mito," *El Nacional,* July 13, 1991, p. D4; Villegas (1992); Linares (1992); García (1992); "Celli: No tenemos a nadie en el gabinete económico," *El Nacional,* January 12, 1992, p. A1; Ojeda Reyes (1992); Garnica (1992); Azocar (1992); "Piñerúa Ordaz no aceptó Ministerio del Interior," *El Nacional,* February 25, 1992, p. D1; "Copei no acepta participar en el gobierno de Pérez," *El Nacional,* February 25, 1992, p. D2; "Hoy será juramentado nuevo gabinete de unidad nacional," *El Nacional,* March 10, 1992, p. A1; Vincenzo (1992); Durán (1992).

Variable Construction

The variables below were constructed for use in the regressions reported in chapter 6.

Presidential preference

It was assumed that the president's preference for partisanship in appointments, irrespective of the wishes of his or her supporters, would depend on how much the president's future political power was tied to a particular party organization. Presidents were placed in one of four categories as a rough indication of their dependence: party builder; conventional nomination; nomination opposed; independent.

Party builders were defined as presidents who had founded their parties or movements during the campaign for the presidency and needed to build the actual organization while in office. Appointments play a large role in building a party machine. For a few presidents, there was some ambiguity about whether they should be placed in the party builder category or not. Three were especially difficult to classify, Peruvian Fernando Belaúnde and two Brazilians, José Sarney and Getúlio Vargas. Belaúnde organized a proto-party to support his campaign for president in 1956. This proto-party served as the nucleus for Acción Popular, which he organized to support himself in the 1962 and 1963 presidential campaigns. In my judgment, however, Acción Popular was not sufficiently or extensively organized before the beginning of the 1962 campaign to count as an established party. Therefore I counted Belaúnde during his first administration as a party builder.

The classification of Sarney is discussed in chapter 6, note 17. I did not classify Vargas as a party builder. The PSD and PTB were both organized by Vargas allies to compete in the 1946 election. Since the formation of the PSD involved more a formalization and naming of the political machine created by

217

Vargas during the dictatorship than the creation of a new political movement, and since its candidate won the 1946 election, I did not treat it as a new party in 1950. The PTB, which drew most of its activists from Vargas supporters who had not held appointments during the dictatorship, probably should be treated as a new party at the beginning of the second Vargas government, even though it was formally organized earlier. Because his supporters were divided between two parties, however, with more in the PSD, Vargas's future did not depend heavily on building up the PTB machine. Therefore I did not place him in the party builder category.

Presidents were put in the conventional nomination category if they were nominated by established parties and supported by most of the leadership of the party. Most presidents fall in this category. It was assumed that their interests would be served by an appointment strategy that both rewarded loyal party supporters and increased competence in the bureaucracy, and that they would therefore prefer to follow a mixed strategy. The few presidents nominated by established parties without the support of most of the party leadership were put in the nomination opposed category. It was assumed that presidents who had been opposed by most established party leaders would use fewer appointments to maintain the party machine—whose loyalty they could not count on—and more to try to achieve high levels of economic performance in an effort to maintain personal popularity despite opposition from within their own parties.

Presidents were considered independents if they ran as independents (whether or not they were also nominated by one or more parties) or if they ran at the head of movements that they made no effort to transform into permanent organizations. These presidents won elections as a result of personal popularity, not party loyalty, and their futures did not depend on building up the party organizations—if any—that supported them during the campaign.

Presidential power

It was assumed that presidents would have more ability to pursue their own preferences if they had more power relative to supporters—whose preferences often differ from the president's.

Presidents can be expected to have greater power if they face no serious rivals within their own party. It was not possible to make a judgment about whether each president had close competitors within his or her party, but, in general, party founders do not face much competition for leadership. Party founder was therefore used as a crude indicator of the power of the president relative to other party leaders. It was coded one if a president had founded the party and zero otherwise.

Presidents can also be expected to have more power relative to party allies in highly disciplined parties. The president's party or coalition was coded zero, one-half, or one, depending on the amount of discipline generally exercised by party leaders.

Presidents can be expected to have more power relative to coalition partners when they are backed by large parties. The president's party size was measured as the percentage of seats controlled by the party most closely associated with the president in the Chamber of Deputies. Because I am concerned with presidents' power relative to that of their allies, I used the seats controlled by their parties alone, not the share controlled by their coalitions. For Allende, for example, I used the number of seats controlled by the Socialist party, not the Unidad Popular coalition. There was some ambiguity about which party's seats to count, especially for the independent presidents. For Bustamante, I counted all the seats won by the Democratic Front coalition, made up more of individuals than of organizations, except those won by members of APRA. For Alessandri, I counted the Liberal party; for Ibáñez, the PAL; for Quadros, the UDN; for Sarney, the PFL; and for Fujimori, Cambio 90. Where midterm elections occurred, I averaged the two legislative terms. Where presidential and legislative elections were on different schedules, I averaged if the legislative election occurred near the middle of the presidential term, and I used only one legislative session when the same legislature sat for most of the president's term.

The presidential power variable was created by adding one to each of the variables above (founder, discipline, and party size) and multiplying them. A multiplicative scale seems to capture the concept aimed for here better than an additive one, since party discipline would not be expected to have much effect on the overall situation if the president's party were very small, and the size of the president's party might not matter that much if he or she could not exercise discipline over it. The multiplicative scale also reduces multicollinearity.

The variables for pact and first time in office are described in the text, as is the interaction variable, conventional nomination × presidential power, created by multiplying presidential power times conventional nomination (coded one if president was nominated by an established party with support from party leadership and zero otherwise).

The raw data are shown in table 23.

TABLE 23
RAW DATA FOR ANALYSIS OF APPOINTMENT STRATEGIES

	Appoint. strategy	Pres. pref.	Party founder	Party size	Party discipline	First time in office	Pact	Pres. power	Conv. nomin.
J. Perón	2	0	1	.69	1	1	0	6.76	0
J. Perón II	1	0	1	.91	1	1	0	7.64	0
Frondizi	6	1	1	.64	1	1	0	6.56	1
Illia	2	1	0	.37	1	1	0	2.74	1
J. Perón III	3	1	1	.60	1	1	0	6.40	1
I. Perón	2	1	0	.60	1	1	0	3.20	1
Alfonsín	3	1	0	.49	1	1	0	2.98	1
Menem	6	2	0	.43	1	0	0	2.86	0
Dutra	3	1	0	.53	.5	0	0	2.30	1
Vargas	5	2	1	.17	.5	0	0	3.51	1
Café Filho	7	1	0	.10	.0	0	0	1.10	1
Kubitschek	4	1	0	.35	.5	0	0	2.03	1
Quadros	7	3	0	.22	0	0	0	1.22	0
Goulart	1	1	0	.28	0	1	0	1.28	1
Sarney	1	0	1	.24	0	1	0	2.48	0
Collor	4	0	1	.07	0	1	0	2.14	0
González	3	1	0	.25	.5	0	0	1.88	1
Ibáñez	7	3	0	.18	0	0	0	1.18	0
Alessandri	7	3	0	.20	.5	0	0	1.80	0
Frei	4	1	0	.56	1	1	0	3.12	1

Allende	1	1	0	.10	.5	1	0	1.65	1
Aylwin	4	1	0	.32	1	1	0	2.64	1
Lleras C.	5	1	0	.50	1	1	1	3.00	1
Valencia	5	1	0	.50	1	0	1	3.00	1
Lleras R.	5	1	0	.50	1	0	1	3.00	1
Pastrana	4	1	0	.50	1	0	1	3.00	1
López	4	1	0	.56	1	0	0	3.12	1
Turbay	3	1	0	.56	1	0	0	3.12	1
Betancur	3	1	0	.42	1	0	0	2.84	1
Barco	3	1	0	.48	1	0	0	2.96	1
Gaviria	4	2	0	.59	1	0	0	3.18	0
Bustamante	7	3	0	.25	0	0	0	1.25	0
Prado	4	1	1	.40	0	0	0	2.80	1
Belaúnde I	2	0	1	.36	.5	1	0	4.08	0
Belaúnde II	4	1	1	.54	.5	0	0	4.62	1
García	1	1	0	.59	1	1	0	3.18	1
Fujimori	8	3	0	.18	0	0	0	1.18	0
Betancourt	5	1	1	.48	1	0	1	5.92	1
Leoni	5	1	0	.31	1	0	1	2.62	1
Caldera	5	1	1	.24	1	1	1	4.96	1
Pérez I	4	1	0	.51	1	0	0	3.02	1
Herrera	3	1	0	.43	1	0	0	2.86	1
Lusinchi	4	1	0	.56	1	0	0	3.12	1
Pérez II	7	2	0	.48	1	0	0	2.96	0

Bibliography

Acuña, Marcelo Luis. 1984. *De Frondizi a Alfonsín: La tradición política del radicalismo.* 2 vols. Buenos Aires: Centro Editor de América Latina.

Alexander, Robert. 1964. *The Venezuelan Democratic Revolution.* New Brunswick: Rutgers University Press.

Amaral, Carlos Veríssimo do. 1966. "As Controvertidas Nomeações para a Previdência Social em 1963: Estudo de um Caso." In Carlos Veríssimo do Amaral and Kleber Nascimento, *Política e Administração de Pessoal: Estudos de Dois Casos.* Cadernos de Administração Pública 60. Rio de Janeiro: Fundação Getúlio Vargas.

Ames, Barry. 1973. *Rhetoric and Reality in a Militarized Regime: Brazil after 1964.* Sage Professional Papers in Comparative Politics, vol. 4. Beverly Hills: Sage.

———. 1987. *Political Survival: Politicians and Public Policy in Latin America.* Berkeley. University of California Press.

Amorim Neto, Octávio. 1991. "Formação Ministerial em Sistemas Presidencialistas Multipartidários: O Caso Brasileiro (1946–1964)." Masters thesis, Instituto Universitário de Pesquisas do Rio de Janeiro.

Arinos, Afonso. 1953. "A Conjuntura Nacional," given at the Escola Superior de Guerra, Rio de Janeiro. Mimeo.

———. 1965a. *A Escalada (Memórias).* Rio de Janeiro: José Olympio.

———. 1965b. *A Evolução da Crise Brasileira.* São Paulo: Editora Nacional.

Arinos Filho, Afonso. 1976. *Primo Canto (Memórias de Mocidade).* Rio de Janeiro: Civilização Brasileira.

Arnold, R. Douglas. 1979. *Congress and the Bureaucracy: A Theory of Influence,* Yale Studies in Political Science 28. New Haven: Yale University Press.

Ascher, William. 1975. "Planners, Politics, and Technocracy in Argentina and Chile." Ph.D. dissertation, Yale University.

Axelrod, Robert. 1970. *Conflict of Interest: A Theory of Divergent Goals with Applications to Politics*. Chicago: Markham.

———. 1984. *The Evolution of Cooperation*. New York: Basic Books.

Azocar, Gustavo. 1992. "AD no está satisfecha con los cambios del Gabinete." *El Nacional*, January 12:D2.

Bamat, Thomas. 1977. "Relative State Autonomy and Capitalism in Brazil and Peru." *The Insurgent Sociologist* 7:74–84.

Banks, Arthur S., ed. 1975–90. *Political Handbook of the World: Governments and Intergovernmental Organizations*. New York: McGraw-Hill.

Bardawil, José Carlos. 1990. "O apito de Collor." *Istoé Senhor*, October 31:28–29.

Barrero Restrepo, Efren. 1991. *Los círculos del poder en Colombia*. Bogotá: Documentos ESAP.

Barros, Alexandre de Souza Costa. 1978. "The Brazilian Military: Professional Socialization, Political Performance and State Building." Ph.D. dissertation, University of Chicago.

Barry, Brian, and Russell Hardin, eds. 1982. *Rational Man and Irrational Society?* Beverly Hills: Sage.

Bastos, A., and Thomas Walker. 1971. "Partidos e Forças Políticas em Minas Gerais." *Revista Brasileira de Estudos Políticos* 31:128–54.

Bates, Robert. 1981. *Markets and States in Tropical Africa: The Political Basis of Agricultural Policies*. Berkeley: University of California Press.

———. 1988. "Macro-Political Economy in the Field of Development." Duke University Program in International Political Economy Working Paper No. 40.

———. 1989. *Beyond the Miracle of the Market: The Political Economy of Agrarian Development in Kenya*. Cambridge: Cambridge University Press.

Beloch, Israel, and Alzira Alves de Abreu. 1984. *Dicionário Histórico-Biográfico Brasileiro*. 4 vols. Rio de Janeiro: Forense Universitário/Finep.

Benevides, Maria Victória de Mesquita. 1976. *O Governo Kubitschek: Desenvolvimento Econômico e Estabilidade Política, 1956–1961*. Rio de Janeiro: Paz e Terra.

———. 1981. *A UDN e o Udenismo: Ambigüidade do Liberalismo Brasileiro (1945–1965)*. Rio de Janeiro: Paz e Terra.

———. 1989. *O PTB e o Trabalhismo: Partido e Sindicato em São Paulo (1945–1964)*. São Paulo: Editora Brasiliense.

Berman, Paul. 1974. *Revolutionary Organization: Institution Building within the People's Liberation Armed Forces*. Lexington, Mass.: D. C. Heath.

Berquó, Urbano C. 1938. "Eficiência Administrativa e Sabotagem Burocrática." *Revista do Serviço Público* 2:5–8.

Berry, R. Albert, Ronald G. Hellman, and Mauricio Solaún, eds. 1980. *Politics of Compromise: Coalition Government in Colombia*. New Brunswick: Transaction Books.

Biles, Robert. 1972. "Patronage Politics: Electoral Behavior in Uruguay." Ph.D. dissertation, Johns Hopkins University.

———. 1978. "Political Participation in Urban Uruguay: Mixing Public and Private Ends." In John A. Booth and Mitchell A. Seligson, eds., *Political*

Participation in Latin America. Vol. 1, *Citizen and State*. New York: Holmes & Meier.

Black, Duncan. 1958. *The Theory of Elections and Committees*. Cambridge: Cambridge University Press.

Blanco Bugand, Josefina, H. Calderón, A. Castro, M. Cortés, C. De la Torre, E. García, M. T. Gómez, M. Fidel Vargas, R. Herrera, E. Muñoz, A. Pereira, M. Rodríguez, and G. Sandoval. 1991. *Los gabinetes ministeriales como élites políticas - Colombia (1930–1990)*. 2 vols. Bogotá: Universidad Javeriana.

Blank, David Eugene. 1984. *Venezuela: Politics in a Petroleum Republic*. New York: Praeger.

BNDE (Banco Nacional de Desenvolvimento Econômico). 1955. *Exposição sobre o Programa de Reaparelhamento Econômico*. Rio de Janeiro.

Bortot, Ivanir José, and Eumano Silva. 1992. "SDR privilegia governistas." *Folha de São Paulo*, August 14.

Bourricaud, François. 1970. *Power and Society in Contemporary Peru*. Translated by Paul Stevenson. New York: Praeger.

Bray, Donald. 1961. "Chilean Politics during the Second Ibáñez Government, 1952–1958." Ph.D. dissertation, Stanford University.

Brewer-Carías, Allan Randolph. 1975a. *Cambio político y reforma del Estado en Venezuela*. Madrid: Tecnos.

———. 1975b. "La reforma administrativa en Venezuela (1969–1973): Estrategias, tácticas, y criterios." In Primer Seminario Interamericano de Reforma Administrativa, *Reforma administrativa: Experiencias latinoamericanas*. Mexico City: Instituto Nacional de Administración Pública.

———. 1985. *El estado incomprendido: Reflexiones sobre el sistema político y su reforma*. Caracas: Vadell Hermanos.

———. 1988. *Problemas del Estado de partidos*. Caracas: Editorial Jurídica Venezolana.

Buchanan, James, and Gordon Tullock. 1962. *The Calculus of Consent*. Ann Arbor: University of Michigan Press.

Bustamante i Rivero, José Luis. 1949. *Tres años de lucha por la democracia en el Peru*. Buenos Aires: Bartolomé U. Chiesino.

Cain, Bruce, John Ferejohn, and Morris Fiorina. 1987. *The Personal Vote: Constituency Service and Electoral Independence*. Cambridge, Mass.: Harvard University Press.

Campos, Roberto. 1975. "O Poder Legislativo e o Desenvolvimento." In Cândido Mendes, ed., *O Legislativo e o Tecnocracia*. Rio de Janeiro: Imago/Conjunto Universitário Cândido Mendes.

Capriles Ayala, Carlos, Axel Capriles Méndez, Ruth Capriles Méndez, and Fanny Díaz, eds. 1989 and 1990. *Diccionario de la corrupción en Venezuela*. Vol. 1 (1959–1979) and vol. 2 (1979–1984). Caracas: Consorcio de Ediciones Capriles.

Cardoso, Fernando Henrique. 1969. "Hegemonia Burguesa e Independência Econômica: Raizes Estructurais de Crise Política Brasileira." Chapter 2 in *Mudanças Sociais na América Latina*. São Paulo: Difusão Européia do Livro.

———. 1971. *Ideología de la burguesía industrial en sociedades dependientes (Argentina y Brasil)*. Mexico City: Siglo Veintiuno.

————. 1978. "Partidos e Deputados em São Paulo." In Bolívar Lamounier and F. H. Cardoso, eds., *Os Partidos e os Eleições no Brasil*. Rio de Janeiro: Paz e Terra.

————. 1979. "On the Characterization of Authoritarian Regimes in Latin America." In David Collier, ed., *The New Authoritarianism in Latin America*. Princeton: Princeton University Press.

Carvalho, Getúlio. 1976. *Petrobrás: Do Monopólio aos Contratos de Risco*. Rio de Janeiro: Forense-Universitária.

Castillo, René. 1974. "Lesson and Prospects of the Revolution." *World Marxist Review* 17:83–95.

Caviedes, César. 1979. *The Politics of Chile: A Sociographical Assessment*. Boulder, Col.: Westview Special Studies on Latin America.

Cleaves, Peter. 1974. *Bureaucratic Politics and Administration in Chile*. Berkeley: University of California Press.

Cleaves, Peter, and Henry Pease García. 1983. "State Autonomy and Military Policy Making." In Cynthia McClintock and Abraham Lowenthal, eds., *The Peruvian Experiment Reconsidered*. Princeton: Princeton University Press.

Collier, David. 1976. *Squatters and Oligarchs: Authoritarian Rule and Policy Change in Peru*. Baltimore: Johns Hopkins University Press.

Collier, David, and Ruth Berins Collier. 1977. "Who Does What, to Whom, and How: Toward a Comparative Analysis of Latin American Corporatism." In James Malloy, ed., *Authoritarianism and Corporatism in Latin America*. Pittsburgh: University of Pittsburgh Press.

————. 1979. "Inducements Versus Constraints: Disaggregating 'Corporatism'." *American Political Science Review* 73:967–86.

Conselho Nacional de Economia. 1962, 1963, 1964, 1965. *Exposição Geral da Situação Econômica do Brasil*. Rio de Janeiro.

Coppedge, Michael. 1988. "Strong Parties and Lame Ducks: A Study of the Quality and Stability of Venezuelan Democracy." Ph.D. dissertation, Yale University.

————. 1991. "Institutions and Cleavages in the Evolution of Latin American Party Systems." Paper presented at American Political Science Association meetings, Washington, D.C.

Corke, Bettina, ed. 1984. *Who Is Who in Government and Politics in Latin America*. 1st ed. New York: Decade Media Books.

Countries of the World and Their Leaders. 1975. Detroit: Gale Research Co.

Cova, Antonio, and Thamara Hannot. 1986. "La administración pública: Otra forma de ver a una villana incomprendida." In Moisés Naím and Ramón Piñango, eds., *El caso Venezuela: Una ilusión de armonía*. Caracas: Ediciones Instituto de Estudios Superiores de Administración (IESA).

Cowey, Peter. 1990. "'States' and 'Politics' in American Foreign Economic Policy." In John Odell and Thomas Willett, eds., *International Trade Policies: Gains from Exchange between Economics and Political Science*. Ann Arbor: University of Michigan Press.

Cox, Gary. 1986. "The Development of a Party-Oriented Electorate in England, 1832–1918." *British Journal of Political Science* 16:187–216.

————. 1987. *The Efficient Secret: The Cabinet and the Development of Polit-*

ical Parties in Victorian England. Cambridge: Cambridge University Press
Series on Political Economy of Institutions and Decisions.

―――. 1990. "Centripetal and Centrifugal Incentives in Electoral Systems."
American Journal of Political Science 34:903–35.

Crain, W. Mark, and Robert Tollison, eds. 1990. *Predicting Politics: Essays in
Empirical Public Choice.* Ann Arbor: University of Michigan Press.

Crassweller, Robert D. 1987. *Perón and the Enigma of Argentina.* New York:
W. W. Norton.

Currie, Lauchlin. 1966. *Accelerating Development: The Necessity and the Means.*
New York: McGraw-Hill.

D'Araújo, Maria Celina Soares. 1982. *O segundo governo Vargas, 1951–1954.*
Rio de Janeiro: Zahar Editores.

Delfim Netto, Antônio, A. C. Pastore, P. Cipollari, and E. Pereira de Carvalho.
1965. *Alguns Aspectos da Inflação Brasileira.* São Paulo: Associação Nacional de Programação Econômica e Social (ANPES).

Demsetz, Harold. 1990. "Amenity Potential, Indivisibilities, and Political Competition." In James Alt and Kenneth Shepsle, eds., *Perspectives on Positive
Political Economy.* Cambridge: Cambridge University Press.

Departamento de Imprensa Nacional. 1960. *Colleção das Leis.* Vol. 5. Rio de
Janeiro.

Diccionario biográfico de Chile, 1948–49, 1953–55, 1972–74.

Dimenstein, Gilberto. 1988. *A República dos Padrinhos: Chantagem e Corrupção em Brasília.* São Paulo: Editora Brasiliense.

―――. 1992. "Collor opta por políticos da antiga Arena." *Folha de São Paulo,*
April 10:7.

Dix, Robert. 1967. *Colombia: The Political Dimensions of Change.* New Haven: Yale University Press.

―――. 1980. "Consociational Democracy: The Case of Colombia." *Comparative Politics* 12:303–21.

Downs, Anthony. 1957. *An Economic Theory of Democracy.* New York: Harper.

Dreifuss, René Armand. 1981. *1964: A Conquista do Estado: Ação Política,
Poder e Golpe de Classe.* Petrópolis: Vozes.

Duff, Ernest. 1971. "The Role of Congress in the Colombian Political System."
In Weston Agor, ed., *Latin American Legislatures: Their Role and Influence.*
New York: Praeger.

Durán, Milagros. 1992. "Hoy será juramentado el nuevo gabinete." *El Nacional,* March 10:D2.

Eastman, Jorge Mario. 1982. *Seis reformas estructurales al régimen político:
Resultados electorales de 1930 a 1982.* Bogotá: Ministerio de Gobierno,
Colección Legislación, Doctrina y Jurisprudencia.

Eckstein, Alexander. 1958. "Individualism and the Role of the State in Economic
Growth." *Economic Development and Cultural Change* 6:81–87.

Elster, Jon. 1979. *Ulysses and the Sirens: Studies in Rationality and Irrationality.*
Cambridge: Cambridge University Press.

Emmerich, Herbert. 1972. "Informe sobre un estudio preliminar acerca de
posibilidades de mejoras en la administración pública de Venezuela (May
1958)." In Comisión de Reforma de la Administración Pública, *Informe*

sobre la reforma de la administración pública nacional, vol. 1. Caracas: Comisión de Administración Pública (CAP).

Evans, Peter. 1979. *Dependent Development: The Alliance of Multinational, State, and Local Capital in Brazil.* Princeton: Princeton University Press.

Evans, Peter, Dietrich Rueschemeyer, and Theda Skocpol, eds. 1985. *Bringing the State Back In.* Cambridge: Cambridge University Press.

Fabregat, Julio T. 1950–63. *Elecciones Uruguayas.* Vols. 1–6. Montevideo: Corte Electoral.

Fiorina, Morris. 1977. *Congress, Keystone of the Washington Establishment.* New Haven: Yale University Press.

Fiorina, Morris, and Roger Noll. 1978. "Voters, Bureaucrats and Legislators: A Rational Choice Perspective on the Growth of Bureaucracy." *Journal of Public Economics* 9:239–54.

Fishlow, Albert. 1971. "Origins and Consequences of Import Substitution in Brazil." In Luis Di Marco, ed., *International Economics and Development.* New York: Academic Press.

———. 1980. "Brazilian Development in Long-Term Perspective." *American Economic Review* Papers and Proceedings 70:102–8.

Frohlich, Norman, Joe Oppenheimer, and Oran Young. 1971. *Political Leadership and Collective Goods.* Princeton: Princeton University Press.

Gabeira, Fernando. 1992. "Dinossauros continuam vivos." *Folha de São Paulo,* April 10:7.

Gamonal, Germán. 1987. *Jorge Alessandri: El hombre, el político.* Santiago: Holanda Comunicaciones.

Garay, Fernando. 1989a. "CAP juramenta hoy su nuevo Gabinete." *El Nacional,* August 27:D1.

———. 1989b. "Lograr la normalidad y confianza pide Pérez a su nuevo Gabinete." *El Nacional,* August 28:D4.

García, Graciela. 1989. "Las caras nuevas." *El Nacional,* August 27:D1.

———. 1992. "Antonio Ledezma por primera vez en cargo público." *El Nacional,* January 11:C2.

Garnica, Hercilia. 1992. "No habrá borrón y cuenta nueva en el MTC." *El Nacional,* January 12:D2.

Geddes, Barbara. 1990. "How the Cases You Choose Affect the Answers You Get: Selection Bias in Comparative Politics." *Political Analysis* 2:131–50.

———. 1991. "Political Institutions and Economic Policy: How Politicians Decide Who Bears the Costs of Structural Adjustment." Paper presented at American Political Science Association meetings, Washington, D.C.

———. 1992. "Case Studies in Path Dependent Arguments." Paper presented at American Political Science Association meetings, Chicago.

———. 1993. "Democracy, Structural Adjustment, and Labor." Paper presented at workshop on the Social Consequences of Liberalization in Comparative Perspective, Berkeley-Stanford Joint Center for African Studies, Berkeley.

Geddes, Barbara, and Artur Ribeiro Neto. 1992. "Institutional Sources of Corruption in Brazil." *Third World Quarterly* 13:641–61.

Gerschenkron, Alexander. 1966. *Economic Backwardness in Historical Perspective.* Cambridge, Mass.: Harvard University Press.

Goldberg, Ellis. 1986. *Tinker, Tailor, and Textile Worker: Class and Politics in Egypt, 1930–1952.* Berkeley: University of California Press.

Gómez, Rudolph. 1969. *The Peruvian Administrative System.* Boulder: University of Colorado, Bureau of Governmental Research and Service.

González G., Fernán. 1980. "Clientelismo y administración pública." *Enfoques Colombianos* 14:67–106.

Graham, Carol. 1989. "APRA 1968–1988: From Revolution to Government—the Elusive Search for Political Integration in Peru." Ph.D. dissertation, St. Anthony's College, Oxford University.

Graham, Lawrence. 1968. *Civil Service Reform in Brazil: Principles vs. Practice.* Latin American Monographs No. 13, Institute of Latin American Studies, University of Texas. Austin: University of Texas Press.

Greenfield, Sidney. 1972. "Charwomen, Cesspools, and Road Building: An Examination of Patronage, Clientage, and Political Power in Southeastern Minas Gerais." In Arnold Strickon and Sidney Greenfield, eds., *Structure and Process in Latin America: Patronage, Clientage and Power Systems.* Albuquerque: University of New Mexico Press.

Groves, Roderick. 1967. "Administrative Reform and the Politics of Reform: The Case of Venezuela." *Public Administration Review* 27:436–45.

———. 1974. "The Colombian National Front and Administrative Reform." *Administration and Society* 6:316–20.

Guillén Martínez, Fernando. 1963. *Raíz y futuro de la revolución.* Bogotá: Ediciones Tercer Mundo.

Guimarey, Mario, and Martín Garay. 1986. *Quién es quién: Congreso de la república, 1985–1990.* Lima: Atlantida.

Haggard, Stephan. 1986. "Newly Industrializing Countries in the International System." *World Politics* 38:343–70.

———. 1990. *Pathways from the Periphery: The Politics of Growth in the Newly Industrializing Countries.* Ithaca: Cornell University Press.

Haggard, Stephan, and Tun-jen Cheng. 1987. "State and Foreign Capital in the East Asian NICs." In Fred Deyo, ed., *The Political Economy of the New Asian Industrialism.* Ithaca: Cornell University Press.

Haggard, Stephan, and Robert Kaufman. 1989. "The Politics of Stabilization and Structural Adjustment." In Jeffrey Sachs, ed., *Developing Country Debt and Economic Performance: Selected Issues.* Chicago: University of Chicago Press.

Hagopian, Frances. Forthcoming. *Traditional Politics and Regime Change in Brazil.* Princeton: Princeton University Press.

Hall, E. F. 1884. "Civil Service Reform." *New Englander* 43:453–63.

Hamilton, Nora. 1982. *The Limits of State Autonomy: Post-Revolutionary Mexico.* Princeton: Princeton University Press.

Hardin, Russell. 1982. *Collective Action.* Baltimore: Johns Hopkins University Press.

Hartlyn, Jonathan. 1988. *The Politics of Coalition Rule in Colombia.* Cambridge: Cambridge University Press.

Hartwig, Richard. 1983. *Roads to Reason: Transportation, Administration, and Rationality in Colombia.* Pittsburgh: University of Pittsburgh Press.

Hayes, Margaret Daley. 1975. "Policy Performance and Authoritarianism in Brazil: Public Expenditures and Institutional Change, 1950–1967." Ph.D. dissertation, Indiana University.

Head, John G. 1982. "Public Goods: The Polar Case." In Brian Barry and Russell Hardin, eds., *Rational Man and Irrational Society?* Beverly Hills: Sage.

Hellinger, Daniel C. 1991. *Venezuela: Tarnished Democracy.* Boulder: Westview.

Herman, Donald L. 1980. *Christian Democracy in Venezuela.* Chapel Hill: University of North Carolina Press.

Hippólito, Lúcia. 1985. *De Raposas e Reformistas: O PSD e a Experiência Democrática Brasileira.* Rio de Janeiro: Paz e Terra.

Hirschman, Albert. 1958. *The Strategy of Economic Development.* New Haven: Yale University Press.

———. 1968. "The Political Economy of Import Substituting Industrialization in Latin America." In *Quarterly Journal of Economics* 82:1–32.

———. 1973. *Journeys toward Progress: Studies of Economic Policy-Making in Latin America.* New York: W. W. Norton.

Hopkins, Jack W. 1967. *The Government Executive of Modern Peru.* Gainesville: University of Florida Press, Latin American Monographs.

IBRD (International Bank for Reconstruction and Development). 1950. *The Basis of a Development Program for Colombia.* Washington, D.C.: International Bank for Reconstruction and Development.

———. 1961. *The Economic Development of Venezuela.* Baltimore: Johns Hopkins University Press.

Imaz, José Luis de. 1970. *Los que mandan.* Translated by Carlos Astiz. Albany: State University of New York Press.

Institute for Comparative Study of Political Systems. n.d. *Methods of Electing National Executives and National Legislatures in South America.* Washington, D.C.: Operations and Policy Research.

Instituto Brasileiro de Geografia e Estatística—Conselho Nacional de Estatística. 1957, 1962. *Anuário Estatístico do Brasil.* Vols. 18 and 23. Rio de Janeiro.

Jacobson, Gary, and Samuel Kernell. 1983. *Strategy and Choice in Congressional Elections.* 2d ed. New Haven: Yale University Press.

Jaguaribe, Hélio. 1956. "Sentido e Perspectivas do Governo Kubitschek." *Cadernos do Nosso Tempo* 5:1–18.

———. 1958. *Condições Institucionais de Desenvolvimento.* Rio de Janeiro: Ministério de Educação e Cultura, Instituto de Estudos Brasileiros.

Jowitt, Kenneth. 1971. *Revolutionary Breakthroughs and National Development: The Case of Romania, 1944–1965.* Berkeley: University of California Press.

———. 1975. "Inclusion and Mobilization in Leninist Regimes." *World Politics* 28:69–96.

Juárez, Carlos. 1992. "The Politics of Trade and Development in Colombia: Export Promotion and Outward Orientation, 1967–1991." Paper delivered at Latin American Studies Association, Los Angeles.

Kalt, Joseph, and Mark Zupan. 1984. "Capture and Ideology in the Economic Theory of Politics." *American Economic Review* 74:279–300.

———. 1990. "Apparent Ideological Behavior of Legislators: Testing for Principal-Agent Slack in Political Institutions." *Journal of Law and Economics* 33:103–31.

Kantor, Harry. 1966. *The Ideology and Program of the Peruvian Aprista Party.* Washington, D.C.: Savile Books.

Karl, Terry. 1982. "The Political Economy of Petrodollars: Oil and Democracy in Venezuela." Ph.D. dissertation, Stanford University.

Katznelson, Ira. 1985. "Working-Class Formation and the State." In Peter Evans, Dietrich Rueschemeyer, and Theda Skocpol, eds., *Bringing the State Back In.* Cambridge: Cambridge University Press.

Keesing's Contemporary Archives. 1945–1992. London: Keesings Publishers.

Kirkpatrick, Jeane. 1971. *Leader and Vanguard in Mass Society: A Study of Peronist Argentina.* Cambridge, Mass.: MIT Press.

Kline, Harvey. 1976. "Political Parties." In Gary Hoskin, Francisco Leal, and Harvey Kline, *Legislative Behavior in Colombia.* Vol. 2. Buffalo: Council on International Studies, State University of New York.

———. 1988. "From Rural to Urban Society: The Transformation of Colombian Democracy." In Donald Herman, ed., *Democracy in Latin America.* New York: Praeger.

Koster, R. M. 1972. *The Prince.* New York: William Morrow.

———. 1975. *The Dissertation.* New York: Harper & Row.

Krasner, Stephen. 1978. *Defending the National Interest: Raw Materials Investments and U.S. Foreign Policy.* Princeton: Princeton University Press.

Krueger, Anne. 1980. "The Political Economy of the Rent-Seeking Society." In James Buchanan, Robert Tollison, and Gordon Tullock, eds., *Toward a Theory of the Rent-Seeking Society.* College Station: Texas A&M University Press Economics Series No. 4.

Kuczynski, Pedro Pablo. 1977. *Peruvian Democracy under Economic Stress: An Account of the Belaúnde Administration, 1963–1968.* Princeton: Princeton University Press.

Lacerda, Carlos. 1961. *A UDN na Encruzilhada.* Rio de Janeiro: n.p.

———. 1977. *Depoimento.* Rio de Janeiro: Editora Nova Fronteira.

Láfer, Celso. 1970. *The Planning Process and the Political System: A Study of Kubitschek's Target Plan, 1956–1961.* Ithaca: Cornell University Latin American Studies Program Dissertation Series, No. 16.

Lago, Pedro Aranha Correa. 1965. "A SUMOC como Embrião do Banco Central: Sua Influência na Condução da Política Econômica, 1945–1965." Master's thesis, Department of Economics, Pontifícia Universidade Católica.

Lanzetta, Mónica, F. Leal, M. Latorre, P. Pinzón, G. Murillo, R. Pardo, F. Cepeda, R. Sánchez, E. Ungar, R. Archer, and D. Röthlisberger. 1987. *Colombia en las urnas: ¿Qué pasó en 1986?* Bogotá: Carlos Valencia Editores.

Lapp, Nancy. 1994. "The Extension of Suffrage and Land Reform in Latin America." Paper presented at Latin American Studies Association, Atlanta.

Leal, Victor Nunes. 1949. *Coronelismo, Enxada e Voto: O Município e o Regime Representativo no Brasil.* Rio de Janeiro: Revista Forense.

Leal Buitrago, Francisco. 1984. *Estado y política en Colombia.* Bogotá: Siglo Veintiuno.

Leal Buitrago, Francisco, and Andrés Dávila. 1990. *Clientelismo: El sistema político y su expresión regional.* Bogotá: Tercer Mundo Editores.

Leal Buitrago, Francisco, and León Zamosc, eds. 1990. *Al filo del caos: Crisis política en la Colombia de los años 80.* Bogotá: Tercer Mundo Editores.

Leff, Nathanial. 1968. *Economic Policy-Making and Development in Brazil, 1947–1964.* New York: John Wiley & Sons.

Leite, Mauro Renault, and Luiz Gonzaga Novelli Junior, eds. 1983. *Marechal Eurico Gaspar Dutra: O Dever da Verdade.* Rio de Janeiro: Nova Fronteira.

Lessa, Carlos. 1964. "Fifteen Years of Economic Policy in Brazil." *Economic Bulletin for Latin America* 9:153–213.

Levi, Margaret. 1988. *Of Rule and Revenue.* Berkeley: University of California Press.

Levy, Fred D., Jr. 1968. *Economic Planning in Venezuela.* New York: Praeger.

Linares, Yelitza. 1992. "El hombre privatizador quiere simplificar el MTC." *El Nacional,* January 11:C2.

Lipset, Seymour Martin, and Stein Rokkan, eds. 1967. *Party Systems and Voter Alignments: Cross-National Perspectives.* New York: Free Press.

López Pintor, Rafael. 1972. "Development Administration in Chile: Structural, Normative, and Behavioral Constraints to Performance." Ph.D. dissertation, University of North Carolina, Chapel Hill.

Machiavelli, Niccolo. 1950. *The Prince and The Discourses.* New York: Random House, The Modern Library.

Mainwaring, Scott, and Timothy Scully, eds. Forthcoming. *Building Democratic Institutions: Party Systems in Latin America.* Stanford: Stanford University Press.

Malán, Pedro. 1977. *Política Econômica Externa e Industrialização no Brasil.* Rio de Janeiro: Instituto de Planejamento Econômico e Social.

Mallory, Walter H., ed. 1956–62. *Political Handbook of the World: Parliaments, Parties, and Press.* New York: Harper & Brothers.

———. 1963–70. *Political Handbook and Atlas of the World: Parliaments, Parties, and Press.* New York: Harper & Row.

Malloy, James. 1979. *The Politics of Social Security in Brazil.* Pittsburgh: University of Pittsburgh Press.

Maram, Sheldon. 1992. "Juscelino Kubitschek and the 1960 Presidential Election." *Journal of Latin American Studies* 24:123–45.

March, James, and Johan P. Olsen. 1984. "The New Institutionalism: Organizational Factors in Political Life." *American Political Science Review* 78: 734–49.

Mares, David. 1990. "Domestic Institutions and Shifts in Trade and Development Policy: Colombia 1951–68." In John S. Odell and Thomas D. Willett, eds., *International Trade Policies: Gains from Exchange between Economics and Political Science.* Ann Arbor: University of Michigan Press.

———. 1993. "State Leadership in Economic Policy: A Collective Action Framework with a Colombian Case." *Comparative Politics* 25:455–73.

Margolis, Howard. 1982. *Selfishness, Altruism, and Rationality: A Theory of Social Choice.* Cambridge: Cambridge University Press.

Martz, John D. 1992. "Party Elites and Leadership in Colombia and Venezuela." *Journal of Latin American Studies* 24:87–121.

Mayhew, David. 1974. *Congress: The Electoral Connection*. New Haven: Yale University Press.

McDonald, Ronald H., and J. Mark Ruhl. 1989. *Party Politics and Elections in Latin America*. Boulder, Col.: Westview.

McGuire, James. 1992. "Union Political Tactics and Democratic Consolidation in Alfonsín's Argentina, 1983–1989." *Latin American Research Review* 27: 37–74.

Ministério da Indústria e do Comércio, Superintendência da Borracha. 1969. *Anuário Estatístico: Mercado Nacional*. Vol. 3. Rio de Janeiro.

Ministério do Planejamento e Coordenação Econômica. 1967. *Plano Decenal de Desenvolvimento* (Versão Preliminar). Rio de Janeiro.

Miranda Ontaneda, Nestor, and Fernán González G. 1976. "Clientelismo, 'democracia' o poder popular." *Controversia* 41–42, Centro de Investigación y Educación Popular, Bogotá.

Moe, Terry. 1984. "The New Economics of Organization." *American Journal of Political Science* 28:739–77.

Moran, Theodore. 1974. *Multinational Corporations and the Politics of Dependence: Copper in Chile*. Princeton: Princeton University Press.

Morcillo, Pedro Pablo. 1975. "La reforma administrativa en Colombia." In Primer Seminario Interamericano de Reforma Administrativa, *Reforma administrativa: Experiencias latinoamericanas*. Mexico City: Instituto Nacional de Administración Pública.

Mossri, Sonia, and Gustavo Krieger. 1992. "BB distribui verbas a parlamentares." *Folha de São Paulo*, August 13:1.

Motta, Paulo Roberto. 1968. *O Grupo Executivo como Instrumento Administrativo de Implementação Econômica*. Rio de Janeiro: Fundação Getúlio Vargas/EIAP.

Mourão, Milcíades M. 1955. *Dutra (História de um Govêrno)*. Rio de Janeiro: n.p.

Murillo, Gabriel, and Javier Torres 1991. "Elección y partidos políticos en la transición de los países andinos: Retos para la superación de la crisis en la década de los noventa." In Rubén Sánchez David, ed., *Los nuevos retos electorales—Colombia 1990: antesala del cambio*. Bogotá: Editorial CEREC.

Nascimento, Kleber. 1965. "Personnel Administration in Brazil and France: An Attempt to Use the Prismatic Model." In Richard W. Gable, instructor, *Papers in Comparative Administration*. Los Angeles: International Public Administration Center, School of Public Administration, University of Southern California. Photocopy.

———. 1966. "O Aumento de Vencimentos do Funcionalismo Federal in 1963: Estudo de um Caso." In Carlos Veríssimo do Amaral and Kleber Nascimento, *Política e Administração de Pessoal: Estudos de Dois Casos*. Cadernos de Administração Pública 60. Rio de Janeiro: Fundação Getúlio Vargas.

Nash, Nathaniel C. 1992. "Poor Buenos Aires! Can Paris Be Like This?" *New York Times*, November 4:A26.

Nordlinger, Eric. 1981. *On the Autonomy of the Democratic State*. Cambridge, Mass.: Harvard University Press.

North, Douglass. 1979. "A Framework for Analyzing the State in Economic History." *Explorations in Economic History* 16:249–59.

———. 1981. *Structure and Change in Economic History*. New York: W. W. Norton.

Nunes, Edson de Oliveira. 1984. "Bureaucratic Insulation and Clientelism in Contemporary Brazil: Uneven State Building and the Taming of Modernity." Ph.D. dissertation, University of California, Berkeley.

Nunes, Edson de Oliveira, and Barbara Geddes. 1987. "Dilemmas of State-Led Modernization in Brazil." In John Wirth, Edson Nunes, and Thomas Bogenschild, eds., *State and Society in Brazil: Continuity and Change*. Boulder: Westview.

O'Donnell, Guillermo. 1973. *Modernization and Bureaucratic-Authoritarianism: Studies in South American Politics*. Berkeley: University of California Institute of International Studies, Politics of Modernization Series, No. 9.

Ojeda Reyes, Yolanda. 1992. "Aprobar el IVA este año se propone Pedro Rosas." *El Nacional*, January 12:D1.

Olavarría Bravo, Arturo. 1962. *Chile entre dos Alessandri: Memorias políticas*. Vol. 2. Santiago: Editorial Nascimento.

Oliveira, Lucia Lippi de. 1973. "O Partido Social Democrático." Master's thesis, Instituto Universitário de Pesquisas do Rio de Janeiro.

Olson, Mancur. 1965. *The Logic of Collective Action: Public Goods and the Theory of Groups*. Cambridge, Mass.: Harvard University Press.

Osterling, Jorge P. 1989. *Democracy in Colombia: Clientelist Politics and Guerrilla Warfare*. New Brunswick: Transaction Publishers.

Page, Joseph A. 1983. *Perón: A Biography*. New York: Random House.

Payne, Arnold. 1968. *The Peruvian Coup d'Etat of 1962: The Overthrow of Manuel Prado*. Washington, D.C.: Institute for the Comparative Study of Political Systems.

Pease García, Henry. 1981. *A un año del segundo belaundismo: Un perfil del proceso político peruano*. Lima: DESCO-Centro de Estudios y Promoción del Desarrollo.

———. 1988. *Democracia y precariedad bajo el populismo aprista*. Lima: DESCO-Centro de Estudios y Promoción del Desarrollo.

Pécaut, Daniel. 1989. *Crónica de dos décadas de política colombiana, 1968–1988*. Bogotá: Siglo Veintiuno.

Penniman, Howard R., ed. 1980. *Venezuela at the Polls: The National Elections of 1978*. Washington, D.C.: American Enterprise Institute for Public Policy Research.

Peña, Alfredo. 1978. *Democracia y reforma del Estado*. Caracas: Editorial Jurídica Venezolana, Colección Estudios Políticos No. 1.

Petkoff, Teodoro. 1978. *La corrupción administrativa*. Caracas: Ediciones Fracción Socialista.

Petras, James. 1969. *Politics and Social Forces in Chilean Development*. Berkeley: University of California Press.

Pinto, Rogério Feital S. 1969. *The Political Ecology of the Brazilian National*

Bank for Development. Washington, D.C.: Public Administration Unit, Department of Economic Affairs, Organization of American States.

Pisarello Virasoro, Roberto Gustavo, and Emilia Edda Menotti, eds. 1988. *Arturo Frondizi: Historia y problemática de un estadista.* Vol. 4, *El Gobernante.* Buenos Aires: Ediciones Depalma.

Polsby, Nelson. 1983. *The Consequences of Party Reform.* New York: Oxford University Press.

Poulantzas, Nicos. 1975. *Political Power and Social Classes.* London: New Left Books.

———. 1976. "The Capitalist State: A Reply to Miliband and Laclau." *New Left Review* 95:63–83.

Powell, John Duncan. 1971. *Political Mobilization of the Venezuelan Peasant.* Cambridge, Mass.: Harvard University Press.

Presidência da República. 1958. *Programa de Metas do Presidente Juscelino Kubitschek.* Rio de Janeiro: Serviço de Documentação.

Price, Robert. 1975. *Society and Bureaucracy in Contemporary Ghana.* Berkeley: University of California Press.

Quem É Quem no Brasil, 1955–1967. Vols. 4–9. 1967.

Quién es quién en Colombia: Biografos contemporáneos. 1962–63. Bogotá: Colombia Editorial Temis Librería.

Quién es quién en la Argentina: Biografías contemporaneas. 1955, 1958–59, 1963. Buenos Aires: Kraft.

Quién es quién en la sociedad argentina. 1982. Buenos Aires: Ediciones Elite.

Ramírez, Cayetano. 1989. "Al reiterar equipo económico se confirma política de paquete." *El Nacional,* August 27:D1.

Rapoport, Anatol, and Albert Chammah. 1965. *Prisoner's Dilemma: A Study in Conflict and Cooperation.* Ann Arbor: University of Michigan Press.

Real, Alberto Ramón. 1965. *Las estructuras políticas y administrativas uruguayas en relación con el desarrollo.* Montevideo: n.p.

Remmer, Karen. 1984. *Party Competition in Argentina and Chile: Political Recruitment and Public Policy, 1890–1930.* Lincoln: University of Nebraska Press.

———. 1990. "Democracy and Economic Crisis: The Latin American Experience." *World Politics* 42:315–35.

———. 1993. "The Political Economy of Elections in Latin America, 1980–1991." *American Political Science Review* 87:393–407.

Rial, Juan. 1985. *Uruguay: Elecciones 1984: Un triunfo del centro.* Montevideo: Ediciones de la Banda Oriental.

Rojas Samanez, Alvaro. 1984. *Partidos políticos en el Peru: Manual y registro.* 3d ed. Lima: Centro de Documentación e Información Andina.

Rose-Ackerman, Susan. 1978. *Corruption: A Study in Political Economy.* New York: Academic Press.

Rosenberg, Hans. 1966. *Bureaucracy, Aristocracy, and Autocracy: The Prussian Experience, 1660–1815.* Boston: Beacon Press.

Rossi, Clóvis. 1992. "Reforma marca a volta da 'era biônica'." *Folha de São Paulo,* April 10:6.

Ruddle, Kenneth, and Philip Gillette, eds. 1972. *Latin American Political Sta-*

tistics: Supplement to the Statistical Abstract of Latin America. Los Angeles: UCLA Latin American Center.

Rueschemeyer, Dietrich, and Peter Evans. 1985. "The State and Economic Transformation: Toward an Analysis of the Conditions Underlying Effective Intervention." In Peter Evans, Dietrich Rueschemeyer, and Theda Skocpol, eds., *Bringing the State Back In*. Cambridge: Cambridge University Press.

Salisbury, Robert H. 1969. "An Exchange Theory of Interest Groups." *Midwest Journal of Political Science* 13:1–32.

Sánchez, Alba. 1990. "Privatización es la prioridad del nuevo equipo ministerial." *El Nacional*, July 28:D4.

Sánchez, Pedro. 1983. *Las presidencias radicales: La presidencia de Illia*. Buenos Aires: Editor de América Latina.

Santos, Wanderley Guilherme dos. 1979. "The Calculus of Conflict: Impasse in Brazilian Politics and the Crisis of 1964." Ph.D. dissertation, Stanford University.

———. 1986. *Sessenta e Quatro: Anatomia da Crise*. São Paulo: Editora Revista dos Tribunais.

Schattschneider, E. E. 1942. *Party Government*. New York: Rinehart & Winston.

Schelling, Thomas C. 1978. *Micromotives and Macrobehavior*. New York: W. W. Norton.

———. 1984. *Choice and Consequence: Perspectives of an Errant Economist*. Cambridge, Mass.: Harvard University Press.

Schmidt, Steffen. 1974. "Bureaucrats as Modernizing Brokers?" *Comparative Politics* 6:425–50.

Schneider, Ben. 1991. *Politics within the State: Elite Bureaucrats and Industrial Policy in Authoritarian Brazil*. Pittsburgh: University of Pittsburgh Press.

Schneider, Mark, and Paul Teske. 1992. "Toward a Theory of the Political Entrepreneur: Evidence from Local Government." *American Political Science Review* 86:737–47.

Schumpeter, Joseph. 1975. *Capitalism, Socialism and Democracy*, 3d. ed. New York: Harper & Row.

Schwartzman, Simón. 1975. *São Paulo e o Estado Nacional*. São Paulo: Difusão Européia do Livro.

Selznick, Philip. 1957. *Leadership in Administration: A Sociological Interpretation*. Evanston, Ill.: Row, Peterson.

———. 1960. *The Organizational Weapon: A Study of Bolshevik Strategy and Tactics*. Glencoe, Ill.: Free Press.

Shackleton, J. R. 1978. "Corruption: An Essay in Economic Analysis." *The Political Quarterly* 49:25–37.

Shepsle, Kenneth, and Barry Weingast. 1981. "Political Preferences for the Pork Barrel: A Generalization." *American Journal of Political Science* 25:96–111.

Shugart, Matthew, and John Carey. 1992. *Presidents and Assemblies*. New York: Cambridge University Press.

Shugart, Matthew. Forthcoming. "The Effects of Timing of Elections for President and Assembly." In Scott Mainwaring and Matthew Shugart, eds., *Presidentialism and Democracy in Latin America*.

Siegel, Gilbert. 1963. "The DASP: A Study in the Deterioration of an Organizational Power Base." In Robert T. Daland, ed., *Perspectives of Brazilian*

Public Administration. Vol. 1. The Comparative Series in Brazilian Public Administration. Los Angeles: University of Southern California and Fundação Getúlio Vargas, Escola Brasileira de Administração Pública.

———. 1966. "The Vicissitudes of Government Reform in Brazil: A Study of the DASP." Ph.D. dissertation, University of Southern California.

Sigmund, Paul. 1977. *The Overthrow of Allende and the Politics of Chile*. Pittsburgh: University of Pittsburgh Press.

Sikkink, Kathryn. 1988. "State Autonomy and Developmentalist Policy Making in Argentina and Brazil: Frondizi and Kubitschek Administrations Compared." Paper delivered at Latin American Studies Association, New Orleans.

Singer, Paulo. 1965. "A Política das Classes Dominantes." In Octávio Ianni, P. Singer, G. Cohn, and F. Weffort, eds., *Política e Revolução Social no Brasil*. Rio de Janeiro: Civilização Brasileira.

Skidmore, Thomas. 1976. *Politics in Brazil, 1930–1964: An Experiment in Democracy*. London: Oxford University Press.

Skocpol, Theda. 1979. *States and Social Revolutions: A Comparative Analysis of France, Russia and China*. Cambridge: Cambridge University Press.

Skocpol, Theda, and Ellen Kay Trimberger. 1977–78. "Revolutions and the World-Historical Development of Capitalism." *Berkeley Journal of Sociology* 22:101–13.

Skowronek, Stephen. 1982. *Building a New American State: The Expansion of National Administrative Capacities, 1877–1920*. Cambridge: Cambridge University Press.

Smith, Peter. 1969. *Politics and Beef in Argentina: Patterns of Conflict and Change*. New York: Columbia University Press.

———. 1974. *Argentina and the Failure of Democracy: Conflict among Political Elites, 1904–1955*. Madison: University of Wisconsin Press.

Smulovitz-Parellada, Catalina. 1991. "Oposición y Gobierno en Argentina: Las administraciones de Frondizi e Illia." Ph.D. dissertation, Pennsylvania State University.

Snow, Peter. 1965. *Argentine Radicalism: The History and Doctrine of the Radical Civic Union*. Iowa City: University of Iowa Press.

———. 1971a. *Argentine Political Parties and the 1966 Revolution*. Buffalo: Council on International Studies, State University of New York.

———. 1971b. *Political Forces in Argentina*. Boston: Allyn & Bacon Series in Latin American Politics.

Solaún, Mauricio. 1980. "Colombian Politics: Historical Characteristics and Problems." In R. Albert Berry, Ronald G. Hellman, and M. Solaún, eds., *Politics of Compromise: Coalition Government in Colombia*. New Brunswick: Transaction Books.

Souza, Maria do Carmo Campello de. 1976. *Estado e Partidos Políticos no Brasil*. São Paulo: Alfa-Omega.

Stallings, Barbara. 1978. *Class Conflict and Economic Development in Chile, 1958–1973*. Stanford: Stanford University Press.

Stebbins, Richard P., and Alba Amoia, eds. 1970–73. *Political Handbook and Atlas of the World: Governments and Intergovernmental Organizations*. New York: Simon & Schuster.

Stepan, Alfred. 1971. *The Military in Politics: Changing Patterns in Brazil*. Princeton: Princeton University Press.

———. 1978. *The State and Society: Peru in Comparative Perspective*. Princeton: Princeton University Press.

Stewart, Bill. 1978. *Change and Bureaucracy: Public Administration in Venezuela*. Chapel Hill: University of North Carolina Press.

Suleiman, Ezra. 1974. *Politics, Power, and Bureaucracy in France: The Administrative Elite*. Princeton: Princeton University Press.

Taagepera, Rein, and Matthew Shugart. 1989. *Seats and Votes: The Effects and Determinants of Electoral Systems*. New Haven: Yale University Press.

Tapia-Videla, Jorge Iván. 1969. "Bureaucratic Power in a Developing Country: The Case of the Chilean Social Security Administration." Ph.D. dissertation, University of Texas.

Taylor, Michael. 1987. *The Possibility of Cooperation*. Cambridge: Cambridge University Press.

Taylor, Michael, and Hugh Ward. 1982. "Chickens, Whales, and Lumpy Goods: Alternative Models of Public Goods Provision." *Political Studies* 30: 350–70.

Taylor, Philip B. 1952. "The Uruguayan Coup d'Etat of 1933." *Hispanic American Historical Review* 32:301–20.

———. 1960. *Government and Politics in Uruguay*. New Orleans: Tulane University Press, Tulane Studies in Political Science, Vol. 7.

Thompson, J. D. 1967. *Organizations in Action: Social Science Bases of Administrative Theory*. New York: McGraw-Hill.

Trimberger, Ellen Kay. 1977. "State Power and Modes of Production: Implications of the Japanese Transition to Capitalism." *Insurgent Sociologist* 7: 85–97.

———. 1978. *Revolution from Above: Military Bureaucrats and Development in Japan, Turkey, Egypt and Peru*. New Brunswick: Transaction Books.

Tsebelis, George. 1990. *Nested Games: Rational Choice in Comparative Politics*. Berkeley: University of California Press.

Tugwell, Franklin. 1975. *The Politics of Oil in Venezuela*. Stanford: Stanford University Press.

United Nations. 1962, 1963, 1967, 1968, 1971. *Statistical Yearbook*. New York: Statistical Office of the United Nations, Department of Economic and Social Affairs.

Urzúa Valenzuela, Germán. 1968. *Los partidos políticos chilenos*. Santiago: Editorial Jurídica de Chile.

Urzúa Valenzuela, Germán, and Anamaría García Barzelatto. 1971. *Diagnóstico de la burocracia chilena (1818–1969)*. Santiago: Editorial Jurídica de Chile.

Uzal, Francisco Hipólito. 1963. *Frondizi y la oligarquía*. Buenos Aires: Cia. Argentina de Editores.

Valenzuela, Arturo. 1977. *Political Brokers in Chile: Local Government in a Centralized Polity*. Durham: Duke University Press.

———. 1978. *The Breakdown of Democratic Regimes: Chile*. Baltimore: Johns Hopkins University Press.

———. 1984. "Parties, Politics, and the State in Chile: The Higher Civil Service."

In Ezra Suleiman, ed., *Bureaucrats and Policy Making: A Comparative Overview*. New York: Holmes & Meier.

———. 1985. "Origins and Characteristics of the Chilean Party System: A Proposal for a Parliamentary Form of Government." Woodrow Wilson Center Latin American Program Working Paper No. 164.

Van Riper, Paul P. 1958. *History of the United States Civil Service*. Evanston, Ill.: Row, Peterson.

Vargas, Getúlio. 1938. *A Nova Política do Brasil*. Vol. 3. Rio de Janeiro: José Olympio.

Venturini, Angel R. 1984. *Estadísticas electorales: Elecciones nacionales 1926–1982, elecciones internas 1982*. Montevideo: Ediciones de la Banda Oriental.

Vidal Perdomo, Jaime. 1982. "La reforma administrative de 1968 en Colombia." *International Review of Administrative Science* 48:77–84.

Vieira, Astério Dardeau. 1938. "O Interesse Público e o Interesse Privado na Administração de Pessoal." *Revista do Serviço Público* 2:9–12.

———. 1967. *A Administração de Pessoal Vista pelos Chefes do Serviço*. Rio de Janeiro: Fundação Getúlio Vargas.

Villegas, Mario. 1992. "Seis nuevos miembros al Gabinete de CAP." *El Nacional*, January 10:D4.

Vincenzo, Teresa de. 1992. "Copei participará en el Gobierno." *El Nacional*, March 10:D1.

Vinogradoff, Ludmila. 1989. "Humberto Celli: Ministros salientes no fracasaron." *El Nacional*, August 27:D1.

Viotti, Ilara. 1990. "Fim de festa." *Istoé Senhor*, December 19:32.

Wahrlich, Beatriz de Souza. 1955. "An Analysis of the DASP—A Contribution to the Study of Comparative Administration." Paper prepared for the Public Administration Clearing House, Chicago. Cited in Gilbert Siegel, "The Vicissitudes of Governmental Reform in Brazil: A Study of the DASP," Ph.D. dissertation, University of Southern California, 1966, p. 64.

———. 1957. "O Sistema do Mérito na Administração Federal Brasileira." *Revista do Serviço Público* 3:23/–54.

———. 1964. *Administração de Pessoal: Princípios e Técnicas*. Rio de Janeiro: Fundação Getúlio Vargas.

Waisman, Carlos. 1987. *Reversal of Development in Argentina: Postwar Counterrevolutionary Policies and Their Structural Consequences*. Princeton: Princeton University Press.

Wilkie, James, and Enrique Ochoa, eds. 1989. *Statistical Abstract of Latin America*. Vol. 27. Los Angeles: UCLA Latin American Center.

Wilkie, James, and Adam Perkal, eds. 1984. *Statistical Abstract of Latin America*. Vol. 23. Los Angeles: UCLA Latin American Center.

Willis, Eliza. 1986. "The State as Banker: The Expansion of the Public Sector in Brazil." Ph.D. dissertation, University of Texas, Austin.

Wise, Carol. 1990. "Peru Post-1968: The Political Limits to State-Led Economic Development." Ph.D. dissertation, Columbia University.

———. 1992. "Post-War Peru: State Policy and Social Conflict." Manuscript, Claremont Graduate School.

Woy-Hazelton, Sandra, and William A. Hazelton. 1987. "Sustaining Democracy in Peru: Dealing with Parliamentary and Revolutionary Changes." In George A. López and Michael Stohl, eds., *Liberalization and Redemocratization in Latin America.* New York: Greenwood Press.

Wynia, Gary. 1978. *Argentina in the Postwar Era: Politics and Economic Policy Making in a Divided Society.* Albuquerque: University of New Mexico Press.

Index

AD (Acción Democrática, Democratic Action), 110–11, 118n. 12, 119, 147n. 11, 150; and Betancourt, 153; and land reform, 36, 37n; pact with COPEI, 151; party discipline in, 153, 189; seats in Chamber of Deputies, 111 table 3. *See also* Betancourt; Lusinchi; Pérez

AP (Acción Popular, Popular Action), 162; formation, 161n. 18, 217. *See also* Belaúnde

APRA (Alianza Popular Revolucionaria Americana, American Popular Revolutionary Alliance): Bustamante government, 153, 174, 219; 1962 election 161n. 18; party discipline in, 153, 189; rivalry within, 147n. 11

Acción Democrática. *See* AD

Acción Popular. *See* AP

Administrative reform: under authoritarianism, 190–94; in Brazil, 20–21, 43–45, 51–55, 61–74, 79–81, 83–98, 115–16; as collective action problem, 19–20, 27–35; in Colombia, 104–8, 123–25; in Chile, 111–15; demand for, 24–26, 44–45, 93–95, 104, 141; reversal of, 55–61; 74–78; 115, 119–30; role of legislature in, 21, 56, 60, 80, 83–98, 183–84; role of presidents in, 21–22, 43–45, 51–78, 80–81, 145–46, 184; in Uruguay, 109–10, 123–25; in Venezuela, 110–11, 119–20. *See also* bureaucratic competence; civil service

reform; compartmentalization strategy; insulation; state capacity

Aguirre Cerda, Pedro (president of Chile), 112

Alessandri, Arturo (president of Chile), 112

Alessandri, Jorge (president of Chile), 148, 161, 162, 219

Alianza Popular Revolucionaria Americana. *See* APRA

Allende, Salvador (president of Chile): appointments, 17–18, 151; coalition supporting, 17 18, 162; election of, 152; land reform, 36; military threat, 21, 151, 169, 170, 174; Socialist party, 219

Appointment Strategy Index, 155–68, 210–16

Argentina, 3n; electoral rules and party system, 11n, 132n, 163n, 188; military threats and intervention, 132n, 169, 170–71, 176–77, 195; Perón, 132n, 147; Peronist Party, 132n, 137. *See also* Frondizi; Illia; Menem; Perón; Peronist Party; UCRP

Authoritarianism, 7, 22–23, 52, 54–55, 190–96

BNDE (Banco Nacional de Desenvolvimento Econômico): early history, 61–63; under Goulart, 60, 75–76, 77; under Kubitschek, 63–64, 68, 78

Belaúnde, Fernando (president of Peru),

241

Compositor: Terry Robinson & Co., Inc.
Printer: Thomson-Shore, Inc.
Binder: Thomson-Shore, Inc.
Text: 10/13 Sabon
Display: Sabon

maque! (4:762). Yet once Sophie has entered the sexual bond she will control her lover, and Émile's governor is determined to help her establish her sway. What the illusory charms of the sciences and the arts do for the ties of civil society, love, that "sweet illusion," will do for the tie that links the married couple—"entwine with flowers and garlands the happy bond that unites them till the tomb" (4:790).

In advising mothers on feminine education, Rousseau licenses girls in the use of a certain amount of cunning. Since "trickery is a natural talent of the sex" and "all natural tendencies are good and right in themselves. . . . It is only a matter of preventing their abuse" (4:711). Having brought Émile and Sophie together, Jean-Jacques watches Émile "drink in long draughts the poison" with which the "girl enchantress" intoxicates him (4:776). As soon as they are married, the governor will use all his influence to persuade Émile that neither of the couple should owe sexual favors to the other, so that Sophie can refuse her husband whenever and as often as she likes. She tests her powers on the very first night, and Émile goes into despair.

The rationale for this regime is that, preserving their freedom, it will allow the couple to go on as lovers in the married state. This liberal idea is a façade. The governor is scheming to help Sophie establish her regime. And this, of course, is his own regime too. He has preached independence and reliance only on things while exercising an absolute personal control. Now, having pretended to expose all of his projects so that his pupil can accept the results of education and make them his own, he is really handing him over to another secret governor. Émile is under supervision and control from the cradle to the grave. His experience of Nature and necessity are contrived from beginning to end. He is a happy victim of control answering to the needs of his inventor, who was an unhappy victim of chance and the gaze of others.[8]

Freedom and the Noble Lie

In educating Émile, Rousseau recognized that he was following in the footsteps of a great predecessor, Plato, author of the *Republic*—"the most beautiful treatise on education ever made," as he calls it. (4:250). The two thinkers have some traits in common: both of them are exemplary in considering politics in psychological terms, both see the problems of political association as an overcoming of private interest and an attachment to a higher good, and both think of the solution as a sublimation of eros toward a new object. Most important for our purposes, both see the establishment of the right relation of individuals to realities outside themselves as a matter of such importance that it justifies any measure, even systematic deception and

[8] In *Émile et Sophie, ou les solitaires,* the sequel to *Émile,* composed some time later in the distress of Rousseau's full-blown paranoia, Émile's happiness is destroyed by Sophie's weakness and he experiences all the torments of Rousseauvian betrayal.

Vicar, which will show him not only the limits of our knowledge but also the sacredness of conscience, leaving him to admire the beauty and perfection of the creation. Above all, Émile will be taught the key to Rousseau's Stoic conception of happiness—that, since happiness is the excess of power over need, one must learn to confine one's desires to the limit imposed by necessity (4:819). Because he has been raised in dependence only upon things and has learned to define his desires only in relation to his own estimate of their objects, Émile will experience no temptation to seek his happiness in the eyes of others. He will live among them as part of necessity and without dependence (4:856).

By the end of the story, all of these sentiments, and these alone, have become second nature to Émile through rigorous training and constant deception. But when the governor finally reveals the covert means by which he has carried out Émile's education, the pupil does not rebel. He accepts what has been done for him with gratitude and wants to remain what his governor has made him (4:651–52). After this education, knowledge of good and evil cannot spoil him. Émile is like a savage who has learned to think and to judge others yet remain very much himself (4:534). He is free and can be happy anywhere.

From One Master to Another

In the education of *Émile*, then, it seems as if Rousseau has finally succeeded in solving, at least for himself, the problem of how one might preserve the goodness of Nature in a social individual. The education of single individuals is a more hopeful project than the education of a people because individuals can be controlled from birth; hence it is possible for them to become wise, which can never be the condition of an entire people. But even Rousseau did not maintain for long that *Émile* showed anything more than that, if such an accomplishment were possible at all, this is how it must be done.[2] For the extraordinary efforts of the governor, like those of the lawgiver before him, seem to testify not so much to the redeemable nature of humankind as to the practical implausibility of the venture. And even if the obstacles to education could be overcome by a virtuous and wise governor, where, given the already corrupt state of civil society, were such governors to be found?

The practical difficulties raised by the scheme of *Émile*, however, are not as troubling as the doubts that emerge from within the text. Even when the educated Émile is equipped with all the natural and intellectual instruments he needs for freedom, Rousseau still cannot imagine him without a governor.[3] When, near the end of the story, the governor Jean-Jacques takes Émile

[2] *Lettre à Christophe de Beaumont,* 4:937.

[3] See Judith N. Sklar, chap. 4 in *Men and Citizens: A Study of Rousseau's Social Theory* (London: Cambridge University Press, 1969).

up on the mountaintop finally to expose to him the methods of his education—to reveal to him the facts of sex, relinquish his authority over him, and become his friend—Jean-Jacques has already anticipated that his pupil will refuse this freedom and ask for continued guidance, and he is prepared to agree only reluctantly so that Émile will later have no doubts about his decision. "It is in this moment," he says, "that reserve and gravity are in their place" (4:652). The governor is still contriving to strengthen his hold on Émile even as he pretends to set him free. He will continue to command, only now he will provide explanations if they are wanted. He will also continue to deceive Émile. He even chooses Émile's bride, Sophie, long before Émile ever sees her, and he orchestrates their courtship step by step, including the requirement of a grand tour that will keep them from coming together while they are still in the first transports of love. At the end of the story, Émile is still begging the governor to continue his reign (4:867–68). It is a strange vision of freedom.

What is still stranger, though, and perhaps even more significant, is that, although Émile is ready himself to become a governor and unite the figure of the father and the governor, he himself will have another governor, for though Jean-Jacques has been able to insulate Émile from unequal relations with society, there is one unequal relation that he cannot do without, and that is his relation with his wife. One of the important tasks of the governor is to keep the child in ignorance of sexual matters until he has reached the age in which he is ready to begin courtship. Rousseau believes that this moment should be postponed as long as possible, and there is deep significance in the fact that the governor takes Émile up on the mountaintop to learn two truths at once—the truth of sex and of their own relationship. It is as if in relinquishing his own governance he is also handing Émile over to his new master. And, as we have seen, Jean-Jacques will preside over the transition.

In the state of nature, Rousseau tells us in the *Second Discourse,* differentiation between the sexes is confined to biological functioning, and only gradually do broader gender differences emerge. The sentiment of romantic love based on them is one of the first products of inequality and *amour-propre,* an "artificial feeling" that women foster "with great skill and care in order to establish their empire, and make that sex dominant which ought to obey" (1:158). Love is a symptom of dependence and a cause of violence. Like the pleasures of the sciences and the arts, its sweetness is a disguise for enslavement.

Rousseau sees the domination of women as one of the essential elements of social inequality. Men are what women would have them be. Woman is the chief witness of male *amour-propre,* and because women are corrupt, men are corrupt. Women's great weapon lies in their weakness, and they do everything to enhance it. By giving men the pride of dominating them, and yielding themselves only unwillingly, they exert a secret control. Behind these feminine arts, of course, lies a profound intelligence, an intelligence that Nature has given women to make up for their lack of strength (4:702). They

make a profound study of the men around them in order to manipulate them.[4] That they should do so is necessary because Nature has not given them the means to provide for themselves and their children without the help of men. But the effect is pernicious, since their feminizing influences separate men from the rigors of Nature. Because they cannot become men, women try to make men into women.[5]

Relations between the sexes, therefore, are for Rousseau the very essence of unfreedom. They exemplify paradigmatically the fact that the sensation of power over others is always a disguise for weakness. Woman, as Rousseau likes to call her, embodies, in fact, the paradox of power: behind her apparent weakness lies a veritable strength. If "to rule is to obey,"[6] as Rousseau tells us, then for woman, to obey is to rule. In her charms she has her own special form of violence (4:694). And if freedom lies in confining one's desires within one's means of satisfaction, so that one's power always answers to one's need (4:695–96), then the raison d'être of women is to deprive men of this freedom, for it is in the nature of the relations between the sexes that women incite more desire in men than they satisfy, and that it is in their interest to do so. The great panoply of feminine weapons aims toward this purpose: "Modesty is in their faces and libertinage at the bottom of their hearts" (4:740). Rousseau has carefully observed their seductive ways. They even take pride in kissing each other in the presence of men in order to incite their desires! (4:719). The theater is a great pageant of feminine corruption and so are the salons of Paris. Rousseau's defense of the innocent purity of Geneva against the temptations of the theater is largely a plea for the autonomy of the sexes.[7] Rousseau would like to confine the influence of women to the home, but this is, of course, their citadel. In times when virtue reigns, their rule is benevolent and necessary to the virtue of men. Rousseau admits the ascendancy of women in history, and he pities the century in which "women can make nothing of men." Women are the great movers of history; they were the epitome of Roman and Spartan virtue as they are the epitome of modern corruption. "All the great revolutions were brought about by women" (4:742).

How, then, does Émile's governor cope with the problem of marriage when there is no longer a polis which modern women can inspire their men to serve? Will he create for Émile an enlightened woman who will have her own freedom and allow him to have his, or will he instruct Émile about the ruses of women so that he can avoid the sweet enslavement of sex? Surprisingly, he does neither. Sophie will be a virtuous woman who will love only a virtuous man. Before she meets Émile she is in love with the idea of Télé-

[4] It is in a Baconian spirit that Rousseau apportions the labor of developing "la moralité expérimentale" between men and women: "It is for women to discover, so to speak, the morality of experience, for us to reduce it to a system." *Émile,* 4:737.

[5] *Lettre à d'Alembert,* 5:92.

[6] *Lettres écrites de la montagne,* 3:841–42.

[7] See *Lettre à d'Alembert,* 5:92–98.

covert manipulation. There is, however, an important difference. For Plato, the alignment of the soul with truth and the good, necessary for individual and civic happiness, is a matter of ultimate value. To be so aligned is to be in touch with the ultimately real, the highest and most permanent aspect of being. The right relation to the good simply is the good, just as, in most religions, to be in the right relation to a god or ultimate reality simply is the good. While there may be more and less proper ways to achieve this good, there is no substitute for it and no other value that can compete with it. If a "noble lie" is necessary, then, to sustain the order of the state upon which the good of the citizens depends, it is justified on that onto-theoretic basis. This is what Isaiah Berlin called a "positive" notion of freedom, and he objected to such a notion on the basis that it can logically justify coercion on the part of those who believe they hold the truth.[9]

Rousseau, however, does not hold a positive conception of freedom, even though *Émile* is full of Platonic formulas. Rousseau's freedom is an absence of dependency. Its value does not lie in itself; rather, it is one of the necessary components of happiness, which derives from one's sense of the excess of power over need. What such a condition promises is the experience of bliss, or the greatest possible "feeling of one's own existence," a key notion for Rousseau. It is the benison of Nature, and freedom is only the removal of the obstacles that prevent it. Émile, in his socially alienated and semi-Stoic self-containment, is encouraged to develop a love of order, and the Savoyard Vicar stresses the force of conscience and the satisfactions of virtue, but these passions do not rest upon an ultimate psychological or ontological ground. Émile's Stoic detachment is for Rousseau an inferior substitute for the benefits of true citizenship and union with the general will, and the general will is an inferior and insecure substitute for the freedom of the state of nature.[10] Rousseau's own religion and his commitment to optimism comprise a passionate preference and a consolation but they do not provide the ultimate ground of his thought. They have the strangely hypothetical idealization that is typical of Rousseau. "The essential worship is that of the heart," the Savoyard Vicar teaches (4:627), but in Rousseau's fancy the heart may have its own reasons for worshiping otherwise. Julie's heart is full of God but this does not keep her love of Saint-Preux from killing her. Émile's governor knows this too when he inducts Émile into the cult of Sophie, yet he lets him "drink in . . . the poison."

The difference between Plato and Rousseau—that one has a positive, the other a negative conception of freedom—puts the key element they share, a

[9] See Isaiah Berlin, *Four Essays on Liberty* (New York: Oxford University Press, 1969), 121–45.

[10] This does not mean that Rousseau fails to see the advantages of departing from the impercipient state of nature to acquire the wider thoughts and nobler sentiments of civilized life. Were it not for the degradations that society inflicts, man would have to "bless without ceasing the happy moment in which he was snatched" from the state of nature, the moment that "made a stupid and limited animal into an intelligent being and a man." *Du contrat social*, 3:364.

stomach for the "noble lie," in a very different light. Plato's conception of freedom (in calling it such I am employing a convenient anachronism) gives license to the kind of manipulation he advocates because the fact that one finally comes to the truth, according to this way of thinking, is far more important than the manner in which one does it. Rousseau, however, is not primarily seeking a truth. Power and independence are his primary values, as they lead directly to happiness and the sense of existence. But in his view of things, one cannot have the sense of power and independence except as the prisoner of a political mythology. Rousseau's negative conception of freedom can only be fulfilled by the removal of power and independence altogether.

For a negative conception of freedom to be coherent, it must recognize that freedom is not the only good, but Rousseau often pursued it as if it were. Toward the end of his life he could characterize all of education, not just the education of the child, as "éducation négative."[11] Pursuing a negative as if it were an ultimate goal led him finally to a condition of paradox. Rousseau accused the Abbé de Saint-Pierre of counting, in a modern political context, upon the existence of virtues that belonged only to the ancients and to "a few modern men who have antique souls."[12] It was not his virtues but his intellectual vices that Rousseau borrowed from the ancients, habits of thought that became vices in the context to which he imported them. Rousseau imbibed from the ancient authors a taste for necessity—both the bold practical necessity that motivated the discipline of the ancient martial cultures described by Thucydides and Plutarch and the intellectual and social necessity that motivates Plato. He sought to find grounds for similar authority working within the skeptical boundaries of a modern intellectual vocabulary that had largely been designed to eliminate this kind of authority in the first place.

Paranoid Self-defense

The third and last phase of Rousseau's career is the saddest, strangest, and, oddly, the most influential. After years of attacking society and its most cherished practices and beliefs, Rousseau himself became increasingly the object of attack. The pose of the virtuous Citizen of Geneva brought him mockery from many of his friends among the *philosophes*. Voltaire, in an anonymous pamphlet, maliciously exposed the surrender of Rousseau's five infant children to the orphanage. "The Profession of Faith of the Savoyard Vicar" led *Émile* to be condemned, forcing the author to flee to England. He had al-

---

[11] See *Rousseau juge de Jean-Jacques*, 1:687. This represents a change from *Émile*, where Rousseau clearly enunciates the principle, "Use force with children, reason with men; that is the order of nature" (4:320). *Émile* still leaves us with the question, though, of whether the student will ever be grown up enough to use his own reason without a master or mistress.

[12] "Jugement sur *La Polysynodie*," 3:643.

ready begun to suffer from delusions about Jesuits tampering with his work while he was writing *Émile*, but the condemnation that followed exacerbated his paranoid tendencies. Later, Jansenists and Oratorians also appeared among his persecutors. While in England he turned against his benefactor David Hume, accusing him of systematic deception, leading to a painful public quarrel. Rousseau gradually derived the conviction that not only the world of the intellectuals but all of France was united in conspiracy against him, a conspiracy of silent manipulation, ostracism, and condemnation which he could never penetrate and which would keep his works from reaching posterity. He undertook his shattering autobiographical work, *The Confessions of J.-J. Rousseau,* to convince others of his essential goodness in spite of this system of conspiracy and accusation, but when he read it to an audience of friends who did not collapse into tears, Rousseau became further embittered and isolated.

Thwarted now in the method of direct confession, Rousseau attempted to dramatize an investigation of himself from the point of view of external observers. The strange book that resulted, *Rousseau Judges Jean-Jacques,*[13] involves three characters—first "Jean-Jacques," the real-life author Jean-Jacques Rousseau; then "Rousseau," a man who has read the published works of "Jean-Jacques" and found his own good nature echoed there; and finally "a Frenchman," who is in on the conspiracy against "Jean-Jacques." Together they seek to discover the truth about him. Once "Rousseau" the reader has gone to meet "Jean-Jacques" and the conspirator has read his works, the two men decide to help him escape from his tormentors.

The real Jean-Jacques was again disappointed with the response to his work. His friend Condillac would give him only literary advice about the manuscript, showing that he too was part of the plot, and when the desperate author tried to lay the work upon the high altar of Notre Dame, with the inscription "Deposit Handed Over to Providence," in the hope that this would bring it to the attention of the king, he found himself blocked by a railing he had never seen before. At this point he concluded that God too was against him.[14] Saddest of all, hungering for a single understanding soul and believing that those who conspired against him might be less able to control his contact with complete strangers than with his pretended admirers, he composed a leaflet giving a brief version of his side of the case (assuming they knew the other). With this instrument he attempted to approach people on the street, but the Frenchmen mocked him with an "ingenuity" that made him "laugh in the midst of his pain," saying that the leaflet, which was addressed "To all Frenchmen who still love justice and truth," was not meant for them (1:984). Defeated in his last attempt to communicate with others, Rousseau's final strategy was to retreat entirely into Nature and imagination,

---

[13] The title can also be translated as "Rousseau the Judge of Jean-Jacques."

[14] See the "Histoire du précédent écrit" ("History of the Foregoing Document") attached to the end of the *Dialogues,* 1:980–81.

and his last work, *The Reveries of the Solitary Walker,* purports to be merely an exercise of private self-diversion and consolation. It too is largely taken up with the vast conspiracy. Rousseau was simply too obsessed to leave the subject alone.

In Rousseau's confessional works, we see him struggling mightily to cope with what he himself takes for an astonishing fact—the existence of an all-powerful conspiracy focused in hostility against him in order to remove him from the sight of posterity. Rousseau believes in this conspiracy—the evidence is all around him—but he is unable truly to make sense of it. In fact, just as he is going to lay before his reader his defendant's case regarding the prosecution against him, so he also hopes that some reader may be able to go beyond him in the comprehension of the plot itself, which he presents not as a certainty but as a mystery of the highest order, the effect of an agent whose being he is unable to conceive.

> Here begins the work of shadows in which I found myself buried for eight years, without any hope of piercing its frightening obscurity. In the abyss of evils in which I have been submerged, I feel the effect of blows that have been delivered upon me, I perceive the immediate instrument of them, but I can see neither the hand that directs them nor the means it puts into effect. Blame and misfortunes fall upon me as of themselves and without being seen. When my tattered heart lets out a moan, I look like a man who complains without a cause, and the authors of my ruin have discovered the inconceivable art of making the members of the public complicit in their plot without them suspecting it or noticing the effect. In narrating, then, the events that concern me, the treatment I have suffered and all that has happened to me, I am not in position, in telling the facts, to trace them back to the guiding hand and to assign them to their causes. The primitive causes have all been observed in the three preceding books [of the *Confessions*]; there all the interests relating to me, all the secret motives are shown. But to say into what form these diverse causes combine to bring about the strange events of my life, that is impossible for me, even by conjecture. (1:589)

This terrifying and elusive conspiracy is a double of the one, unmasked in the *Second Discourse,* that contrived the institutions of civil society in favor of the rich, but now the plot is focused specifically upon Rousseau himself.[15] Just as suspicion of society and skepticism about the power of reason leads Rousseau the political theorist back to the fantasy of a god-like lawgiver who makes up for all of the obstacles that stand in the way of social cooperation, so now an equally manipulable society, guided by an evil genius, takes its revenge upon him and proves that it is capable of just the kind of concerted

---

[15] Starobinski notes the similarity between the operations of Rousseau's all-controlling enemies and those of Émile's governor. *La transparence et l'obstacle,* 258.

action he denied. What particularly outrages Rousseau is the unwillingness of the conspirators to confront their victim and give him the chance to defend himself. He finds himself trying to surrender in an acceptable way to this stronger opponent, or to build a smaller, narrower line of defense against what remains an invisible accusation. As Starobinski puts it, the *Confessions* are the "work of a man retrenched to his ultimate defensive positions."[16]

The eerie third-person descriptions of the plight of Jean-Jacques in *Rousseau Judges Jean-Jacques* reveal the scope of Rousseau's delusion and the detail with which he developed it. The Frenchman explains to the character Rousseau that "wise people" are maintaining a surveillance over Jean-Jacques

> "such that he cannot say a word that is not recorded, nor take a step that is not marked, nor form a project that has not been penetrated from the moment it was conceived. They have made it so that, apparently free in the midst of men, he has no real contact with anyone; he lives alone in the crowd and knows nothing of what is done, what is said around him, nothing above all of what affects and interests him the most, so that he feels everywhere weighed down with chains the least vestige of which he can neither display nor see. They have raised around him walls of shadow impenetrable to his view; they have buried him alive among the living. Behold what must be the most singular, the most stunning undertaking that has ever been achieved. Its complete success attests to the power of the genius who conceived it and of those who have directed its execution; and what is no less stunning is the zeal with which the entire public has leant itself to it, without being able to appreciate the grandeur, the beauty of the plan of which it is the blind and faithful expression." (1:706)

Again many themes of Rousseau's vision are echoed in this passage—the chains of civilization, the great, ingenious plot, the shadows of social deception, the force of continuous scrutiny, the manipulating genius of the lawgiver, and the innocent collaboration of the citizens.

What we have, then, in the confessional works, is Rousseau's attempt to represent his personal psychology and history in response to accusations that he believes have been made against him. The unity of the narratives is one of negation—they disprove or undermine another life-narrative hostile to the author. Like Luther, Rousseau is struggling with a burden of responsibility and, rather than defending himself in the terms in which that responsibility was initially conceived, he attempts to revise the moral vocabulary altogether. This, of course, had been his intellectual strategy all along, only now his general defense of humanity becomes a particular defense of his own

---

[16] "Jean-Jacques Rousseau et le péril de la reflection," in *L'œil vivant: Corneille, Racine, La Bruyère, Rousseau, Stendhal*, edition augmentée (Paris: Gallimard, 1961), 138.

character and nature. Rousseau the lawgiver becomes Rousseau the victim, the plaything of inner and outer forces. Rousseau's confessional narratives may not give us a sound account of how he came to acquire his personality, but they do allow us to assess what is personal in his point of view. Among his contemporaries, the paranoid element of Rousseau's confessional writings served to isolate him from readers who knew him, but for later generations who would encounter Rousseau only in the pages of a book, its psychological perspective would become one of the most attractive elements of the work. Even for the makers of the Revolution, where Rousseau's authority was cited on every side of the debate, it was his personal story, his heroism as the martyr of liberty, that constituted the source of his appeal.[17]

If the content of Rousseau's paranoia seems a comic version of his system, the tone in which he presents it is equally recognizable as his own. From the beginning of his career and in spite of extraordinary applause, Rousseau's stance toward his audience was hostile and defensive. In the Preface to the *First Discourse,* his first published work of speculation, he anticipates "universal blame" (3:3). Even before the outlines of the master conspiracy against him had begun to appear, he was particularly disturbed by two accusations, both having to do with his preference for solitude—that it marked him as a misanthrope, and that it betokened an unhappiness incompatible with his account of himself as the man who had overcome the denaturing influence of society. He never ceased to rankle over the reproach leveled against a character in one of Diderot's plays, a man exemplifying Rousseau's virtues: "Only the wicked man is alone" (1:455).

Rousseau's fullest self-defense before the *Confessions* appears in a private document, the *Letters to Malesherbes,* in which, writing to an important patron, he attempts to explain the peculiarities of his nature and habits. Remarkably, he cites as the key fact of his life his reading of Plutarch at the age of six. By the time he was eight, the stories of the noble Greeks and Romans had infused him with a "taste for the heroic and romantic" that never ceased to grow and finally left him "disgusted with everything around him that did not resemble his follies."[18] All the involvements of his youth were activated by vain hopes of finding himself among men like the ones he had read about, until, "embittered by the injustices" that he experienced and witnessed, and thrown into disorder by the force of events, he "came to despise his century and his contemporaries." Knowing that his heart would find no happiness among them, he became "little by little detached from the society of men" and made for himself "another in my imagination which charmed me all the more in that I could cultivate it without pain and without risk, and in that I would always find it secure and such as I needed it to be."[19]

---

[17] Blum, *Republic of Virtue,* 33–35, and Joan McDonald, *Rousseau and the French Revolution, 1762–1791* (London: Athlone, 1965), esp. 155–73.

[18] *Lettres à Malesherbes,* 1:1134. Rousseau repeats the account in the *Confessions,* 1:9, and in *Les rêveries du promeneur solitaire,* 1:1024.

[19] *Lettres à Malesherbes,* 1:1134–5. Consider in this context the following dialogue with

If we take his account at face value, this was Rousseau's life nearly until the age of forty, the life of a Quixotic dreamer who was neither content with himself nor with others, until a "happy accident," the question from the Academy of Dijon, showed him what he had to do to overcome the contradictions of his existence.

> If ever there was something like a sudden inspiration, it was the movement that was made in me at that reading; all at once I felt my intellect dazzled with a thousand illuminations; crowds of vivid ideas presented themselves to me at once with a force and confusion that threw me into an inexpressible commotion; I felt my head taken by a dizziness like being drunk. A violent palpitation oppressed me, made me inhale; no longer able to breathe while walking, I let myself down under one of the trees by the road, and I spent a half hour there in such an agitation that in getting up I noticed I had soaked all the front of my vest with tears without having felt that I had spent them. O Monsieur, if I had ever been able to write a quarter of what I saw and felt under that tree, with what clarity I would have depicted all the contradictions of the social system, with what force I would have exposed all of the abuses of our institutions, with what simplicity I would have shown that man is naturally good and that it is through these institutions alone that he becomes wicked. (1:1135–36)

This was the dawning of Rousseau's central insight and it brought about a great and powerful inner transformation. On the spot, Rousseau composed the speech of Fabricius that is the centerpiece of the *First Discourse,* in which the noble Roman hero returns in a later age to denounce the corruption of his city. As late as January of 1762, when the *Letters to Malesherbes* were written, Rousseau still thought of this moment as the happiest of his life, the one that liberated him from the tyranny of other men and enabled him to take up his position "against the current" (1:1136). It led him to depart from Paris, "where a black bile gnawed upon" his heart (1:1131). For the first time he began truly to live.

The Vincennes epiphany brought Rousseau an enormous sense of power, a release of long-held tensions, and the speech of Fabricius that was the core of the *First Discourse* became the first expression of a new-born self. As Carol Blum puts it, "one of the Plutarchan identifications which had been his source of strength in childhood had broken through to him and provided him with an ecstatic experience of internal unification."[20]

Rousseau reported by James Boswell: ROUSSEAU: "Sir, you don't see before you the bear you have heard tell of. Sir, I have no liking for the world. I live here in a world of fantasies, and I cannot tolerate the world as it is." BOSWELL: "But when you come across fantastical men, are they not to your liking?" ROUSSEAU: "Why, sir, they have not the same fantasies as myself." *Boswell on the Grand Tour: Germany and Switzerland, 1764,* ed. Frederick A. Pottle (New York: McGraw Hill, 1928), 223–24.

[20] Blum, *Republic of Virtue,* 41.

O Fabricius! what would your great soul have thought if, called back
to life for your unhappiness, you had seen this Rome saved by your
arm and that your honored name had made more illustrious than all
of its conquests had done. "God," you would have said, "what has become of those roofs of straw and rustic hearths that once housed mod-
eration and virtue? What fatal splendor supplanted Roman simplicity?
What is this strange language? What are these effeminate manners?
What is the meaning of these statues, these Paintings, these buildings?
Madmen, what have you done? You the Masters of Nations, you have
made yourselves the slaves of the frivolous men you have vanquished."
(3:14)

Here is Rousseau's essential voice, the knowing moralist who returns from
the virtuous past as a stranger to denounce the corruption of the ages, the
cumulative perversities of time. Like Quixote, Rousseau is overwhelmed by
the fantasy of an imaginary self derived from a heroic model, only here the
model represents a potent ideal, a vision of antique virtue that no modern
soul could live up to. And as with his knight-errant predecessor, it is through
rhetoric that the influence permeates his sensibility. Throughout his life
Rousseau would maintain this elevated and grand style, full of long periods
and ironic periphrases, the ideal instrument of virtuous indignation.

In Rousseau's account, it was full of this noble spirit of reform that he
composed the works of his critical phase—the two explosive discourses and
the arch and caustic responses to them, as well as the *Discourse on Political
Economy* and the *Letter to d'Alembert on the Theater*. In them Rousseau
treats his contemporaries like deluded children or weaklings who have given
in to the softening influence of women and the arts. "The scorn that my profound meditations had inspired in me for the mores, principles, and preju-
dices of my century made me insensible of the raillery of those who held
them, and I crushed their little *bon-mots* with my sentences as I would crush
an insect between my fingers" (1:417). Rousseau's new persona gave him
more than an intellectual or rhetorical stance. Upon learning that he had
been awarded the prize of the Academy of Dijon, he undertook a revolution
in his entire mode of life and manner, stripping himself of all ornaments of
dress and relinquishing all sources of income except what he could gain from
the mechanical copying of music. He even threw away his watch, as if to signify that he would no longer live in step with his contemporaries. No longer
an aspirant for success among the *philosophes* and sophisticates of Paris, he
became the good and simple Jean-Jacques, exiled but faithful Citizen of
Geneva, a land uncorrupted, he then claimed, by the ways of the modern
world. For six years he lived, according to his own later account, "intoxi-
cated with virtue" (1:416), in a mania of moral superiority, and it was in this
guise that he achieved a string of unparalleled successes with the public. His
opera, *The Village Soothsayer,* created a sensation, and his reputation grew
in the aftermath when he refused a pension from the king. The final gesture

of this heroic period was his departure from Paris and withdrawal into the solitude of the country. It is this solitude to which Rousseau ascribes his happiness in the *Letters to Malesherbes*. It was the true meaning of his revelation.[21]

Until January of 1762 and the completion of his middle phase, Rousseau could still think of his Vincennes experience as a "happy accident," one that set him in a different direction from the "fatal chance" that had been determining human fate since our first wanderings from the state of nature. By the time he came to write the *Confessions,* this attitude had been completely reversed. The illumination of Vincennes now marks for Rousseau the beginning of all the unhappiness associated with his role as an author, the role that had extracted him from humble insignificance and brought him under the malign influence of the public eye. This makes for the great difference in perspective between the *Confessions* and Rousseau's writings up to that time. Until this point, Rousseau has been a prophet of the ideal, denouncing all compromise with the weaknesses of human nature. He has been playing the role of the natural man who is uniquely above compromise, who has rejected the society of his fellow men, preferring to love mankind in general while keeping his distance from the particular. If Swift loved John, Peter, and Thomas but hated mankind, Rousseau was equally implacable in the opposite direction. But now the man who had once "set aside all the facts" in order to revive the essential truths of human history, and who advocated a "general will" to subsume all particulars, becomes the advocate of the particular, of the exception that preempts the rule and keeps it from being applied. Whereas Rousseau had established himself as a judge of men and Nature, now his primary concern is to control, defuse, and evade judgment. And where he had shown himself as master educator and manipulator, controlling the influences that shape the human personality and taking supreme responsibility for the happiness and unhappiness of others, now he will show himself being miseducated, misshaped, manipulated, and made incapable of happiness.

In the "Sketches" of the *Confessions,* it is clear that self-rehabilitation and self-justification in the face of his enemies were from the beginning the chief motives of the work, and though he accuses earlier practitioners of the art of self-portrait, including Montaigne, of being mere apologists for themselves (1:1149), Rousseau, far more than Montaigne, is a responder to calumny. It is not in mischaracterizing his deeds so much as his feelings that his enemies have done him ill, and this emphasis upon feeling gives Rousseau

---

[21] Rousseau's solitude and independence were, of course, largely a fiction the main point of which was his rejection of Paris and all it represented. For years he was hardly ever without his female companion, Thérèse, and the members of her large family. His refusal to profit from his works or to accept a pension from the crown left him only more constantly in need of aristocratic patrons and their servants. He was beloved by readers and haunted by visitors, and for a solitary man who claimed that he could only write with great difficulty, the volume of his correspondence was prodigious.

the authority to speak of himself. His attempt at self-depiction, he claims, will be of great philosophical importance because it is for lack of a point of comparison that men have failed to comprehend themselves. That is the "unique and useful thing" his purely objective self-description will provide (1:1153). And although the attempt is a supremely difficult one, no one could have been better situated for it. "When it comes to evaluating experience and observation, I am in the most advantageous position, perhaps, in which a mortal has ever found himself, since without having any social position myself, I have known all of them; I have lived in all of them, from the lowest to the highest, excepting only the throne." Men of each rank can claim to know their own natures, but "the nature they have in common, man, escapes them all equally. As for me, being careful to remove the mask, I recognize it everywhere. . . . Being nothing, wanting nothing, I burden or importune no one; I gain entry everywhere without becoming attached anywhere, sometimes dining with Princes in the morning and supping with peasants in the evening" (1:1150). At this point, Rousseau still occupies the persona of the all-seeing lawgiver, or of de Wolmar, the "living eye." It is from nowhere and without reciprocity that Rousseau observes most comfortably.

The task of his *Confessions,* he warns us, is such a novel one that he will have to invent a new language in order to complete it, a language that can shift with his moods and "follow the thread" of his "secret disposition" (1:1152). The narrative must be absolutely complete, for it is only in the context of the whole that each particular detail of "this bizarre and singular collection" can be understood (1:1153). It is above all the secret origins that Rousseau will be unveiling for his reader.

> In order to know a character properly it is necessary to distinguish the acquired along with the natural, to see how it was formed, what occasions have developed it, what chain of secret affections has made it what it is, and how it shifts in order sometimes to produce the most contradictory and unexpected effects. What is seen is only the least part of what is; it is the appearance the internal cause of which is hidden and often very complicated. (1:1149)

This claim will be repeated in the body of the posthumously published version of the *Confessions* (1:174–75). The need to follow the chains of cause and to see each detail in the context of the whole justifies the fullness of Rousseau's narrative, including the most trivial, absurd, and embarrassing details.[22] In book 9 Rousseau mentions an abandoned project called "The Materialism of the Sage" in which he planned to lay out a complete program for accomplishing the total conditioning of the human being through the control of environmental influence (1:409). Had he completed it, the world

[22] Michael Sheringham, *French Autobiography: Drives and Desires: From Rousseau to Perec* (Oxford: Clarendon, 1993), 42.

might have received an even more detailed and perhaps more widely applicable program of control than the one envisioned by the governor of Émile, one that could have been the model for Bentham, Helvétius, or even B. F. Skinner. Instead, what Rousseau provided was the demonstration of his own nature being accidentally conditioned, making himself an example of the hidden effects of haphazard and premature education upon the sensitive soul.

In the final manuscript of the *Confessions,* the grand rationalizing prologue of the "Sketches" has largely been suppressed, though the claim to provide "the first comparison piece for the study of men" is retained in a prefatory paragraph in which, on behalf of the manuscript, Rousseau begs the mercy of his "implacable enemies" (1:3). The *Confessions* begins far more dramatically, with the author pledging his readiness to go before the Last Judgment with this book in his hand, defying anyone who has read it to stand before God and say, "I was better than that man." The opening words proclaim the revolutionary nature of the project.

> I have conceived an enterprise that has no example, and of which the execution will have no imitator. I want to show to my fellow men a man in all the truth of nature; and that man will be me.
>
> Me alone. I know my heart and I know men. I am not made like any of them that I have seen. I dare to believe that I am not like any that exist. If I am not worth more, at least I am different.

In these opening sentences we can grasp the energizing contradiction of the *Confessions.* Its object will be a man of nature ("un homme dans toute la vérité de la nature)," but at the same time a man who is "autre"—different, otherwise, other. "Je suis autre" will be the key to the story. *I am different from what you have heard about me, different from what my enemies claim. I am different from what Nature made me but in a way that can be traced through the hazards of circumstance back to Nature. I am so different from you and from all others that you cannot understand me without reading every word of my confessions and withholding judgment till the last. I am the subject of a story that I alone can tell, but you cannot understand yourselves without understanding me. I am the other of every other, the only "pièce de comparaison," the only man whose story will ever fully be told, the only man who will ever be able to maintain his clear-eyed dignity in the midst of the full and complete triviality, shamefulness, irrationality, absurdity, and blamelessness that constitute a man.*

With this logic, Rousseau set out to play a role that has been repeatedly reinvented among modern authors, from Montaigne and La Rochefoucauld to Nietzsche, Freud, and beyond—the role of the first honest man. It is in the courage to show himself ridiculous that Rousseau distinguishes himself. The flamboyant pathology he exposes in the process has made the late works a central point of reference for modern psychiatry, and there is hardly a term in the history of pathology that has not been applied to Rousseau at one time or another.[23] The narrative of the *Confessions* brilliantly conveys the story of a man as he achieves the discovery of a nature that is always surprising and paradoxical both to himself and to others. By the perverse junctures of inclination, society, and destiny, we see Jean-Jacques driven to mad impulses in every aspect of his life and making a spectacle of them all: self-exposure and masochism, obsessive masturbation and petty theft, the ecstasies and torments of the life of fantasy. We see him taking on numerous personae not his own, being trapped in every role he occupies, committing pitiful crimes and howling absurdities, but we never see him convicted of an ill intent.

Some of the psychological tendencies displayed in the *Confessions* throw into relief the intellectual patterns of the earlier books. The tendency to invest every important development with the absolute decisiveness and irreversibility of the Fall is apparent throughout the *Confessions,* just as it is in the *Second Discourse.*[24] Rousseau's childhood reading, we are told, corrupted his nature forever; his earliest sexual experiences stamped him as a masochist; being locked outside the walls of Geneva separated him from his destiny; his debut as an author fixed his inexorable fate. The language of destiny serves only to underwrite the possibility of these dramatic moments, each one of which undoes what came before. Rousseau's temporal consciousness has become a kind of lapsarian machine, registering Fall after Fall, but because Rousseau himself always remains in an ultimate state of innocence, his character and destiny can never be fixed. The lapsarian structure of the life narrative becomes nothing more than an obsessional topos. The state of loss makes no demands upon the agent; it provides a contemplative distance that does not burden the will.[25] Indeed, Rousseau is freest when he feels himself close to death, when the demands and possibilities of the future have been finally foreclosed. Death leads Rousseau not toward an afterlife but toward the release from desire and from the need to negotiate with others.[26] Death is the only true reversal of his fall into society.

Closely linked to this theme is a peculiarity Rousseau himself observes—that he cannot accept any qualification of the absolute. In his imagination there is no space between perfection and corruption. He finds the hidden key to his nature in the sudden horror inspired in him by the beautiful Venetian

[23] Claude Wacjman's *Fous de Rousseau: Le cas Rousseau dans l'histoire de la psychopathologie* (Paris: Éditions Harmattan, 1992) is a lesson in how many aspects of a person's behavior can be understood in pathological terms, including, in the case of Rousseau, his love of walking ("la dromomanie" or "manie ambulatoire"—42) and his love of solitude ("le robinsonisme"—121). Wacjman's volume has a splendid epigraph from Jean Cocteau: "The posterior of Jean-Jacques was Freud's moon on the rise."

[24] On this theme and Rousseau's tendency toward polarized judgments, see *L'œil vivant,* 182–83.

[25] As Starobinski puts it, Rousseau's archetypal objects of desire are displaced into the past to give them "a detached future." *L'œil vivant,* 163.

[26] See Ann Hartle, *The Modern Self in Rousseau's "Confessions": A Reply to St. Augustine* (Notre Dame: University of Notre Dame Press, 1983), 48–60.

prostitute Zulietta, in whose body he discovered a single flaw.[27] All of Rousseau's human relationships seem to be marked either by idealization or disillusionment, and it is so even in his relation to Nature itself, which can only be considered in its inviolate and perfect form, the first sign of departure from which ensures an inevitable progress of decay. Whereas we saw in *Gulliver's Travels* an insistence on the painful emptiness of the middle space between ideal and actual, with nothing to bridge them, in the *Confessions* this gap has been made subjective and temporal. It is set in motion in an unstable oscillation, like the charms of Zulietta, which are one moment dazzling, then monstrous, then dazzling again. The accidental has become fatal, the fatal has become accidental and unstable but endlessly repeatable.

One of the admitted purposes of the *Confessions* was to free Rousseau's guilty conscience of certain despicable crimes. His defense is always to immerse these crimes among contingent and temporary circumstances. In his telling, Rousseau's acts of duplicity, like the fatal accidents that determine his destiny, always occur in a moment and are the result of irresistible impulse. They represent no settled intention or plan and can be connected in no way to the general dimension of his character. He is overtaken by "moments of inconceivable delirium" in which he is "no longer himself" (1:148). Frequently the shame of standing before witnesses keeps him from admitting the damning truth. Rousseau is more afraid of being thought ridiculous than evil. In the most famous of his crimes, the affair of Marion and the ribbon, in which he blames a young housemaid for having taken a ribbon that he himself had stolen with the intention of wooing *her*, it was the fact that the ribbon reminded him of her, and not that he wanted to hurt her, that made him attribute the theft to the unfortunate young woman. Thus it was not hostility but his feeling of friendship that was cause of his crime! (1:86).

Because hurting Marion was not his aim, Rousseau believes he is not really guilty of having hurt her. That this seems like a defense is itself disturbing,[28] but it exemplifies a general tendency of Rousseau's apologies—that the protagonist is never to blame for anything that is not the motivating purpose of his action. Outcomes of an action that are accidental in relation to its purpose do not count as morally definitive, even if they are its predictable results. Once Rousseau is responding even partly to external circumstances, he is no longer responsible. By this all-or-nothing logic, his good will always remains above the squalor of his actions. It is on such general grounds that he defends himself in *Rousseau Judges Jean-Jacques*—as a man "rather without malice than good, a soul healthy but feeble, who adores virtue without practicing it, who ardently loves the good and hardly does any of it" (1:774). In this essential moral passivity we see the import of the "great maxim of morality, and perhaps the only one useful in practice" that Rousseau for-

---

[27] *Confessions*, 1:317–22. Zulietta's reply is one of the most apt in history—"lascia le Donne, e studia la matematica"—"Give up Women, and study mathematics" (1:322).

[28] Sheringham, *French Autobiography*, 51.

mulates for himself in the *Confessions:* never to put himself in a situation in which his duties conflict with his interests (1:56). It is useless, that is to say, to resist temptation, or to make any attempt to weigh another person's interests in balance with one's own.[29]

As Rousseau shows himself moving between the two poles of paranoid eccentricity—from self-inflated idealist to puppet-victim—he makes little attempt to preserve his dignity. Or perhaps it would be more accurate to say that indignity is the proving ground of his indestructible self-esteem. What he hopes for is that others will be driven to admit that they are as much the victims of their own nature and the circumstances of their lives as he is of his and that this admission will move his tormentors to release him from the enchantments of conspiracy. His aim is to make his passivity and subjectivity normal and natural, to dethrone himself as an exception in order to make exceptions the rule. And as we have seen, there is even a further hope—that his readers will be able to find more in the details of the conspiracy than he does and so be able to trace it to the ultimate cause he is unable to fathom.

To analyze Rousseau's narrative of his behavior in the manner I have done above is necessarily to take up a satirical view toward it, to turn him back into a Quixote whom we observe with a combination of sympathy and irony, an attitude that can easily be extended to his uncritical admirers. But however inevitable that gesture may be, it is more important to see that Rousseau in a sense courts this satiric treatment in order to turn it back upon the reader, not in the sardonic and detached manner of La Rochefoucauld or Freud but with his personal helplessness and suffering fully on display. Rousseau is hoping to prove that no matter how ridiculous, petty, and inadvertently destructive he may have been, he still does not deserve the ultimate punishment that is being inflicted upon him by his enemies. In *Rousseau Judges Jean-Jacques* he argues that even if the entire case against him were true, he still would not deserve to be treated as he has been. It is only from within the extremity of Rousseau's paranoid assumptions that we can grasp the absurdly permissive casuistry he applies to his behavior.

The final irony of Rousseau's paranoid condition is that the principle object of the conspiracy against him is to deprive him of the one thing his philosophy should teach him to renounce—his concern for the regard of others. His tormentors intend him no physical harm. What they want is to block his access to literary posterity, but this was a sacrifice of *amour-propre* that Rousseau for a long time could not bear. He preferred to depict himself more and more pitifully, strip himself of every claim to dignity and reveal every

---

[29] In assessing these episodes it is impossible, of course, to know how completely they correspond even with Rousseau's current beliefs about his own experience, not to mention that experience itself. In the *Reveries* he looks back at the *Confessions* and admits he has touched up his image there, that "the profession of truthfulness that I have made has its foundation more in feelings of rightness and equity than in the reality of things, and that in practice I have rather followed the moral directions of my conscience than abstract notions of true and false. I have often recited fables, but I have rarely lied" (1:1038).

one of his follies in the hope of placating his accusers, rather than pass into posterity in a version created by others. Until his very last work, Rousseau continues to struggle for the control of his image in the eyes of future generations. Even as he renounces every shred of his heroic identity, he clings to the essential Plutarchan value, fame. Having begun by throwing off both the Christian sense of depravity and the heroic need for admiration, he ends up humiliating himself like a sinner in order to preserve a scrap of social dignity for his work. He even thinks it just that his reputation should expiate his crimes, since it was his desire to preserve his reputation that had brought them about in the first place.[30] Like Gawain in his temptation, Rousseau is still wavering between systems of virtue and the differing claims to excellence and depravity that they admit.

Last Resorts

In the grip of paranoid delusion, Rousseau was unable to grasp the fact that it was his belief in the conspiracy against him, and not that conspiracy itself, that was cutting him off from his friends and contemporaries. When readers failed to be moved in the way he expected by his *Confessions* and *Rousseau Judges Jean-Jacques*, it was not because they could not credit his account of his own actions but because they could not accept the existence of the conspiracy Rousseau had built around them. It was not his crimes that were unacceptable but his punishment. No degree of candor, it seemed, could disarm these imaginary enemies. It did not help Rousseau to recognize the similarity of his situation with the plot of *Don Quixote*; it was only the more humiliating that he was being treated as a puppet for other people's amusement, as the aristocratic enchanters treated Sancho when he was the governor of an island (1:716).[31] There was no Knight of the White Moon to enter into the spirit of Rousseau's delusion and help him play it out, though that is precisely what he was seeking both in the composition of the *Confessions* and *Rousseau Judges Jean-Jacques*.

The exemplary self-condemnation of the paranoid victim was not, however, to be the end of the story. In his final literary work, *The Reveries of the Solitary Walker*, we see Rousseau to some degree making his peace with his fate and returning to a more positive view of his conduct and philosophy. He accepts the fact that his enemies have triumphed over him, that he will be forever an outcast even to posterity, and that, as he now sees, God himself must have chosen this destiny for him in spite of his innocence (1:1010). He also recognizes at this point that by caring about other people and what they

[30] *Ébauches*, 1:1155.

[31] In *Rousseau juge de Jean-Jacques*, the "Frenchman" who has become convinced of the justness of Rousseau's cause still does not want to "play Don Quixote" by going on a crusade to help him (1:946).

think of him even in posterity, he was committing the cardinal sin of *amour-propre,* whereas he would be free of his enemies if only he could forget their existence. Having surrendered the real world to enemies of his own creation, Rousseau once more takes up the challenge of living on the resources of his imagination. He flees his imaginary enemies by *pretending* that they do not exist.

In contriving this last escape, Rousseau was only rededicating himself to the embrace of solitude and idealizing fantasy which had allowed him to produce the works that made him famous—the grand stroll in the woods that produced the vision of Nature in the *Second Discourse,* for example, or the ecstatic reverie of *The New Eloise,* in which he lived for months among the shades of his noble and sensitive heroines and heroes. In the *Letters to Malesherbes,* Rousseau describes the innocent happiness of solitude, which had induced him to leave the disturbances of the world behind in favor of higher satisfactions.

> But in what, finally, did I take pleasure when I was alone? In myself, in the entire universe, in everything that is, in everything that could be, in everything beautiful in the world of the senses, in everything imaginable in the world of the intellect: I gathered around me all that could flatter my heart, my desires were the measure of my satisfaction. No, never have the voluptuous known such delights, and I have enjoyed my chimaeras a hundred times more than they have enjoyed their realities. (1:1138–39)

Rousseau felt no embarrassment in the admission that he preferred the company of the chimerical to the real, for it provided him with a strong form of self-justification—that he did not care enough about real people to intend them any harm. Only unhappiness could accuse him, only a complaint about his enemies could provide the evidence that he had not achieved pure and perfect self-love, without dependence on the regard of others. In the *Reveries,* the perfecting of self-love has become Rousseau's central concern. All the pleasures of his solitary life fulfill this purpose—the use of his intellect and his senses, the emotional nourishments he gains from the "children of [his] fantasy," his own self-contentment, and the feeling that he deserves it. "In all of this," he adds, "the love of myself does everything, *amour-propre* plays no part" (1:1081). His happiness, his being, have no point of reference other than himself, and this is his salvation. The man who had once offered himself as the "pièce de comparaison" for the human race has now found happiness in severing himself from all comparison.

At this point of the story, Rousseau believes that his being has reached perfect passivity and solitude. He requires no effort and no thought—his thought is all sensation. There are no other moral beings but him. His fellow human beings all belong to "a frenetic generation" which has given itself over "entirely to the blind fury of its leaders against an unfortunate who neither did, nor wished, nor returned evil" (1:1077–78). He can no longer think of them as human. They are "mechanical beings" who act "only according to physical impulse and whose actions I could only comprehend using the laws of motion" (1078). Surrounded by automata, he no longer needed to resent the blows they aimed at him: "The wise man who sees in all the evils done to him only the blows of blind necessity does not experience these senseless agitations" (1:1078). In the last analysis, Rousseau was not solitary only because he was alone or because other men were against him but because, truly, there were no other men, only instruments of "blind necessity."

In the *Letters to Malesherbes,* Rousseau emphasizes the delights he owes to his imaginary friends as his compensation for the loss of real ones, and in *Rousseau Judges Jean-Jacques* he gives an enthusiastic defense of the good fortune of one who can commune six hours a day with sociable chimaeras of the highest quality (1:814–15). This motif appears again in the *Reveries,* but in the later work the pleasures of Nature emerge as the more significant compensation. Rousseau's *promenades* show no reveling in beauty but rather a hard-won and difficult self-extrication from the miseries of society. Rousseau seeks the forest, following "Wherever nature led," like the speaker of Wordsworth's "Tintern Abbey," "more like a man / Flying from something that he dreads, than one / Who sought the thing he loved."[32]

I climb the rocks, the mountains, I plunge in valleys, in woods, in order to remove myself as much as possible from the memories of men and the attacks of the wicked. It seems to me that under the forest shades I am forgotten, free and peaceful, as if I no longer had enemies or that the foliage of the forest could shield me from their blows even as it had removed them from my memory, and I imagine in my stupidity that, not thinking of them, they will not think of me. I find such great sweetness in this illusion that I would give myself over to it entirely if my situation, my weakness, and my needs permitted me to do so. The deeper the solitude in which I live, the more it is necessary that some object fill the void of it, and those that my imagination or memory refuses me are furnished by the spontaneous productions that the earth, uncoerced by men, offers everywhere to my eyes. The pleasure of going to some deserted place to seek new plants augments that of escaping from my persecutors, and when I arrive in one of these places where I see no traces of man I breath more at my ease, as in a retreat where their hatred cannot pursue me. (1:1070)

Reading this sad passage, we can see Rousseau's delusional struggle to escape from the enemies he himself has unknowingly invented along with what

[32] "Lines composed a few miles above Tintern Abbey," in *The Poetical Works of William Wordsworth,* 2 vols., ed. E. de Selincourt (Oxford: Clarendon, 1944), lines 70–72.

we may take to be his semi-rational attempt to distract himself from his own *idée fixe* so that he can experience for himself the pleasures of Nature. Rousseau is perfectly aware that, given his capacity for self-gratifying fantasy, he ought to be disposed toward solitude. What he is unable to see, however, is that, of all men, he is the least capable of a solitude without witnesses. His fantasies demand words and an audience in order to live. It is the solitude not of a Creator but of an author. It ultimately depends upon the existence of other morally adequate beings, but, like the Hegelian Master, Rousseau, in dehumanizing others, has left himself without an adequate reflection of his own consciousness.

This leads us directly back to the fundamental paradox of Rousseau's system, which is that its vision of natural happiness can only be achieved by a denaturing of the human being, a process that turns him or her back into a thing. From the beginning Rousseau has staked his claim to happiness on his power to be sufficient unto himself, and to rejoice in his nature without concern for the admiration of other men. Thus he remains faithful to his original vision when, in his last state of distress, he declares himself alone in a world in which there are no other significant moral beings and in which he can be happy only as long as he can keep other human beings out of mind. He withdraws from the company of imaginary friends, the shadow of social life, to a state in which Nature is his only other, a state like God's before the creation. Rousseau's illness brought him to live out in an ironic and desperate way that credo of the beautiful soul that he enunciated in identical words in two of his chief works: "Except for the single Being existing alone, there is nothing beautiful except that which is not" (2:693; 4:821). Rarely has a vision been lived out with such exactitude in all the fullness of its consequences.

I have been emphasizing the hazards of the isolation envisioned by Rousseau in his last work, and the desperation that drives him to it, and that is one of its persistent notes, for the author himself sees his victory over the real world to be a fragile and fleeting one, and his protests of independence are clearly part of a defensive routine. At the same time, the ecstasies of Nature also lead Rousseau toward the grandiose dimensions of his personality. It was not only God's solitude to which he aspired but the infinity that comes with it. Perfect solitude and absence of comparison could bring him to a freedom from self that was also an expansion of the self to the scale of the natural world. "I never meditate," he insists, "I never dream more deliciously than when I forget myself. I experience ecstasies and transports that make me dissolve, so to speak, into the system of beings, and identify myself with the whole of nature" (1:1066–67). At the moment when Rousseau has achieved the most total isolation and the most complete reduction of being, he is also in the moment of greatest ecstasy, having reached

a state in which the soul finds a solid enough position to rest upon completely and gather all of its being there, without having need to recall the past or venture toward the future; where time is nothing for it, or where the present lasts forever without marking its duration and with no trace of succession, without feeling any sentiment of privation or enjoyment, pleasure or pain, desire or fear other than that of our existence alone. If this one sentiment could fill the soul completely, then, as long it lasts, the one who has found it can call himself happy, not with a poor, relative, and imperfect happiness such as one finds in the pleasures of life, but with a happiness sufficient to itself, complete, and perfect, leaving in the soul no emptiness to fill. (1:1046)

It would be natural to compare this description of the *sentiment d'existence* with mystical experience, for it touches upon tropes of the *via negativa* such as timelessness and emptiness. The editors of the Pléiade edition recommend comparison with Fénelon (1:1799). They also mention Henri Bergson, and there is no doubt that Rousseau's sense of the primacy of the phenomenal was both forward-looking and influential. Lionel Trilling considered the "sentiment of being" to be the signature element of modern "authenticity."[33] What Rousseau envisions here, though, is something different from either mystical transport or the authenticity of worldly experience. Unlike the mystic, Rousseau emphasizes the primary absence of privation, when consciousness has been stripped down to mere feeling, detached from all worldly experience, all ethical content, all sense of transition or movement. What is revealed is an original fullness of self that leaves no void. The mystic seeks an emptiness and a timelessness that will lead to the entrance of God. Such self-reduction is an attempt at conversion. But Rousseau's soul has no emptiness to fill and experiences no need for God. Its self-sufficiency is god-like in itself and beyond temporality.

What is it we enjoy in a situation of this kind? Nothing that comes from outside ourselves, nothing other than ourselves and our own existence, so that while this state lasts we are sufficient unto ourselves, as God is. The sentiment of existence stripped of all other feeling is by itself a precious sentiment of contentment and peace that suffices to make existence precious and sweet only to those who know how to distance themselves from all earthly and sensual impressions, which come ceaselessly to distract us and trouble our joys here below. (1:1047)

It is fascinating to see that while Rousseau has promoted himself to the role of God, a consciousness that is all-powerful and self-sufficient, fully absorbed in its own existence, he retains nevertheless a contempt for "earthly and sensual impressions," symptoms of enslavement to what we can still recognize as a descendant of Augustine's City of Man and therefore a distrac-

---

[33] See Lionel Trilling, chaps. 3, 4, and 5 in *Sincerity and Authenticity* (Cambridge: Harvard University Press, 1972).

tion from the new City of God which has as its sole occupant Rousseau's self-transported consciousness.

Rousseau is above the authenticities of the real world. In the course of the *Reveries,* we see him recalling with pleasure those times in his life when he had the opportunity to play God by performing acts of kindness in which he was not recognized by the beneficiary and therefore could not become entrapped in those relations of dependence that always took away the pleasure from his acts of charity.[34] We even see him trying on the Ring of Gyges in his imagination in order to certify the goodness of his heart by the purely benevolent fantasies it evokes. "Perhaps in moments of gaiety I would have had the childishness to accomplish prodigies now and again, but only ones that were perfectly disinterested with regard to myself and having for their rule only my natural inclinations; for each severe act of justice I would have performed a thousand of mercy and equity" (1:1058). Through all of his life, it was only on account of "weakness and slavery" that Rousseau had ever been capable of an act of wickedness. "If I had been invisible and all-powerful like God, I would have been beneficent and good like him" (1:1057). The same relation held between Rousseau and other men. His failure to surpass them in moral terms was directly related to his inferiority in force. "I would have been the best and most merciful of men," he insists, "if I had been the most powerful" (1:1053). It was a strange denouement for the prophet of equality.

The Beauty of That Which Is Not

The story I have been telling is, it is impossible to deny, the story of an extreme and fragile temperament gradually verging into madness, a temperament that made Rousseau aggressive and superior toward others yet too weak and preoccupied with his own feelings to accept responsibility for the results. Adored during his lifetime as no author had been, only his critics mattered to him, and the more famous he became, the more urgently he needed to escape from society. The hostility he attributed to his contemporaries confirmed his suspicion that, addicted to the corruptions of civilization, they could not bear to have their life of slavery exposed. At the height of his reforming zeal, his ostracism from France and condemnation by his beloved Geneva turned his original conception of society as a form of enslavement into a new and fantastic conception—that it was a universal conspiracy directed at *him.* His first impulse was to placate his demons by showing that he too was a victim, both of society and fatal chance, and that he did not deserve the absolute retribution inflicted by his enemies. In his final days he struggled to accept and rise above his fate, clinging to the insight that his contemporaries were nothing but mechanical contrivances. Alone in

---

[34] This is the burden of the ninth *Promenade* of the *Reveries.*

creation, he could finally revel in the God-like transports of true solitude and self-sufficiency. This, at least, was his final consoling fiction.

Rousseau has been the subject of many extreme and contrary judgments.[35] There are professional scholars who treat him as psychologically unique and others who take his way of thinking as definitive for Western culture.[36] By the generation that succeeded him, he was greeted as a liberator of mankind, while more recently he has been blamed for instigating the spirit of the French Revolution and even of twentieth-century totalitarianism.[37] Such attributions of personal but indirect responsibility for historical events seem to me to be without genuine clarifying value. My attempt in the foregoing pages has been to show that Rousseau was the inheritor of a specific set of problems about human agency and its place in the world to which he made a powerful and original response. He never abandoned his original faith in God, that "omniscient and just Eye," as Starobinski puts it, "inseparable from the sky of Geneva."[38] In addition, he adopted both Locke's skeptical and passive empiricism and Pope's optimism about Nature and the cosmic order, each of them central elements of Enlightenment opinion. At the same time, he held society up to an ideal standard justified by his reading of history and romance and by the intuition of his own natural goodness, which he extended to humankind. The application of this ideal led him to deeply suspicious views of social existence, views that undoubtedly drew upon the Calvinist atmosphere of his youth but were also powerfully buttressed by his reading of Hobbes, Pascal, La Rochefoucauld, Mandeville, and others. Seeing the social bond as inherently irrational and degrading and reason as impotent but being prepared to accept neither the Christian resignation of Pascal and Fénelon nor the grimacing affirmation of Pope, Rousseau spent his life imagining how human agency could be removed from every domain of existence so that men could enjoy a simple dependence upon things alone, a life regulated by necessity but not the will of others.[39] In every area of his

[35] For some of the reasons see Arthur M. Melzer, *The Natural Goodness of Man: On the System of Rousseau's Thought* (Chicago: University of Chicago Press, 1990), 1–9.

[36] Jean Guéhenno, one of Rousseau's best biographers, is so concerned to stay within the lived experience of his subject that he attempts to "reconstruct" Rousseau's life from day to day without himself knowing what will come next. Michel Foucault, on the other hand, in his preface to *Rousseau Judges Jean-Jacques,* frames a dialogue (like one of Rousseau's own) between a psychologizing reader and himself in order stress his conviction that, while madness may be part of the work, the psychology of the author is of no interest. Jean Guéhenno, *Jean-Jacques: Histoire d'un conscience,* 2 vols. (Paris: Gallimard, 1962), 12; Michel Foucault, introduction to *Rousseau juge de Jean-Jacques* (Paris: Librairie Armand Colin, 1962), xxiii–iv. See also my remarks on de Man, Derrida, and Starobinski in the introduction.

[37] A well-known example is J. L. Talmon, *The Origins of Totalitarian Democracy* (London: Secker & Warburg, 1955), 38–49. Jan Marejko considers Rousseau both the inventor of modern totalitarianism and its first victim. See *Jean-Jacques Rousseau et la dérive totalitaire,* 19–20.

[38] Starobinski, *L'oeil vivant,* 138.

[39] Starobinski argues that the demonizing of reason distinguishes the later, paranoid Rousseau from his earlier self and shows the signs of his illness. As I have noted, however, for Rousseau, reason was always the possession only of the few, and it was largely an ineffectual

thinking, he sought the elimination of the human hand. His account of human history offers hope only in the suppression of the effects of choice; his political philosophy is a philosophy of reification, in which the absolute power of the law makes human interactions as reliable as the laws of physics; his mode of education is an "éducation négative"; and his final psychological recourse, as he imagined it from within the paranoid struggle with his enemies, was to recognize that his fellow creatures were mere "mechanical beings" whose actions he could "only comprehend using the laws of motion" (1:1078). In all of this, Rousseau's personal psychology and his intellectual inheritance played an inseparable part in determining his fate, and his failure to escape from moral engagement with others predictably led him to the relations of dominance and submission he feared. Just as his political philosophy envisioned only all-seeing lawgivers and deluded citizens, so in his paranoid distress he oscillated between exposing the shaping powers that had deformed his nature and asserting his still-potent capacity to rise above human comparison to the scale of Nature and God. Pascal's rhetorical questioning—"Shall I believe that I am nothing? Shall I believe that I am God?"— became for Rousseau a intractable conundrum.

Irrelevance was Rousseau's last defense, his devotion to "that which is not." All of his solutions were counterfactual, based upon the assumption of nonexistent or impossible conditions—the state of nature, unquestioning love, a general will. Reforming the world in such terms became a way of escaping from it. It may have been personal weakness, and finally madness, that made Rousseau unable to negotiate with the world of others, but what gave this weakness such astonishing influence was its grounding in a denial of the rational ideals that could have governed such negotiations and made them anything other than contests of power.

---

instrument, with more power to corrupt than to illuminate or guide. Cf. *La transparence et l'obstacle*, 247–48.

Epilogue

Paranoia and Postmodernism

Wheels have been set in motion, and they have their own pace, to which
we are . . . condemned. Each move is dictated by the previous one—that is the
meaning of order. If we start being arbitrary it'll just be a shambles: at least, let us
hope so. Because if we happened, just happened to discover, or even suspect, that
our spontaneity was a part of their order, we'd know that we were lost.
—*Rosencrantz and Guildenstern Are Dead*

It has long been believed, both by the opponents of modernity and by its
advocates, that a fragmentation of the human identity and an uprooting of
human values came as the inevitable result of the findings of science and the
progress of modern technology. The deracination of the modern spirit and
the loss of a sense of agency or its displacement have been treated as side-
effects, unintended consequences of the benefits of modernity. I have been
attempting to show that these developments were deliberate achievements of
the makers of modern culture. They fostered a sequence of modes of thinking that made the denial of agency into a virtue and the assertion of agency
into folly or vice. The makers of modernity established the denial of agency
as a central form of agency, and their accounts of agency stood in a deter-
minate relation to each other. Each was an attack upon and in some measure
an inversion of the one that came before. The founding figures of Protes-
tantism inherited a religious paradigm of action that saw agents choosing
freely, though with the help of God, and accepting responsibility for the
degree to which their actual behavior and the world they lived in approached
an accessible ideal. Luther and his successors, attempting to free themselves
simultaneously from the yoke of Catholicism and from its burden of responsibility, turned this model on its head, making the renunciation of
agency and the subverting of its claims into the chief criteria of faith. The dimension of the ideal was thus severed from agency and given over to the de-

graded realm of the other, leaving agents to strive only toward the acceptance of their actual state of failure. The phase of Hobbesian and Augustan irony that followed the Reformation achieved the deflation even of this demand. Differences between religious positions came to seem like mere choices of delusion, and the paranoid extravagances of Quixote, a venial form of amusement in Cervantes' conception, came to look like a universal form of insanity. Michel Foucault argued that the Enlightenment brought about the exclusion of madness as an other. It would be more accurate to say that it began with the undermining of the difference between sanity and madness, taking madness and delusion into its own identity.

The optimistic trend of Enlightenment naturalism was a rejection both of religious pessimism and reactionary irony, with an attempt to establish a new ideal based upon Nature. As we have seen, however, naturalism of the Enlightened sort did not succeed in producing a viable conception of agency. Whereas in the Augustan model, the space of agency between actual and ideal had become either unbridgeable or illusory, in the mode of Nature it collapsed altogether. The actual was already the ideal, and any human action that made a difference could only do so for the worse. The self, insofar as it was an agent, became its own other. The Protestant and Hobbesian displacement of agency toward a higher power was succeeded in this model by the new enshrinement of a collective agency, society itself. Rousseau's adaptation of this model shows its full potential to accommodate and foster paranoia. In his version, society, with its intrusive and unnatural ideals, becomes the all-powerful other, while the practice of individual agency can only lie either in resistance to society, in the renunciation of the world in favor of an imaginary omnipotence, in ideals unsullied by relevance to real life, or in the fictive agency of a hidden lawgiver.

The modern suspicion of agency brought a remarkable cast of characters to prominence, characters whose personalities throve on their ability to see through the façades of human power and to conjure up enemies answering to their need for conflict. Their peculiar endowments of pathology and genius gave a decisive stamp to modern culture. Once the mode of heroic unmasking had been established, it was perennially available to be taken up by new and still more daring rhetoricians. Each offered freedom from the one that came before, even if it in turn demanded further renunciations of intellect and power. Standing upon narrower and narrower grounds of their own, they could always boast of having taken more and more territory from the enemy. Ideology is typically considered an idealizing instrument, but the ideology of the modern has been relentlessly negative. The power of its aggressive demystification, as applied to past ideologies, has served as a compensation for the self-repressive aspect of its own.

It is important to note that the changes in culture I have been describing did not depend primarily either upon the decline of religion or upon skepticism about the accessibility or reality of truth. Even Hobbes professed to believe both in God and in the truth. Skepticism, so often considered the signature of modernity, plays a marginal role in this line of development. Denial of agency, rather, is the key. Only later would the Baconian attack on past cultures widen into questioning the very existence of truth. At the same time, while we underline the relentless negativity of modern views of agency, it is important to stress once again the central paradox of this study, that the denial of agency constitutes one of chief modes of social action in modern culture. The point does not only apply to world-changing reformers like Luther, Rousseau, and Marx. The most darkly ironic of the authors I treat here, Swift, Pascal, and La Rochefoucauld, engaged in open provocation against the authority of church or state. Hobbes, with whom each of them had so much in common, would have feared every one of them.

It would take a book perhaps longer than this one to carry the story from the place where I must leave it, here on the verge of Stendhal's "age of suspicion," up to the end of the twentieth century. For many thinkers, at that point, not only have agency and ideals become fundamentally other, but the actual too, reality itself, has become the creation of an alien force—capital, power, discourse. Some new factors would enter the analysis along the way. One of them would be the growth of the sense of history, and with it a new self-consciousness about the dynamics of society, the collective other. As both the present and the past become increasingly alien and distant, the force of history not only registers as an ever-mounting threat but also offers more and more radical opportunities for revolutionary idealism and prophetic rhetoric, for grandiose and suspicious characters like Marx, Nietzsche, and Freud to set their achievements in the context of collective time. Following the story after Rousseau, we would also see the increasing importance of clinical diagnoses for the understanding of intellectual activity, so that they gradually lose their abnormal character and acquire a kind of satirical glamour.

Freud was a leader in this regard. He took self-vaunting delight, for instance, in the irony of exposing his own likeness to the psychotically paranoid Schreber, whom he considered superior to his fellow doctors of the mind. Thus he played Quixote to his own Cervantes. With Freud we are well on the way to the clinical nonchalance of the present, in which it seems natural to describe the transition between the art and culture of the mid-sixties and what came after as a movement from paranoia to schizophrenia.[1] Finally, and perhaps most importantly, after Rousseau our story would have to come to grips with the influence of Darwin, an intellectual who does not share the paranoid affinities described in this book but whose work poses

---

[1] It is a sign of the degree to which modern artistic culture has insisted upon the value of escaping the mental standpoint of everyday life, however permissively we define it, that Louis Sass could so productively turn the tables of this procedure. Instead of applying psychiatric findings about schizophrenia to artists, he studies modern art to learn about schizophrenia. Louis A. Sass, *Madness and Modernism: Insanity in the Light of Modern Art, Literature, and Thought* (New York: Basic Books, 1992).

new problems for agency both individual and social.[2] In the aftermath of Darwin and Nietzsche, we would have to grapple with the still-potent modern tendency to reduce truth to power or to seek an entirely naturalized epistemology. I have been careful in this study to distinguish healthy skepticism from suspicion. The writers treated in this book all believed in the potential truth of inquiry even if they brought agency into doubt, while later attitudes toward truth often undermined the possibilities of agency even further.

A continuation of this history, then, would bring some new elements into view, though the satiric aspect of psychology was already visible in the seventeenth century, and the elevation of Quixote as a kind of paranoid everyman had substantially been accomplished by the beginning of the nineteenth, when Milton's Satan, another primal satiric victim, would also have his moment. In the following centuries, liberal spirits like Herman Melville would find invigoration conjuring up the Satanic energies of a paranoid Captain Ahab; Henrik Ibsen would see his own longings for revolt expressed in the supernatural strengths and weaknesses of the mad Masterbuilder; and Franz Kafka would struggle with his impossible idealism by reducing the romantic quest to an inescapable and formally rigorous absurdity.

For the most part, the great masters of suspicion of the next two centuries would integrate and systematize the elements of suspicion already developed by their intellectual predecessors. They would pursue Bacon's Idols of the Mind wherever they could be found, create deeper and more elaborate forms of Hobbesian and Mandevillean egoism, and explore the depths of human self-deception opened up by the Jansenist psychologists and La Rochefoucauld. Along with the utilitarians, Marx would sustain the optimistic side of the Enlightenment project, the hopeful surrender to natural systems, integrating Smith's and Hegel's sense of the benefit of unintended consequences with Rousseau's utopianism and its attendant suspicion. In Marx's vision of the future, the proletariat, like Rousseau's general will and Hobbes' Leviathan, would prevail on account of its universality, admitting of no outside and no other. After 1848, pessimism, the Lutheran note, becomes dominant over the liberal one, and we see Nietzsche performing a new suspicious dissection of human idealism and foible, with an empirical skepticism and unmasking of the self more disabling than Hume's, a classicizing primitivism more strident and historically persuasive than Rousseau's, and a fatalism still more heroic and ostentatiously challenging than Luther's. There is no denying the originality of Nietzsche's genius, but the features of his outlook that have fascinated his admirers to this day remain the paranoid habits of rhetoric and thought he variously shares with Luther, Rousseau, and indeed

---

[2] One way to think about the struggle over agency I have been presenting in this book is to see it as part of a central fault line in post-classical western culture between Augustinian and Pelagian positions on freedom. Until the nineteenth century, almost every Augustine had a Pelagius. Luther had his Erasmus, Mandeville his Shaftesbury, Voltaire his Rousseau, Malthus his Godwin, but Darwin still lacks a worthy antagonist, though the debate continues among Darwinians like E. O. Wilson and Stephen Jay Gould.

Quixote—grandiose self-mythologizing, the displacement of agency, suspicious decoding, heroic renunciation and irony, embattled resistance to self-assigned enemies, and absolute judgments of good and evil (couched in a neo-Darwinian vocabulary of sickness and health, weakness and strength that also echoes Rousseau). All that was left was for Freud to reduce it to a system, recentered to his own personal myth.

It was with Rousseau, nevertheless, that the elements of modern paranoia crystallized, and it is in connection with him that I offer now a speculative sketch linking this study to recent developments, particularly the reported disappearance of the self. Rousseau stands out from among the figures who precede him in these pages in that his model of agency was not connected with the advocacy of any institution or group. Its historical moorings were a by-gone animal past, glimmerings of Nature in Rousseau's own psyche, and the myth of an ideal natural state whose conditions of existence were no longer available. Among our subjects, only La Rochefoucauld was similarly unattached, but authorship for him was a valetudinary pastime, whereas for Rousseau it was a life-long crusade. Rousseau found himself taking up a new stance in opposition to society as a whole. His feelings were his justification and he never doubted that those feelings belonged to him alone. However imitable the romantic self would later prove to be, for its inventor it was unassumingly his own. There was of course an audience for this role. Rousseau cut himself off from society and the *philosophes* only to find a new relation to the reading public, a connection that would allow him to relate to others without losing his individuality or becoming dependent upon any one in particular. At a time when few authors signed their work, he referred to himself in print as "Jean-Jacques." No wonder he feared being cut off from his readers and having the public turn against him. This was the specific nightmare of a self that had been nourished almost entirely in the act of writing.

Rousseau made it clear precisely how the kind of self he had discovered could hope to preserve its integrity. Once again I refer to a key passage of *Émile*.

> There are two kinds of dependence: dependence upon things, which is natural, and dependence upon men, which is social. The dependence upon things, having no moral element, does not harm liberty and engenders no vices. The dependence upon men, since they are in disorder, engenders all of them, and it is on account of it that master and slave bring each other into depravity. (4:311)

Salvation for society depends upon making the law as dependable as a thing, but since that attempt must fail, the self has to look elsewhere for its stability. It has to detach itself from all those things that are full of human arbitrariness and caprice, and fasten upon what comes to it without choice. This is the most important aspect of Nature, its inanimate character. For those who are not omnipotent, or who do not have an omnipotent governor, dependence upon things brings freedom from the degraded realm of human choice. With metaphysical and moral necessity out of the reach of human powers, and social teleology unmasked as a ruse of self-interested ancestors, upon what form of necessity were the boundaries of the self to be fixed? Only by the limits of choice, both our own and others, which is to say, by contingent necessity—all those circumstances of our particular existence that belong to us alone but that we ourselves have not chosen. The private realm of the contingent thus stands over against the degraded realm of the arbitrary and the other.[3] It is this contingent but objective aspect that hallows the things we experience as Nature—their freedom from the stain of the human hand, their ability to confront us with an otherness against which we can define ourselves without introducing the struggle with a foreign will. The encounter with natural contingency—the discovery of who we are, where we are, what we are, the whole range of what Heidegger ingeniously called our *Geworfenheit,* our "thrownness"—defines the writable self, that self which can be expressed for the sake of others as unique to us.

At the same time, then, that he made the arrangements of the social world come to seem arbitrary and unnecessary, Rousseau also located the limit of struggle in the natural contingencies of the particular. He took refuge from the arbitrary in the contingent, and in doing so, he invented the role of the artist as a creature of the particular. Rousseau's *Confessions* was by no means, of course, the first efflorescence of particularity. By the time his career as a writer was getting underway, the novel was beginning to crystallize as a genre, and *Robinson Crusoe,* with its vision of solitary struggle against Nature, provided Rousseau with a utopian model of the undegraded self. He prescribes it as the only appropriate reading for young Émile. We can only imagine how completely Rousseau would have shared Crusoe's terror at the sight of Friday's footprint in the sand announcing the return of the hitherto unsuspected other. It was not Defoe, however, but Rousseau who, struggling with his paranoid impulses, brought together the critique of society and the flight to the particular. The personal narrative of natural contingency that he invented in order to justify himself against his enemies became the defining mode of romantic and modern art, a new genre in all but the denial of its generic character.

The development of the mode of contingency is the history of two centuries of culture, and its varieties are well known. Freud, in a Baconian spirit, gave us a psychological allegory of its tensions with his distinction between the principles of pleasure and reality, reality now being that which contin-

---

[3] In drawing the distinction between the arbitrary and the contingent, it is important to recognize that the two are not contraries. The arbitrary is that species of the contingent that derives from acts of will—others' or even our own—that are not apparently justified by principle. The form of consciousness fostered by Rousseau can accept contingency only when it is not polluted with the human will.

gently resists our desire.[4] Though the power of imagination may be a key modern theme, one that suggests the freedom and creativity of the self and its capacity for self-gratification, every transport of the modern imagination seems also to demand a rededication to the reality principle, a turn back from the "gold mosaic" of Yeats's Byzantium to the "foul rag and bone shop of the heart."[5]

The contingencies of subjectivity provided one of the essential resources of the modern imagination, along with the innocent discovery of human nature in childhood. It is almost a given in modern fiction that a novel which begins with childhood will decline in power as the protagonist grows because it is in childhood that we experience the contingent most constantly and wholly. A child, for the most part, must accept what is given. Only later do arbitrariness and contingency become evident—the strangeness and unreasonableness of *these* people, *these* conditions, as opposed to what they might have been. Premodern cultures offer similar attractions, not only an image of primitive manners—the "childhood of humanity"—but, more important, access to consciousness not yet infected with the arbitrary dimension of choice. Their myths, being innocent, could reflect back to us the loss both of innocence and myth, while their strangeness could exhale a utopian suggestion of freedom—of how different *we* could be—as long as they do not know how different *they* could be. Primitive otherness does not threaten because it does not exercise agency and thus cannot arouse suspicion. It goes without saying that the aesthetic charm of the "primitive" depends upon the pathos of distance created by the perception of a decisive difference in power.

In the twentieth century, the pursuit of the contingent became gradually more arduous and evoked more and more acrobatic exertions from "the performing self."[6] Modernism in its maturity demanded an intensification of authenticity in the direction of the erotic, the pathological, and the criminal. It could present highly personal expressions of impersonality or it could outwit the arbitrary in a purely rational way in games of chance and arbitrarily chosen schemes. It could find concentrated intensity in detached moments—"epiphanies," "intermittences du coeur." The "extinction of personality," to recall Eliot's phrase, would make schizophrenia a potent aesthetic inspiration,[7] while through the end of the century Freud's unconscious

---

[4] "Formulations on the Two Principles of Mental Functioning" (1911), in *The Standard Edition of the Complete Psychological Works of Sigmund Freud,* trans. James Strachey (London: Hogarth Press and Institute for Psycho-Analysis, 1958), 12:213–26.

[5] I am quoting here from line 18 of "Sailing to Byzantium" and line 40 of "The Circus Animals' Desertion." W. B. Yeats, *The Poems: Revised,* ed. Richard J. Finneran (New York: Macmillan, 1983).

[6] The phrase belongs to Richard Poirier, *The Performing Self: Compositions and Decompositions in the Languages of Contemporary Life* (New York: Oxford University Press, 1971).

[7] Schizophrenia, as Louis A. Sass has shown in *Madness and Modernism,* is not a devolution of consciousness into primitive or emotional depths but a kind of intellectual alienation and detachment that has been an attractive model for a culture that, as we have seen, does everything it can to undermine the real-world standpoint of agency.

provided a seemingly inexhaustible source of meaningful contingency that was by definition out of the reach of conditioning choice. And surrealism, of course, with its quest for psychic automatism, was deeply indebted to Freud. All of these strategic reserves, though, even the unconscious, were ultimately vulnerable either to simple exhaustion or to unmasking, and the power of the unmasker grew as the domain of contingency flourished. We can see Rousseau's two great roles, the unmasker of society and its innocent victim, gradually coming apart.

The last stage of the contingent self, near the moment of its vanishing, is epitomized for me in Ernest Hemingway's story "The Snows of Kiliman-jaro," in which a writer on safari, a sportsman and adventurer like the author himself, dying of gangrene on the mountain, recalls with bitterness all of the experiences he has never managed to write about because, having succumbed to the temptations of marriage to a rich woman, he waited too long. We can see in this story the same fear of social comfort, weakness, and feminization that typify not only the heroic adventure mode but also that of the naturalizing moralists like Rousseau and Nietzsche, themes which are richly echoed in the popular culture and sociology of the period.[8] What gives Hemingway's story its charm and power, however, is the collection of epiphanic memories that the character has wasted but that Hemingway himself now poignantly gathers, expressions of natural contingency free from all stain of the arbitrary—memories of love, of war, or of favorite parts of Paris that belong only to the one who has experienced them. We might call them, following Rousseau, the reveries of the solitary writer. Having read the story, one comes back to its mysterious epigraph to find the kernel of the tale.

> Kilimanjaro is a snow-covered mountain 19,710 feet high, and is said to be the highest mountain in Africa. Its western summit is called the Masai "Ngaje Ngai," the House of God. Close to the western summit there is the dried and frozen carcass of a leopard. No one has explained what the leopard was seeking at that altitude.[9]

The mountain personifies an ultimate contingency, the most austere and solid of the epiphanic presences in the story. The fact that it is merely "said," not known, to be the highest mountain in Africa suggests that it has not truly been conquered by westerners. It still belongs to the Masai. But the leopard who has strayed beyond his proper bounds is obviously a figure for the dying writer and his kind. Its death might be a sign of self-destructive heroism and lone seeking or a sign of dispossession, of the encroachment of civilization that drives the strong one, like Zarathustra, into the upper reaches. In connection with Kilimanjaro, the grand symbol of natural contingency, the

[8] See Timothy Melley, chap. 1 ("Bureaucracy and its Discontents") in *Empire of Conspiracy: The Culture of Paranoia in Postwar America* (Ithaca: Cornell University Press, 2000).

[9] *The Short Stories of Ernest Hemingway* (1938; New York: Collier, 1986), 52.

writer's fate is purged of its arbitrariness and acquires a fine purity and strangeness. In the next generation of writers, the possibility for such epiphanic discoveries would narrow and finally seem to have been used up altogether; the performing self will be without a stage. Third World countries would cease by and large to be a colonial playground, and only tourism— travel from which the accidents and contingencies have been removed— would be left, a denouement announced in different ways in Lévi-Strauss's *Tristes tropiques* and Pynchon's *V.*

It was to this post-romantic and postmodernist condition, in which reality and the self disappear amid the products of culture, that Pynchon applies the term *paranoia,* and his novel *Gravity's Rainbow* (1973) gives a most vivid and telling portrayal. The characters in Pynchon's novel inhabit the world of what its narrator calls the "multi-national cartelized state," a multiplicity of sprawling and interlocking markets and technologies perpetrating psychological and political manipulation on an unprecedented scale. It is not only romantic adventure that has been absorbed into the apparatus, but all forms of private contingency. Many of Pynchon's characters give themselves to this system happily, but some, the heroes and heroines of the tales, undertake the quest to understand how this system, controlled by faceless agencies ("Them"), has conditioned and shaped their lives, and how they can fight back against it. These characters want to discover what in themselves is fundamentally their own, their own endowment of natural contingency, so that they can divide it from the desires and responses that have been conditioned in them by others. Pynchon's Émiles want to unmask their governors.

But the search for the self in *Gravity's Rainbow* becomes a terrifying one, for all of the protagonists' deepest wishes turn out to have been manufactured by the forces of capitalism for use in World War Two, which, it turns out, was not a struggle for victory between two groups of combatants but a grand mobilization of markets. Since everything is under the control of Them, the very desire to seek what is one's own, the nostalgia for home and innocence, turns out to be one of Their conditioned reflexes. As Tyrone Slothrop, the book's paranoid anti-hero, pursues the quest for the sources of his self, he finds himself assuming the guise of Rocketman, a character out of comic-book fantasy. Almost from the beginning of his attempt to establish contact with the grounds of his nature, Slothrop is being transformed into an archetype, one that suggests he was serving the building of the V-2 rocket all along. As the quest continues, Slothrop becomes gradually less and less real, until he finally dissipates into the cultural background. He is freed, as the narrator says, from the "albatross" of self, implying that his unfeathered and scattered identity was from the beginning nothing more than a conditioned burden of Puritan guilt.[10] There is a hint of liberation in "plucking the albatross of self" (623), a touch of counterculture Buddhist unselfing,[11]

[10] *Gravity's Rainbow* (1973; New York: Penguin, 1987), 712.
[11] John A. McClure, "Pynchon, DeLillo, and the Conventional Counterconspiracy Narra-

and Slothrop will now be free of Them in the sense that nothing remains of him to be "positively identified and detained" (712). The trouble is that, without this detainable feature, nothing else is left. The mind-body connection dissolves at the nexus of technology and myth, and the middle ground of self, that pineal contrivance where material and intellectual being long held together, simply disperses into the original components of its illusion. "Slothrop" starts off as a self in search of identity and winds up a myth that could be used to condition the identities of others.

It is not mere technology that has accomplished this transformation, not just the final subjection of material existence to the techno-bureaucratic will. There is also an intellectual component, because for Pynchon's paranoids the reality principle that assembles this diagnosis has itself been undermined even while it is preserved as part of a more general sphere of delusion. It goes on operating, struggling to free itself from unreality, but, like a limed bird, involving itself ever more deeply with each spasm. The uncanny persistence of the investigation that discovers Their machinations must itself be either a delusion or a plot: if one's sense of reality continues to go on working at all, only madness or the existence of some sinister human contrivance like the "multi-national cartelized state" could explain the fact. For the self-conscious paranoid, operating upon the principle that all coherence is a delusion and order itself belongs to Them, the moment one begins to make sense of anything, even one's own paranoia, the sole question that can arise is, *Who is responsible?* To put it another way, if all the world is art, a humanly created thing, as Nietzsche believed it to be, and there is no limit to the will, no contingent necessity imposing upon and giving definition to individuals, then the sole important choice left to be made is whether one will live as the hero or heroine in a romance of one's own devising or as a victim in the self-aggrandizing dreams of others.

The uncanny persistence of the will-to-truth for Pynchon's paranoid heroes corresponds with the ironic sense of the inescapability of metaphysics among poststructuralist critics like Roland Barthes and Jacques Derrida. The emergence of *écriture,* of writing without attachment to author, self, or reality, betokens from their perspective the coming to consciousness of the true nature of language. Language in this view is a self-subsistent but unstable system; it has a determining power of its own and cannot be made subservient to anything outside of it. The truth and reality which it can neither designate nor renounce signify an ineffaceable otherness, the seductive power of metaphysical "presence," which constantly tempts us either to accept the terms of our own discourse as more than terms of discourse or to declare them only terms of discourse and so fall back into the illusion of a valid account. The only seeming response to this dilemma, in which both our own discourse and the discourse of others threaten to entrap us, is a refusal

tive," in *Conspiracy Nation: The Politics of Paranoia in Postwar America,* ed. Peter Knight (New York: New York University Press, 2002), 264.

to come to rest in any stable assertion, to cultivate a consciousness that stands aside from consciousness, seeking continuously to undo itself in an attempt not to betray the infinite play of signification, or, for poststructuralist Freudians like Deleuze and Guattari, not to reduce by abstraction the polymorphous perversity of the "body without organs."[12] This is Pynchon's paranoia embraced as a solution to the dilemma it poses. It is in a sense the dying reflex of the author bidding the self adieu. Literary language can no longer escape the abstraction of philosophy and its vocation for unmasking.

We have now reached that period I referred to in my introduction, when paranoid fiction became the norm of social imagination and all-encompassing principles of otherness—especially Foucault's *power*—the dominant resources of explanation among professors in Humanities departments. The arrival of postmodernism coincided with a number of dramatic unmaskings and disappearances. Derrida showed that Lévi-Strauss's version of structuralist anthropology still depended upon Rousseau's naïve conception of Nature.[13] Foucault announced the passing away of that "recent invention," man, an event which, though apocalyptic enough, depended on his peculiar articulation of "epistemes."[14] More telling was Roland Barthes's announcement of the "death of the author" in 1968.[15] This death was a logical outcome of the constructivism of Nietzsche and his academic successors. What was special about it, though, was that it was a philosophical unmasking that coincided with a historical event. Authors were always a myth, we were being told, just like souls or unicorns, and these mythical beings disappeared just a generation ago.

The "death of the author" seemed to surrender an element of reality to which many were still attached, the experiencing and expressive self, yet its claim to be a datable event inside history was in part a convincing one. If we take the practice of high culture as definitive for society as a whole (and this is the key, and questionable, assumption), the model of expressive consciousness seemed to lose its revelatory force sometime during the 1960s in the United States and some other developed countries. Since this time the most vital new forms of artistic practice over a broad range of media had in common a refusal of original expression in favor of the reproduction of already produced images and words. Art became, as Barthes put it, a "tissue of quotations" (63). It seemed hard now to deny that the artistic self had always been a cultural construction and that in the sixties this had simply become apparent in a way it had not been before. For those who were willing to generalize from the character of art to the character of culture as a whole, the death not just of the author but of the self seemed to have occurred. It

[12] See Gilles Deleuze and Felix Guattari, *Anti-Oedipus: Capitalism and Schizophrenia*, trans. Helen R. Lane and Robert Hurley (New York: Viking Press, 1977).

[13] Jacques Derrida, *De la grammatologie*, pt. 2 (Paris: Éditions de Minuit, 1967).

[14] Michel Foucault, *Les mots et les choses: une archéologie des sciences humaines* (Paris: Gallimard, 1966), 398.

[15] Roland Barthes, *Le bruissement de la langue* (Paris: Seuil, 1984), 61–77.

was as if Jean-Jacques Rousseau had finally given up the struggle. His philosophical dissolution coincided with the arrival of new and more powerful enemies than the ones he had faced, the social other built up to a new level of that "perfectibility" he feared.

The most important account of this moment of dispersal has been the Marxist Fredric Jameson's theory of postmodernism.[16] Jameson sees postmodernism as that moment in which capitalism has completed the process of modernization, the moment when the contrast between traditional modes of life and modern ones is no longer possible to discern, the last residual traces of the traditional having finally moved out of sight. In this account, the struggle against nature that had been the energizing force of all previous cultures is simply no longer visible. Everything in our world has been absorbed into the sphere of culture; there is nothing that cannot be traced to the activity of human hands. The space of critical distance has been dramatically foreclosed, as "the prodigious new expansion of multinational capital ends up penetrating and colonizing those very precapitalist enclaves (Nature and the Unconscious) which offered extraterritorial and Archimedean footholds for critical effectivity" (49). Jameson believes, of course, that the struggle with Nature, with its inevitable division of classes, goes on, but the special predicament as well as the defining feature of postmodernism is that it conceals our relation to this struggle. In doing so it conceals our relation to reality; thus, part of the unfreedom of our state is to be cut off from reality itself. The benefit of postmodern art is that it helps us grasp the shock of this confinement, though it leaves us with the problem of imagining an escape from it. For this we need a way of "mapping" the new postmodern landscape, a new cognitive paradigm that will permit a vital and integrated relationship with the structures and forms of multinational capitalism.

There is a certain irony for dialectical thinking in the emergence of culture as an all-inclusive category of experience, for was this not the goal of Hegel's Absolute Spirit in the first place, that the species man should overcome all of its falsely reified objectifications and achieve an awareness of itself as creative spirit? The freedom that arrives at the end of the dialectic was to be the recognition that all of the human responses to necessity had been nothing more than opportunities for self-realization. The end of the dialectic, however, has produced not the full realization of the self but its dissolution, not autonomy but heteronomy and paranoia. At the end of the day, it is not the self but the other that has remained standing. This can occur not because the self is actually separable from us but because, on account of the alienation of agency I have been describing, it subtends a will we no longer recognize as our own. If this is the Absolute, it does not turn out to be the

---

[16] See the title essay of Fredric Jameson, *Postmodernism, or, The Cultural Logic of Late Capitalism* (Durham: Duke University Press, 1991) and also "Periodizing the 60s" in *The Syntax of History*, vol. 2 of *The Ideologies of Theory: Essays 1971–1986* (Minneapolis: University of Minnesota Press, 1988), 178–209.

final expression of freedom in necessity; instead, it is only an ultimate revelation of the arbitrary. Mysteriously, like Rousseau's new subject of im-
putability and Adam Smith's invisible hand, it includes *and* excludes us at
once, while leaving us without a principle of agency of our own.

At the same time, the recognition that all human reality is culturally determined has not made it seem any less determined. For Jameson, the contradiction between the apparent overcoming of Nature and our actual
unfreedom is a Gordian knot that cannot be undone by thought but only by
action, by the great social movement of the future, a global process that will
emerge after capitalism has completed its own revolution through the oper-
ation of global commodification. This Mandevillean confidence remains uncanny as long as our contact with reality and history have been suspended,
and it seems now a more-than-Pascalian act of faith to believe that a further
plunge into commodification, which is to say, into collective illusion, will
bring us closer to freedom. Jameson remains ultimately committed to the
possibilities of thought, but he is willing to surrender these possibilities temporarily as long as he can surrender them to History and Capital. Like an
old soldier, he has become attached to his enemies and cannot do without
them. Indeed, he has found a brilliant way of keeping them in force long after their supposed disappearance.

The theorists I have been discussing are like Pynchon's paranoids in one
important respect: each has accepted the notion that the reality principle that
motivates his investigations is part of the illusion he seeks to dispel. For all
of them, the categories they employ—the Natural, metaphysical "presence,"
"postmodernism," or "late capitalism"—can neither be fully asserted nor
fully demystified. They can only be negated in a way that preserves them as
the only available point of reference. The one imaginable relief, then, from
the effort of negation is a further movement into illusion, in which the spell
of the other will finally be broken or where thought will finally (unimagin-
ably) be relieved of the fantasy of truth that keeps it from indulging in its
other imaginary satisfactions. For Derrida, this is the play of signification;
for Jameson, the completion of global commodification; for Deleuze and
Guattari the abandonment of abstract, "territorializing" thought in favor of
a pure, unself-conscious, undifferentiated or "deterritorialized" experience
like that they attribute to schizophrenics. The homeopathic remedy for paranoia seems to be schizophrenia, and this in fact is the "aesthetic model" that
Jameson very effectively employs to describe the undifferentiating flow of experience aimed at by the postmodernist wave of aesthetic innovation now
divested of the oppositional character of modernist art.[17]

I would like to suggest a more modest historical explanation for the
"death of the author" and the arrival of postmodernism, one that does not
deny the changes in culture and technology that have occurred but situates
them differently with respect to art and the intellectual past. It starts with a

[17] Jameson, *Postmodernism*, 25–31.

recognition, first, that the "death of the author" and the expressive self depends not only upon changes in the situation of artistic production but also upon certain long-held intellectual presuppositions. I am thinking especially of the belief in the arbitrariness of human culture and invention, the dominant attitude among advanced intellectuals for two centuries, in consequence of which Rousseau's pursuit of natural contingency became the primary self-defining, self-justifying, and self-exculpatory resource. What we now see is the final exhaustion of that resource, but what I hope the foregoing analysis will have shown is that it need not have been the only resource, and that postmodernism as a condition is no more inevitable than Rousseau's analysis in the first place.

Rousseau's perfectionistic conception of freedom envisioned an impossible abolition of the other. Nevertheless, Rousseau's redirection of consciousness toward natural contingency provided artists with an important mode of self-defense from the enemies that Hobbes, Mandeville, and Rousseau himself had conjured. Indeed, as the exemplary bearer of self and rebel against society, the artist became a more central cultural figure than ever before. As long as natural contingency was visible and could be the stabilizing element of the self, modern skepticism about language, truth, and value did not take on the drastic consequences of the Nietzschean analysis. Modern art benefited from a repose of skepticism in contingency that was already visible as a possibility in the writings of Montaigne. For the romantic self, teleology and order, the forces of Freud's pleasure principle, could be kept in their place by the resistance of reality, even as that resistance excluded the intervention and control of others. As natural contingency became harder and harder for individuals to confront, however, the artist's role began to show its vulnerability. With the world shot through with images and messages, becoming more and more social, more completely filled with bearers of abstract and therefore arbitrary significance, contingent Nature could no longer particularize. It had been written over, and without being able to orient itself in the sphere of intellectual discourse, it could no longer sustain its existence. The remaining vestiges of contingency became a more and more precious commodity until finally they were depleted, and there was nothing to stave off the recognition that we are entirely social creatures, which is to say, of course, natural and social at once. Rousseau's false distinction between Nature and society was no longer tenable even as a source of imagination.

What were the mechanics of this transformation? It was not, of course, that They, the faceless agencies of the market, now actually began to control our personal thoughts and experiences before we had them. What occurred, rather, was a change in the conditions of specifically artistic production. As the opportunities for private experience dwindle, competition for them increases. There are too many people having the same thoughts and experiences and too many media competing to package and convey them for the artist to maintain personal possession. Natural contingency "up close and personal" is now the possession of journalism, television, radio, movies, and the internet, all of which process their contents much faster than the digestive powers of the writerly self allow. What these media lack in terms of style and artistic enhancement they make up in immediacy, exploiting an ever-increasing proximity to "real time." The artistic self, then, having stabilized itself against its other, the brute resistance of reality, made itself prey to what turned out to be an exhaustible commodity—exhaustible, and also capable of falling into other hands.[18] Cervantes could sustain a beautiful and humorous poise by mocking Avellaneda's knock-off version of *Don Quixote* because his audience could be expected to tell the difference between the original and a cheap imitation. But in a world in which real-time immediacy has replaced originality, this confidence becomes far more difficult for the artist to sustain. This exhaustion of the natural self, which is also the writerly self, shows the ultimate consequence of replacing the older culture of agency and its inexhaustible repertoire of stories with a culture of flight to the particular in which truth has become entirely a private commodity.

Jameson misses the historical point, then, when he says that reality has become unrepresentable in postmodernism. What we have seen, rather, in the arrival of postmodernism is the discounting and remaindering of a specific role for the artist. The practitioners of this role can no longer evade its general and arbitrary character. It is not Nature that has disappeared but Rousseau's peculiar and fragile conception of it, particularized natural contingency, which was from the outset a way of escaping what he set up as the arbitrary world of the social. Natural contingency has not really disappeared, only become public property. As such, it is no longer able to help put off the consequences of a fully Nietzschean attitude toward truth, language, and society. As a further turn of the screw, with the exhaustion of expressive consciousness and the arrival of moral tourism in every sphere, even the personal heroism of the unmasking critique has become a weary academic routine. The hidden purpose no longer sustains the interest of the surface. Reality, then, has not moved out of reach; it has only become tedious when filtered through the sights of expressive individuals deprived of their adventures and unmaskings, individuals much of whose experience is now pro-

[18] Rousseau's political philosophy displays a similar vulnerability to obsolescence and unmasking as arbitrary. As Roger D. Masters put it, "Having defined a logic of civil obedience that is purely formal, Rousseau tacitly admitted that the prudential science defining the good civil society was not an intrinsic or necessary part of his principles of political right, but merely a guide to their successful implementation. Rousseau was therefore forced—along with Machiavelli and Hobbes—to treat the differences between the various forms of government primarily as a technical problem whose solution depends on knowledge of the 'natural tendencies' of politically relevant phenomena. But as soon as the triumph of modern technology permitted man to conquer the natural relationships which Rousseau thought were invincible, his definition of the *necessary* superiority of the simple, agrarian city became an anachronistic and purely personal preference—one is tempted to say, a pious wish—which can be rejected without abandoning his principle of popular sovereignty." *The Political Philosophy of Rousseau* (Princeton: Princeton University Press, 1968), 423.

vided to them by the media themselves.[19] This is not the fate of all human beings but of a narrow intellectual class who have felt history go on without them. Their defenses against an alienated sense of agency no longer seem to work.

As for Foucault and his alien *pouvoir,* imagine an Émile or a Jean-Jacques who can no longer believe in the dependence upon things as morally protective against people because that story is already one of Theirs and he can no longer evade the fact. The curtain has been withdrawn and the horny feet of the lever-pulling legislator at the center of the panopticon finally stick out. Since social being and social agency have always been alien to him, he is now at the mercy of his enemies. Power has always been elsewhere, not because that was where he could actually locate it but because his own natural agency could only be preserved in negativity and resistance, and these accustomed resources have vanished.[20] So he finds himself in a condition of pure passivity and victimization, nakedly exposed to the Sartrean gaze, surging with moral alarm but without responsibility, and playing the fugitive by inventing ever new accounts of modernity. In an attempt to address the surprising changefulness of his thought from book to book and his acrobatic disclaimers of past positions, Foucault asks,

> What, do you imagine that I would take so much trouble and so much pleasure in writing, do you believe that I would stick to my task, head down, if I were not preparing—with a somewhat feverish hand—the labyrinth into which I can venture, . . . in which I can lose myself and appear at last to eyes that I will never meet again. No doubt there are others like me who write so as to have no face. Don't ask who I am and don't ask me to stay the same: that is the morality of the state; it regulates our credentials.[21]

[19] Jameson's way of analyzing this subject is a natural expression of his method. He assumes, in a generally Hegelian fashion, that we do not have direct access to reality and can only achieve access to it through the negation of previous historical conceptions. The price for this method is that all historical conceptions of reality acquire validity as expressions of reality. Their necessity is not open to question. They are not intellectual choices but determined historical effects. Yet the historical narrative conjured up by Jameson, which he presents as a "once upon a time" fairy tale of the dismantling of the sign, has a rather limited historical horizon, more so even than that of Marx. It begins with the "corrosive dissolution of older forms of magical language" and their replacement by "scientific discourse" through a process of "reification" (rationalization, Taylorization, specialization) that is "the very logic of capital itself." Jameson, *Postmodernism,* 95–96. The writing off of the intellectual past as a symptom of "magical language" is a transparently Baconian gesture, its vocabulary updated with the help of anthropology and Freud. As we have seen, though, this gesture does not dissolve the grip of the problems of agency bequeathed to us by the magicians of the past. In fact, it makes them inescapable.

[20] Timothy Melley observes that in projecting the sense of agency onto alien subjects, a process he calls "postmodern transference," authors like Foucault and Pynchon are complying with the demands of narrative itself. *Empire of Conspiracy,* 101.

[21] Michel Foucault, *L'archéologie du savoir* (Paris: Gallimard, 1969), 28.

Writing "so as to have no face" perfectly describes the condition in which expressive consciousness has outlived the notion of agency that could make it cohere or give it power to sustain a narrative. Such writing, if it were truly possible, would not be a form of communication but an escape from communication. The "eyes that I will never meet again" are eyes that cannot recognize or define, eyes that focus on the present without caring for the future. Or, as the metaphor of the labyrinth suggests, are these the eyes of the minotaur, which free us from the future altogether? If to be defined is to be oppressed, destruction is a release, a freedom from the "prison of the body" or the "albatross of self."[22]

It is important to recognize, finally, that the conception of the contingent self, for all of its dependence upon uniqueness and particularity, had a unifying as well as a divisive effect. In a manner of speaking, it represented the survival of intellectual universalism in its opposite, a powerful mode of relating to others, if only through a psychology of difference, resentment, and fear. There is, for this reason, something profoundly instructive about the paranoid fate of the self. The inhabitants of this role resolutely insisted on their uniqueness, but by making resistance to society the sole form of agency, they developed a new, undeniably social role, one that both undermined and usurped the meaningfulness of other ways of life. Only that which did not evidently partake of the social could be socially communicable as art. But this antisocial role required a certain configuration of mass audience and print culture in order to survive, and when its social productivity waned, it waned. Its final resource was to unmask itself. At the moment of its deflation, the modern self, with its latent universalism and disguised social basis, lends a remarkable reminder of the indispensability, indeed, the inescapability of social roles and the conception of agency they demand.

Some Final Questions

At this point, I would like to address two questions I have sometimes encountered when presenting parts of this book to scholarly audiences. The first one is that, having offered this large-scale and critical account of what I take to be a central element of modern culture, what distinguishes the suspicion and interpretive ambition of my own account from paranoia? This question, which takes it for granted that any ambitious attempt at explanation must either seek to undo itself or succumb to Quixotic fantasy, arises naturally from within the set of assumptions I have been attempting to question. My reply

---

[22] Thomas Pynchon, of course, is a fugitive intellectual even more faceless than Foucault, having remained invisible to the public for over forty years since V. made him famous in 1963. Writing "to have no face" makes a perfect description of the schizophrenically detached and inhuman voice that not so much narrates as registers much of the action in V. and Gravity's Rainbow.

is to go back to the specific models of agency I have described as invitations to paranoia and to point out that I do not participate in them. I do not insist, for example, on the supreme ethical value of submitting to necessitarian determinism and renouncing all human fitness for ideals, as did Luther and his intellectual descendants all the way down to Nietzsche and beyond. And as for the closely related Baconian suspicion about the mind's temptation to find more order among the things of the world than really exists, I consider it a valuable methodological principle of caution, but I do not think it should be wielded in a sectarian spirit or made the basis of distinguishing between whole cultures or eras; one cannot find truth merely by avoiding error, and, as many philosophers of science have shown, science does not work simply by factoring out the mind's contribution to inquiry.

Similarly, I understand with Hobbes that the alienation of power is a fundamental human goal because the state needs executive authority, but I naturally do not endorse the egoistic nihilism which justifies making the state an absolute authority. And while I admire the psychological and sociological acuteness of Pascal and La Rochefoucauld, and Swift's ability to see through the truly mechanical stupidity of much human behavior, making insights of this kind the center of one's own claim to intellectual authority, as Swift does, represents to me a failure to learn from one's own lesson. If we were all fundamentally irrational, then it would be irrational to pride oneself upon the recognition, since it would merely be another form of our irrationality. I have mentioned that Pascal takes up this stance explicitly: "Men are so necessarily mad," he says, "that not to be mad would only be another turn of madness." This is superb, and close enough to the truth to be painful, but the use of the term *madness* in this near-absolute sense can only be meaningful in a theological context that relies upon an implicit contract with prelapsarian wholeness.

Regarding the system-building naturalists like Adam Smith, their way of concealing human agency behind the workings of a natural machine, now global in its scope, continues to trigger paranoid reflexes to this day, both in those who want the machine to work and those who want to stop it from working. As for Rousseau, I see him as a person of undeniable genius who was right to protest against the assault on human powers being carried out by the *philosophes* but whose response to it was the greatest invitation to paranoia of all. Asserting his own pure goodness, denying all individual responsibility, and blaming all on society and the past, he essentially rebuilt the Augustinian model of agency inside out and upside down. What is remarkable is how powerfully it functioned and for how long.

I do not, of course, find paranoia everywhere in modern culture and, consequently, I have not written a general history of modernity. Many important modern authors take for granted or seek to strengthen our everyday sense of freedom and responsibility. This can be said of figures as different as Kant, Goethe, Coleridge, Jane Austen, J. S. Mill, George Eliot, Proust, and Czeslaw Milosz. Mill makes a good point of contrast with the authors treated in this book. In *On Liberty*, he expresses a concern about society's suppression of the most creative and unique individuals that is akin to the suspicion of society I have been tracing, but his response is to advocate neither fugue nor fusion, neither an escape into solipsism nor submission to a higher order. Rather, he defends liberty, much as Milton does, for its importance in the discovery and vitalizing of truth. There is a hint of the natural system in Mill's attitude toward inquiry: he sees resistance as necessary for the health of the social body. This is not surprising for a utilitarian. But truth for Mill is more than just an effect of the system. It has independent value, and that value is potentially available to all.

This brings me to the second question. If I reject paranoia about agency and the notion that all thinking is equivalent to it, what would I put in its place? What I offer, simply, is an intuition that I hope this study will have strengthened in my readers. It is the following: as many before me have noted, while the sense of agency that we cannot do without in everyday life tends to be undermined by many theological, sociological, psychological, and mechanistic schemes of explanation, the power to assert these schemes assumes that very sense of agency they attempt to deny. Faced with this dilemma, intellectuals of the paranoid sort have tended to embrace the paradox with exemplary submission or heroic irony. They have given the externally reductive view—what Thomas Nagel instructively calls "the view from nowhere" an extraordinary privilege.[23]

But the shift to the outside and the emphasis upon the controlling power of others has not brought a halt to moralizing, only a more thoroughly hostile, suspicious, and self-assured way of separating Us from Them. It is essential to recognize, therefore, that this response to the dilemma of agency has no special claim to authority. In fact, it is as inconsistent and self-contradictory as could be.

This is not the place for me to offer my own reasoning about the foundations of agency or the freedom of the will, though part of the motivation for this study has been my belief that the denial of causal power in the will is more problematic than its affirmation once we have assumed that there is such a thing as a will at all. So even if we lack the means to solve the problem of freedom on philosophical grounds, we cannot be faulted *on any grounds* for adopting a scheme whose attractions derive from their support of our indispensable sense of our own power rather than one that appeals to us either because it underwrites the impulse to displace responsibility elsewhere, because it discredits some established form of ideology, or because it undermines the idea of responsibility altogether. It remains to be seen whether or not we can develop a better way of understanding and acting in relation to the greater social structures that articulate our lives, of grasping our collective responsibility for them, and of bridging the distance between the way things are and the way we would like them to be without falling back upon the resources of paranoia.

[23] Thomas Nagel, *The View from Nowhere* (New York: Oxford University Press, 1986).

Index

About the Author

John Farrell is Professor of Literature at Claremont McKenna College and is the author of *Freud's Paranoid Quest: Psychoanalysis and Modern Suspicion.*